The Act of Interpretation

The Act of Interpretation

A Critique of Literary Reason

Walter A. Davis

The University of Chicago Press

Chicago and London

The University of Chicago Press, Chicago 60637
The University of Chicago Press, Ltd., London

Printed in the United States of America
82 81 80 79 78   9 8 7 6 5 4 3 2 1

WALTER A. DAVIS is associate professor of
English at Ohio State University.

Library of Congress Cataloging in Publication Data

Davis, Walter Albert, 1942–
    The act of interpretation.

    Includes bibliographical references and index.
    1. Criticism.   I. Title.
PN81.D377   801.95   77–13803
ISBN 0–226–13795–3

For Zandy

for Zandy

Contents

Acknowledgments

Without Robert Marsh and Wayne Booth I would never have written this work. Most of the ideas I develop here first began to take form in courses that I took from Marsh. Wayne Booth read the manuscript on three separate occasions; his extensive comments, on style, structure, and content, helped me clarify myself to myself and his encouragement and support sustained me through several revisions.

And there are so many others to thank: my parents for the many sacrifices that enabled me to get an education; Stephen Lacey and Jon Ramsey for teaching me whatever I know about the process of stylistic revision; H. Porter Abbott and Thomas Steiner for taking the time to read and comment on my work; Gary Heim for conversations and reflections over the years; Frank Thomas for encouragement and wit; my colleagues at the University of California, Santa Barbara—Guy Beckwith, Ron Perring, Howard Beckwith, Clayton Duncan, and Marc Debbaudt—for stimulation and support in difficult times; Julian Markels who was there when it counted. A special word of thanks to Jan Collins and the secretarial staff of the English Department at UCSB, especially Kay Hudson, who not only typed the manuscript but also discovered and corrected many of my errors in the process.

My greatest debt, finally, is reflected in the dedication.

The real "movement" of the sciences takes place when their basic concepts undergo a more or less radical revision which is transparent to itself. The level which a science has reached is determined by how far it is *capable* of a crisis in its basic concepts. In such immanent crises the very relationship between positively investigative inquiry and those things themselves that are under interrogation comes to a point where it begins to totter.

Heidegger, *Being and Time*

Nothing can permanently please which does not contain in itself the reason why it is so and not otherwise.

Coleridge

1 The Act of Interpretation: Faulkner's "The Bear" and the Problems of Practical Criticism

The Logic of Literary Interpretation

Toward the Text: The Concept of Form

What is a literary work and what is the nature of literary interpretation? Is there a single order of questions implicit in literary study and a single order of concepts capable of giving a systematic direction to the diverse investigations that make up the discipline? I am convinced that there is such a logic and that its discovery contains the possibility of unifying everything we can know about a literary work in a synthetic understanding that would be grounded, throughout its operations, in the act of close textual interpretation. Such a logic would enable us to take biographical and historical information, the knowledge of genres and conventions, and the growing number of interdisciplinary concepts that so many critics rely on today and to bring them together in a single order of inquiry. The many investigations that critics are too often prone to regard as discrete topics of separate study might then begin to come together in a way that would enable us to unify our knowledge of literature—and our experience of it.[1]

Let us begin, then, with the notion that the literary work is a *gestalt* in which the intrinsic nature of the whole determines the parts which compose it. For lack of a better word I shall call this concept the principle of form. In contrast to the popular use of *form* to denote artistic techniques and linguistic properties distinguishable from a work's "content,"[2] I employ the term in its traditional philosophic sense to signify that principle of unity which determines the nature of a concrete whole. So understood, form is the synthesizing principle of structure which makes every component in the literary work a functional part of it. Form does not arise out of the mere combination of parts; it is, rather, that prior principle which, imposed on them, determines their relationship—and apart from the function form confers upon it, no component, strictly speaking, has any artistic status. Which is to say no more than that *The Ambassadors*, for example, is not just Henry James' masterful techniques of narration, his intricately constructed plot, and the depth of insight he provides into the mental processes of a character like Strether, but somehow the unity of all these things. We read *The Ambassadors* as a coherent work of art and that experience suggests that the many things that go to make it up function as integral parts of that totality. Put in the simplest and most exacting terms, the task of interpretation is to apprehend the purposive principle immanent in the structure of a literary work which determines the mutual interfunctioning of its component parts.

If he understands it along these lines, the concept of form offers the practicing critic a clear and precise logic for his dealings with the text. Function, structure, and purpose, in that order, become the primary categories of interpretation: for parts function only by serving a purpose and structure is the process through which purpose is actualized. All specific interpretive perceptions and problems are determined by the application of those categories to the particular text under examination. Lacking such a logic, it is hard not to resolve the literary work into its parts as if it were no more than the number of discrete topics it presents for separate analysis. One may discuss, in turn, the author's personal and historical situation, his sources, the conventions and generic properties found in his work, and the noteworthy stylistic and technical innovations he achieves, only to conclude with some general comments on the cultural significance of his major "themes." Style and manner, plot, character, and theme become separate matters, independently intelligible, with the discussion held together, if at all, by a running plot summary or recapitulation of the major "events" that occur in the work.

In opposition to such practices, which in many ways typify critical discourse, the critic of forms takes the knowledge of backgrounds and conventions not as a critical conclusion but as a starting point. The task of interpretation is to discover, through internal analysis, the particular purpose, always potentially new, to which a writer puts the materials, conventions, and generic expectations he derives from his sources. By the same token, it is one thing to identify unit-ideas and philosophic influences, quite another to discover what a particular artist is doing with the thought and commonplaces of his time; one thing to posit the ambiguous possibilities implicit in the nature of poetic language, quite another to understand why a particular writer uses language in the ways that he does; one thing to describe the principles of unreliable narration, quite another to find out why a given writer employs such a narrative technique. Style and technique are not ends in themselves but means: their true artistry lies in their relation to the subject which they shape.

The same principle applies to the question of structure. While many critics treat structure as if it were no more than a mechanical principle for selecting and arranging materials that remain independently intelligible, the critic of forms tries to apprehend structure as the continuous manifestation and development of an organizing purpose. It is one thing to summarize a "plot" as if it were no more than a libretto for the presentation of character or theme, and quite another to grasp the structure of an action from within, thereby apprehending the concrete sequence of events in terms of the immanent purpose which shapes it.[3]

For the critic of forms everything hinges on the discovery of purpose, and the concrete way in which he employs that concept differs sharply from the way the category of purpose is generally handled. Purpose is often the last thing critics consider. Its status is generally no more than that of an abstract category under which to group the discussion of general artistic ends (such as, *utile et dulce*, expression of the imagination) or local aesthetic qualities (such as, beauty, sublimity, wit) which bear little or no relationship to a work's concrete movement and phenomenal integrity. Its connection with the text is of the loosest sort. Purpose floats above and beyond the work or is only present in it from time to time. The critic of forms, in contrast, conceives purpose as an immanent or indwelling rather than transcendent cause. He holds the connection between purpose and structure to be direct and continuous: rather than locating purpose in a disembodied realm of general artistic ends or abstract intentions, he strives to find it at work in the dynamic progression of the text. Purpose coincides with structure because it gives birth to it. It is the most concrete category in criticism because its embodiment is constant and comprehensive: the purpose that shapes a work of art is realized by no more and no less than that entire work of art.

In all its operations the criticism of forms is thus animated by the search for artistic unity. Recently, as part of the ascent of "structuralist" and deconstructionist assumptions in criticism, it has become fashionable to question the very possibility of artistic unity. If by unity we mean the kind of thing the New Critics and other "formalists" talk about, that skepticism was long overdue. For when unity is conceived in radically organismic terms—with the implication that a work lacks form unless literally every word (indeed syllable) in it proves absolutely essential—the literary universe gets divided abstractly into the obviously small number of works which meet such criteria and the remainder which do not. If the notion of organic form is the only concept of artistic purpose we possess, about all we can say about the latter class of works is that we don't know what to make of them: lacking organic form they strike us as a bundle of discrete parts and qualities arranged willy-nilly for no discernible reason. But there is a conceptual irony at work here that is worth careful attention. One may question whether one can know or establish the latter class of works at all. How does one decide that a given work is not unified? One can only make that decision by referring the work to a purpose which it fails to achieve. The same holds for a decision regarding any part or component in the work: a particular part fails to function only because we have posited a purpose to which it does not contribute. Without some concept of form there is, in short, no way to set up the two classes of works distinguished above. The opposite of form, disunity, is a strictly derivative notion and gives us no way to proceed.[4] The New Critics and the deconstructionists are opposite sides of the same abstract dichotomy.

If we equate form with radical organicism, and consequently employ the concepts unity, wholeness, structure, and function in a narrow and restricted way, we force ourselves into the impossible dilemmas described above. But there is no reason to do so. Organic form is merely one instance, and a marginal one at that, of form in art. Fortunately, there are many alternatives between organicism and lack of unity; and the concept of form we are developing is as applicable to Moby Dick and Don Quixote as it is to the poetry of Poe and Mallarmé. Naturally one must distinguish the organic unity of Mallarmé's poetry, where every syllable is essential and nothing can be removed without destroying the whole, from the unity of purpose at work in a book like Moby Dick, where Melville yawns from time to time and includes much that may not be essential. But that distinction is contained within the concept of form, not outside it. An abstract opposition between organic form and the lack of artistic unity blurs the issue, for there are many kinds of unity in art, each appropriate to the kind of artistic purpose which they instance. The kind of unity proper to a complex action such as we find in *King Lear* or *The Brothers Karamazov* is quite different from the lyric unity of mood sought by a poet like Mallarmé. Moreover, the parts essential to the unity of each are quite different: the unity of *Hamlet*, being one of action, resides primarily in "plot" rather than in the sound-values of words on which the unity of a poetry like Mallarmé's depends. In fact we may have done Melville wrong when we granted, even provisionally, that there are most likely many passages and episodes that mar the unity of *Moby Dick*. For it is just as likely that Melville fulfills, in a logically unified way, the demands of a purpose which we have not yet discovered. Until we discover that purpose we are in no position to decide what fits and what doesn't.

If one thinks of artistic unity in organismic terms or in terms of poetic language alone, it is natural to conclude that many literary works, even certain great ones, are not unified wholes, even if that conclusion is tantamount to saying that such works are devoid of artistic purpose. The concept of form I am developing entails no such dilemmas because it does not make the possibility of unity in art a function of poetic language, the attention span of one's audience, or the conditions of heightened sensibility. In a far more empirical spirit, it is a concept derived from the simple observation that when an artist composes he does so with a general purpose or end in view. If he didn't, there is no way he could get started. Progression as well as revision would be impossible and he would never know when he was done. Not knowing what fits and what doesn't he would be unable to cross out this line and write in that; remove such and such an episode and add something else in its place; decide to narrate the story in one way rather than another; and so on.

The concept of form is an attempt to formulate, in conceptual terms, the logic implicit in such processes. The purpose around which the artist organizes his activity manifests itself by creating function, structure, and unity. Those concepts derive from purpose rather than the other way around; they are the basic categories of criticism not because they satisfy some a priori notion of organic form but because criticism is and should be an attempt to apprehend the realized intention of the artist.

Naturally I am not suggesting that the artist could give us a theoretical account of his activity. Nor do I assume that artistic choice is in any way infallible. Deviation from one's purpose, failure to achieve it in the most systematic way, irrelevancy, digression, even downright incompetence are characteristics of artistic labor, and a multitude of factors, many of them nonartistic, enter into the artistic process. Occasional, and sometimes striking, lapses from one's purpose are most likely the rule rather than the exception, especially when a writer is engaged in a fairly complex task. Some artists, like Flaubert, are not content until everything fits; others, like Dostoyevsky and Shakespeare, frequently leave their works cluttered with a number of things that they would willingly have us blot. That does not mean that their works lack artistic unity: all it means is that there is much in their works that does not directly contribute to that unity, much that is not a functional part of the whole. The fact that one deviates from one's purpose does not mean that one lacks a purpose; on the contrary, only when one has a purpose can one depart from it.

Such, in general terms, is the order of concepts required to make practical criticism a rigorous discipline dedicated to preserving the artistic integrity of the phenomenon before it. It is not, I hasten to point out, a program that forces us, in the manner of the New Critics or their opponents, to oppose the criticism of forms to historical criticism or to "approaches" (Freudian, Marxist, etc.) which employ concepts derived from other disciplines, as if there were no way one could root the literary work in time or respond to the complex human problems with which it deals without compromising its aesthetic purity. Instead of setting up a critical division of labor, the concept of form contains the possibility of unifying the entire critical enterprise.

We can, in the words of Kenneth Burke, "use all that there is to use" because we have found a way to use all the knowledge available to us. We can welcome the wealth of historical information at our disposal without fear of reducing the literary work to a bundle of historical facts or historical curiosities. The problem is not to choose between extrinsic and intrinsic criticism in absolute or exclusive terms, but to discover how the work of art orders or fails to order the historical situations from which it derives. Historical inquiry and the criticism of forms complement one another in a definite causal order, with intrinsic considerations of artistic function regulating the use of historical information.

By the same token, there is no reason to oppose the criticism of forms to interdisciplinary considerations as if the only way one could preserve the integrity of art is by depriving it of contact with life. We may, indeed, need to have an intimate knowledge of Marx or Freud, Hegel or Heidegger, Lévi-Strauss or Jung (or all of them) in order to understand the human problems and materials with which art deals. The concept of form alone, however, is what enables us to discover how the artist *qua* artist orders those materials. In the use of Marxist categories, for example, the issue for us must always be one of Marxism and form—as it is in Frederic Jameson's valuable book of that title—and that relationship is strictly one of matter to the form imposed upon it. Just as the artist orders the materials of human experience, giving them what Aristotle terms a form or purpose which they would not by nature assume, so, too, the critic of forms determines the place in his program of the concepts and insights he derives from cognate disciplines by subordinating them to principles which those disciplines do not and cannot provide.[5]

In an analogous way, the concept of form gives a new direction to the classification of critical questions into the traditional triad of author-work-audience. Rather than taking the three topics as distinct areas of critical study, an understanding of form enables us to synthesize all three in a single order of inquiry that is rooted in attention to the text and controlled by its primacy. While past critics often speculated on the creative process apart from the text (and just as frequently derived their understanding of the literary object from that inquiry), the structures realized *in* the text have become for us the true basis for constructing a theory of the poetic faculty. The study of form offers us a way of reasoning toward imagination, creative intuition, and expression rather than from them, and enables us to develop the question of artistic psychology under the category of realized artistic purpose rather than in terms of abstract statements of artistic intention or uncontrolled psychoanalytic speculations.

In a similar fashion the random and general effects diverse audiences find reflected in their "experience" of literature—the multiplicity of local effects and isolated "commotions" it occasions—recede before the possibility of a more rigorous and objective consideration of art as experience. Though it offends the solipsism of some audiences, reading is in fact a highly structured activity.[6] Because the "effects" a literary work is designed to produce are objectively present in its structure, the literary work makes its audience rather than the other way around and shapes our experience in pervasive and subtle ways, even though our subsequent accounts of that experience often do great violence to what, as readers, we already know.

Despite their differences, contemporary critics agree on one fundamental truth: any theory of literature worthy of serious consideration must prove itself in the arena of close textual interpretation. The concept of form I have outlined is our ticket of admission to that field of endeavor, for the order of inquiry it establishes is not one approach among many, but the general logic that organizes all the concepts, facts, and disciplines that are employed in the study of literature.

Judging from the frequency with which critics today employ form and its attendant terms, a casual observer might assume that the concept of form is, in fact, the controlling paradigm of contemporary criticism. But if one compares the exacting interpretive logic implicit in the concept with most of the discussions of literature that are carried on in its name, it is difficult not to conclude that form for the most part is no more than a terminological umbrella, frequently used to propagate the very practices it calls into question. By and large interpretation continues to be little more than the parading of one or two isolated insights through an elaborate pastiche of paraphrase and extended quotation, aided and abetted by a running plot summary which by renewing in us an image or memory of the work we once read asks us, in effect, to supply what should be the business of the interpreter.

Strong words, no doubt—especially since it will not be my purpose here to substantiate them through an extended survey of extant critical writings. Putting the logic of form into practice strikes me as a far more forceful way to make its disruptive implications apparent—indeed, perhaps, the only meaningful way—for an understanding of all that is wanting in contemporary criticism grows in degree as we move toward a more adequate apprehension of our object and is one of the direct, although far from the most important, fruits of that labor.

Toward the Text: Preliminary Observation

To move in that direction let us consider William Faulkner's "The Bear." For purposes of analysis we may distinguish preliminary attention to the text from the act of interpretation proper.[7] In the former, through careful reading and patient attention to detail the critic locates the most important "features" of the text. With Kenneth Burke we may compare this process to an inventory. At this stage of the inquiry the critic notes, for example, the various conventions Faulkner employs, ranging from the tall tale and the hunting sketch to the *bildungsroman* and the myth of initiation. He sees the potential significance of names like Sam Fathers and Isaac. He charts the most important language and image patterns he finds in the work. He becomes attuned to the various possible relations of comparison and contrast among events: he discovers, for example, that recurrent activities of quest, relinquishing, and bequest mark the progress of each section in the tale—and he notes the possible ironies implicit in that pattern. He recognizes that structures of ritual and myth play an important part in defining Ike's development. He takes the many theological and moral issues Faulkner has incorporated into the tale and orders them around central thematic oppositions such as nature and history. He makes a careful study of the different techniques of narration Faulkner employs and has characterized his various styles: thus he is ready to see how both manner and language shape Faulkner's "subject." In striving to define that subject he perceives the structural relationship of sections 1 through 3 to section 4, and both to section 5, as a problem of primary importance: why does Faulkner employ this reversed chronology[8] and what is the intention behind his use of intricate, convoluted time schemes?[9] Finally, in considering the work as a whole, he takes the tragedy of Ike McCaslin and of the wilderness as its primary action.[10] Everything he has so patiently observed he feels must somehow contribute to the realization of that action since it is the one continuous subject of interest and concern that is developed in every episode of the tale.

Not in themselves an act of interpretation, such observations are, however, a necessary prelude to it. And despite the fact that critics often proceed upon insufficient or precariously selective attention to such details, observations of this order are not really open to question, nor do they pose any major epistemological problems. One has to be sensitized to perceive such things, and hard work is the *sine qua non* of criticism, but once one possesses the requisite discipline there is really no point in questioning the possibility, cogency, or validity of such observations. For they are perceptually self-given to attentive reading and need only be pointed out for their existence and importance to be established.

Toward the Text: Percepts and Concepts

The real epistemological problems of interpretation emerge when we try to establish a formal relationship among such perceptions. And that is the essential act. To give coherence to our observations (and to our experience) we must apprehend a functional relationship among the work's components by referring everything we have observed to an informing purpose. But how do we get from the former to the latter?

Once that question arises, interpretation proper begins. And with it all of our observations take on a new, and initially disruptive, focus. For no one observation, nor an indeterminate combination of observations, provides the answer we seek. In fact, once we begin relating observations we become increasingly aware of alternative possibilities which cannot be resolved simply by emphasizing some observations at the expense of others. What are we to make, for instance, of the mythic structures that inform Ike's development in sections 1 through 3 once we juxtapose them with his manifest failures in section 4? Is that relationship melodramatic, tragic, ironic? What is Faulkner's purpose in using ritual and myth? The mere presence of ritual and mythic structures in a work provides conclusive evidence of nothing, and the answer to our question is not given to mere observation.

Discerning the functional relationship among a work's components depends on inferring the purpose which determines their combination. But to make that inference we have to go beyond the parts *qua* parts or their mere sum, for the purpose which informs a work is present in it as an underlying principle of continuous synthesis rather than as one part among many. It is omnipresent within the work but never directly perceived. There is no way we can simply point to it the way we did to any of our preliminary observations, yet until we apprehend it there is no way our observations can cohere and converge.

How do we make such an inference? By an intuitive leap? By critical consensus? Or perhaps through concepts, even, indeed, as a result of theory? Let us consider a fairly typical example. Many critics assume that everything in a literary work somehow contributes to the development of a central theme or "vision." As it is generally employed, the concept of theme is meant to provide a way of relating everything in a literary work to a single end. So understood, theme is not merely one of the "things" one finds in "The

Bear," but the organizing principle of structure which determines everything that one finds there.

But how does one arrive at such a conclusion? Where does the concept of theme as a principle of artistic synthesis come from? Since it is not derived from direct perception, tracking it down requires that we make the Kantian turn. As Kant demonstrated, "percepts without concepts are blind." There are no unmediated perceptions: without theory we should remain forever at the stage of discrete observations awaiting an apperception we can have only if we create. To make the inferences required to relate its constituent parts we must bring a general concept of artistic purpose to the literary work. We can look at the text forever, but, bereft of such a principle, there is no way we can apprehend it as an artistic whole—and since that is so, interpretation must be understood as a conceptual rather than an intuitive or merely perceptual affair.

If there were only one valid theory of form, this realization would not prove particularly troubling. No one objects to using concepts when assured that they are the correct ones or the only ones possible. But do we face such a situation in contemporary criticism? Does theme present the only viable conception of artistic purpose? Is it, self-evidently, the only conceivable way in which the materials of human experience may be organized in art?

Even a casual survey of recent criticism suggests the contrary. In opposition to thematic criticism, R. S. Crane argued that Aristotle's *Poetics* provides the proper critical language for understanding mimetic works such as "The Bear"; following it one may see the particular pleasure such works are designed to produce as the synthesizing principle of their structure. At the same time that Crane wrote, Kenneth Burke was developing a new and more rigorous brand of thematic criticism that enables us to see literary works as "symbolic actions" organized rhetorically to communicate values to an audience; for Burke the Aristotelian concept of "pleasure"—even in as developed an instance as the principle of catharsis—scarcely begins to apprehend the complex rhetorical and social functions that define literary form. Since the Romantic period a significant number of critics have been fascinated by an even richer and more radical possibility: literature is a primary mode of knowing with profound philosophic significance; through literary form alone man is able to attain a nonreductive apprehension of concrete experience in all its existential complexity. The literary work is an immediate realization of the primary cognitive processes through which man apprehends reality. It is a structure of foundational thought directly comparable, as a way of knowing, to science and philosophy.

In schematic terms, some critics conceive form as an emotional *dynamis* imposed upon the matter of experience; others look on it as a structure which gives the content of social life the dramatic form required for its effective communication; while for a third group literary form is the primary mode of concrete knowing and transcends the perspective of social thought. Despite the use of similar terms, contemporary criticism offers us at least three distinct theories of form—and, as a result, three distinct ways of organizing the interpretive enterprise.

If we understand each of the theories rigorously and in its own terms, their fundamental difference becomes their defining characteristic. And that difference presents immense theoretical problems. Let us assume for the moment that we find each theory coherent and plausible and see no way either of eclectically combining them or of giving any one of them a privileged status. Can we accept this situation as such, and, as a consequence, begin moving toward a radical pluralism? It is not easy to do so. A plurality of distinct and exclusive theories of what is presumptively a single entity—in this case literature—has traditionally suggested an antecedent contradiction to philosophic understanding, and stands in the way of the desire for that single grand "theory of literature" that so many of us have been laboring for so long to achieve.

For interpretation it proves even more disruptive, and makes it a problem strictly speaking for perhaps the first time. If there is only one valid conception of artistic purpose, meticulous and patient application of that theory to texts exhausts the problems of interpretation. Once we are faced with a plurality of distinct theories of form, however, the "conflict of interpretations" becomes the primary fact and the ambiguities inherent in any act of interpretation the primary problem. As equally legitimate *hypotheses* each theory must be given its day in court, but how is judgment to be rendered? Since any text is shaped by the concepts we bring to bear upon it, won't the same initial observations provide evidence for disparate inferences? How are we to decide, in a given case, which hypothesis most likely accounts for the "data"? If internal evidence proves to be inherently ambiguous, since it is constituted by the concepts we bring to the text rather than by any privileged perceptions or infallible signs, how can we proceed to test our hypotheses or validate one of them? Just as we were paralyzed without concepts when we tried to move from observation to the apprehension of form, are we not now frustrated by an excess of concepts? If we take seriously the problems implicit in the possibility of a plurality of legitimate theories of form, our initial response must be some mixture of fear and resistance given the multiplication of our questions and tasks. In entering the hermeneutic circle[11] in so radical a manner, we may, in fact, regard it as a tunnel of despair from which there may be no exit.

Toward the Text: The Testing of Hypotheses

Does the logic of interpretation implicit in the general concept of form suggest a way out of these dilemmas? It requires that to be taken seriously any hypothesis must actually account for the text as a whole. It won't do simply to select the "data" one finds most amenable to one's concepts while cloaking that practice with terms like *form, function, structure,* and *purpose.* By demanding that any hypothesis actually live up to the demands of close textual interpretation, shouldn't we be able to discover, in each particular case, sufficient "internal evidence" to justify only one interpretation among many? In the spirit of Wittgenstein, let us "look and see."

To develop the problem I propose the following experiment. Let us view "The Bear" successively in the light of the three distinct theories of form outlined above, beginning each interpretation at the point we reached in completing our preliminary observations about that text. Adopting that procedure will enable us to make the ultimate or synthesizing stage in the act of interpretation our constant focus, thereby making concrete the general concept of form we have advanced. At the same time it will guarantee a discovery of the substantive rather than accidental problems of interpretation, for a genuine "conflict of interpretations" is only possible if critics actually address the same "data" and attempt the same task.

The purpose of the experiment is four-fold: (1) to show what the logic of formal interpretation demands of the critic; (2) to develop three distinct and important theories of form by illustrating how they engage in that common task; (3) to construct, from their battle, a new and radically pluralistic theory of literary form; and, finally (4) to dramatize the problems implicit in any act of interpretation in order to bring us to a new conception of hermeneutics. Taking "The Bear" as our text we will develop all four problems simultaneously in what is, I think, the most concrete way possible.

A final note on procedure. The interpretations which follow are arranged in an order of increasing complexity. Each successive interpretation "begins," in a sense, where the previous one leaves off. And to avoid repetition detailed references to "The Bear" become progressively truncated as we proceed. I discuss "the myth of the birth of the hero," for example, only in the first interpretation yet imply it throughout the second and third interpretations, where, for critics of the latter persuasions, it no doubt takes on its true significance. For these reasons the essay may appear to enact a process of Hegelian *Aufhebung* or progressive uplifting. But that is, as we shall see, only one possibility.

R. S. Crane and the Theory of Emotional Form

Theory

Form for R. S. Crane resides in a work's affective structure. As a mimetic artist, Faulkner's basic problem in writing "The Bear" was to confer a single emotional *dynamis* or power upon the diverse materials of human experience which formed his subject, materials "which would not by nature assume such a particular power to move us."[12] As a principle of artistic synthesis such an emotional *dynamis* provides the rule for selecting and arranging materials as well as the rationale behind their technical manipulation—in this case Faulkner's intricate use of narrative viewpoint, his elaborate style, and his frequently convoluted chronology. As the principle behind the basic artistic choices Faulkner makes in shaping his materials, it is the fundamental cause of the structure his work attains. So understood, our emotional experience of "The Bear" is not a matter of subjective caprice or merely local pleasures, but is a coherent response to a complete action and is determined by William Faulkner far more than it is by us. As a result our emotional response is the index of form, the key whereby we may discover the objectively realized unity of the work's action. It is the principle of the work's plot, if we understand that concept correctly.

To this end Crane lays down the following procedure.[13] To apprehend the form of a mimetic work such as "The Bear" we must analyze the sequence of desires and expectations we are led to form regarding the central character as they are shaped by the complex connection in the work's developing action of three basic evaluations: (1) our perception of the protagonist's moral character in relation to (2) the situation in which he is placed as together they determine our judgment of (3) his responsibility for the actions he initiates. These are the essential causes of our emotional response. The single sequence of interacting desires and expectations they create constitutes the unity of a mimetic work.

Crane's formula contains the conditions of dramatic instability required for an action as well as the moral norms that underlie our emotional involvement in "the fate of characters about whom we are made to care."[14] Thus it is a formula which gives us the only adequate definition of plot: the structuring of those peculiarly artistic emotions—such the tragic catharsis of pity and fear—which are the property of mimetic works as wholes.[15]

Practice

Regarding "The Bear" as the tragic drama of Ike McCaslin's opposing the values he discovers in the wilderness to those of his society only provides a starting point, however. A generic term such as *tragedy*, covering works as different in their emotional effect as *Othello*, *Macbeth*, and *The Death of a Salesman*, is no more than a necessary concession to linguistic limitations. To seize the unique tragic *dynamis* of "The Bear" we need to flesh out that vague designation through a detailed structural analysis of the action which will concretely describe the unified emotional experience the work produces.[16]

If we are correct in seeing Ike's tragedy as the central action of "The Bear"—and it is hard to see any other way of accounting for section 4—two major problems arise. Why do the first three sections in the tale focus on an action with little apparent connection to Ike and why, since his tragedy is completed in section 4, does the story conclude in section 5 with events that occurred several years earlier? These questions are crucial. Any action, by definition, begins by establishing an unstable situation which develops through action and reaction to a conclusion in which, if successful, all the initial instabilities are brought to a resolution. Thus the beginning, middle, and end of the work are the central points around which our moral evaluation and consequent emotional participation turn. Unless we can discover *why* Faulkner structured his materials in the way he did, we can have little assurance that the formula advanced above apprehends the unity of his action.

To see why Faulkner took such a lengthy and circuitous path we must reflect on the immense problems he faced in constructing the character of Ike, a young man devoid of any qualities save aspiration and openness, who will espouse a wholly naturalistic ethic which will bring him into fundamental conflict with his society. Such a character must be constructed from the ground up. And to create the response he is after Faulkner must make us strongly sympathize with Ike's affirmation of that ethic while forcing us at the same time to realize the tragic possibilities implicit in that choice. If he fails to satisfy any of these conditions, the situation will lack tragic potential. Thus while the formation of Ike's character must be the primary focus, that development must continually foreshadow implicit tensions. The former shapes our desires, the latter creates our expectations. Together they form the affective continuity of sections 1 through 3.

Everything connected with the wilderness and the hunt exists, as it were, for the formation of Ike's character. Faulkner presents the wilderness in mythic and ritual terms as a setting of values that are both natural, permanent, and normative. Once there, men are "ordered and compelled by and within the wilderness" to an activity which confers upon them a special dignity and lifts them momentarily above their society—a society which fears and abhors the wilderness and has already begun to destroy it. Because Faulkner so clearly underscores the educational significance of the wilderness for the formation and testing of human character, we desire Ike's "novitiate" to it for the sake of his own moral growth.

Faulkner maximizes that response by describing Ike's initiation in terms strongly reminiscent of "the myth of the birth of the hero." Sam Fathers, as shaman, articulates the conditions Ike must fulfill in his quest for manhood. He must cast off all the trappings of his civilization—gun, watch, and compass—and undergo great hardships merely to enter the numinous presence of Old Ben, who embodies the wild immortal spirit that defines the wilderness.

Thus Faulkner employs ritual and myth as a means of narrative magnification in order to invest Ike's development with ethical significance.[17] His use of point of view performs a similar function. In the first few pages of the story he employs a narrative voice attuned to the mythic, ritual, and heroic aspects of the wilderness in order to increase our sense of the ethical importance of Ike's initiation. Then, by limiting himself to Ike's viewpoint he arranges subsequent events around Ike's meditative participation in them. Seeing the events through Ike's eyes, we are caught up with him in the movement of his finest aspirations. There is perhaps no better way to create an eventual compassion for a character's plight than by establishing such a close initial identification with him. By subsequently developing the hunt through Ike's eyes, Faulkner keeps it focused on his aspiration toward the virtues of courage, pride, humility, endurance, and spirit he finds manifested in it. For all its inherent interest, the final reference of the hunt is to the harsh choice Ike's participation in it will demand of him.

To give the action that focus, Faulkner plants the seeds of future conflict in the midst of Ike's initiation. Always on the horizon of Ike's choice stands his society. More than once Sam Fathers emphasizes that the unalterable opposition between the wilderness and that society presents Ike with a fundamental choice. Moreover, each stage of Ike's development is marked by an implicit rejection of his society. Yet the way Faulkner depicts Southern society serves primarily to reinforce our desire that Ike pursue the wilderness. For except when it vaguely testifies to the greatness of the wilderness, that society is presented in an unflattering light: "puny humans," having lost touch with the wilderness, in a mixture of fear and abhorrence, attempt to destroy it. Our perception of their animating greed and loss of dignity strongly increases our sympathy with Ike's heroic aspirations, while alerting us to the hard consequences implicit in his choice. As this pattern develops we become painfully conscious of a tragic discrepancy between the values to which Ike aspires and the world in which he will have to actualize them. Thus we are deeply concerned over the fate of those values at the very moment in which we are being most powerfully enlisted on their behalf. Being so moved, we experience Ike's initiation as the generation of a potential tragedy. And that is not the whole story.

To make that conflict more than the melodrama of a purely heroic character being frustrated by an evil society, Faulkner must depict Ike's character from yet another angle. His aspiration toward the wilderness must reveal a fundamental instability in his character and this flaw, more than anything else, must be the basis for his later failure. For good reasons Faulkner must keep this concern in the background; emphasizing the defects in Ike's character at the start would undermine the initial sympathy Faulkner wishes to create for him. Yet unless those defects are apparent to some degree, sections 1 through 3 and section 4 will strike us as glaringly discontinuous. The way he alerts us to Ike's defects is one of the subtlest aspects of Faulkner's artistry in sections 1 through 3.

Avoiding any direct authorial commentary which would disrupt the movement of the work, Faulkner has us infer the defects in Ike's character from the limitations in his viewpoint. By noting the discrepancies between what Ike sees and what he fails to see, we become aware of the deficiencies in his character.

We perceive, for example, Ike's benign neglect of the many tensions discussed above. By the end of section 1 Ike has made a choice which required both a total surrender to the wilderness and an equally thoroughgoing rejection of his society. As the hunt develops, both choices grow without reservation—and at the expense of any qualified awareness. Ike remains blind to anything but the most heroic qualities of the hunt. His response to that action, a combination of what he half-creates and half-perceives out of a youthful rush of unqualified affection, finally tells us more about his character than it does about anything else. An instinctive discontent with his society and an equally romantic naivete about the values of the wilderness provide a constant backdrop to Ike's quest. For these reasons his identification with the wilderness develops without check or balance. He assumes that it is a field of elemental values that are to be emulated without modification and honored to the exclusion of any other concerns. At each stage his choice involves, accordingly, a growing rejection of his society *and* a further unquestioning immersion in the wilderness, which leaves him oblivious to the consequences of his choice.

Yet the beginning of section 2 presents him with a dilemma. "So he should have hated and feared Lion." For Lion signifies not only the coming end of the hunt—which Ike would like to see continue forever—but also the need for a more mature and qualified response to the wilderness. Lion is characterized by an "impersonal malignance like some natural force." He loves "no man and no thing," and his "cold and grim indomitable determination" is markedly inhuman. His courage, will, and desire "to endure beyond all imaginable limits of flesh" are too large and too instinctive to provide a model for man, and his singleminded dedication "to overtake and slay" brings out a harshness in marked contrast to the pristine and benign face the wilderness presents in section 1. The romantic quality of the wilderness, however, remains uppermost in Ike's mind. What he cannot understand—or what is disturbing—he simply suppresses. He resolves the dilemma of Lion by passively enduring it.

So he should have hated and feared Lion. Yet he did not. It seemed to him that there was a fatality in it. It seemed to him that something, he didn't know what, was beginning; had already begun. It was like the last act on a set stage. It was the beginning of the end of something, he didn't know what except that he would not grieve. He would be humble and proud that he had been found worthy to be a part of it too or even just to see it too.[18]

Only in section 4 will Ike attempt to conceptualize his experience, and only then will Faulkner make explicit the flaws of character that shaped his response.

Once attuned to these traits in his character, we experience sections 1 through 3 as the initiation of a tragic drama, for we experience a conflict within our moral estimation of the character in whose support our affections have been so strongly enlisted. We see Ike's idealism both positively and negatively. A romantic flight not merely from his society but from any mature frame of conduct informs Ike's aspiration toward the wilderness. He desires a wholly natural ethic that can be had by immersion and that will remain impenetrable to circumstances. The very values to which he aspires, and his understanding of how they relate to conduct, betray the romantic and quixotic naivete at the core of his character. Such controlling flaws of character will make it difficult for him to act significantly upon the manifest wrongs of his society—yet his maturation in the wilderness requires that he assume responsibility for that situation.

Thus within the positive movement of Ike's initiation Faulkner establishes intricate patterns of external and internal conflict. Unless we experience all three structures simultaneously in our reading we shall not have the complex of desires and expectations required for a proper response to section 4. It is not a question—as it is for so many critics—of choosing among these structures, but rather of holding them all together in a single experience. The ethical significance of the wilderness remains the primary, though increasingly ambivalent, emphasis throughout sections 1 through 3. For the most part the negative representation of Ike's society reinforces our desire that Ike pursue the wilderness. But it also foreshadows a possible reversal of Ike's desires. And that tension, in turn, is reinforced by the defects we perceive in his character. As the story proceeds we experience a painful distance between what transpires in the wilderness and the conditions of human, social conduct.

All three patterns coalesce at the end of section 3. When Ike participates, to a deliberately unspecified degree, in the ritual death of Sam—an act which is far from ethically unambiguous—his unquestioning identification with the primitivism of the wilderness is complete. The necessary and direct result is the opposition to his cousin with which the section concludes. Ike's education is complete, and the tragic action proper begun, once the conflict that has been present throughout his development becomes explicit:

> 'Leave him alone!' he cried. 'Goddamn it! Leave him alone!'
>   4.
>   then he was twenty-one.[19]

If we experience these three structures together we move into section 4 strongly disposed in Ike's favor, applauding his desire for responsibility, and hoping he can actualize the values found in the wilderness in a society badly in need of correction, yet expecting that it is not to be and that Ike will bear the primary responsibility for that failure.

To avoid melodrama Faulkner's basic problem in section 4 is to make us experience Ike's defeat as a consequence not merely of the evils he faces but as the issue of his own moral flaws. Failure to dramatize both sides of the matter will disrupt the tragic power of the story. While preserving our sympathy for Ike, we must move from respect for his attempt at atonement through our developing awareness of his defects to the eventually harsh judgment we are led to form of his character, without sacrificing our sympathy for him. Otherwise his defeat will merely be one "in which nobody loses anything of value. . . . and, worst of all, without pity or compassion."[20]

Faulkner's decision to incorporate into the section the entire history of the South and of Ike's family and, moreover, to reveal these materials only in the course of Ike's attempt to explain to Cass his decision to relinquish his inheritance, poses immense problems of orientation for the reader. But it is a brilliant dramatic response to Faulkner's central problem. For in this way the wealth of historical materials that define Ike's situation are given through—and exist in—his moral response to them. Thus the drama of his character remains the center of attention. It is as if the entire history of the South and of his family, carried up into Ike's debate with

Cass, formed a single, grand drama pointed to Ike's attempt at atonement. The movement from Ike's rebuke of Cass at the end of section 3 to its equivalent in the opening lines of section 4 ("then he was 21.") through the one unbroken sentence that contains the tragic history of his people and, from there, to the pathetic conclusion of Ike's marriage thus forms the inseparable sequence of necessary connections that define his tragedy.

By juxtaposing the revelation of Ike's flaws with the evils of his situation, Faulkner assures that we continue to be moved in two ways throughout the section. In view of the enormous wrongs he tries to rectify, we maintain our sympathy for Ike even though his defects become an increasing burden to us. The family ledger and the history of the South trace a recurrent pattern of inhumanity that cries out for restitution and human care. We never doubt the imperative of acting on that situation, and we find Cass' gradualism the unconvincing mask for his fundamental indifference. Our attachment to the values Ike found in the wilderness grow in degree with each revelation we are given of the inhumanity that marks the history of the South. By magnifying that inhumanity, Faulkner reinforces our initial sympathy for Ike's attempt to make restitution. No matter how futile Ike's actions become, his moral desire to reverse that pattern of inhumanity commands our respect while his failure increases our pain.

Yet the evils of that situation are of such a magnitude that we also demand a truly effective action—not one that merely affirms the rectitude of one's intent or the mere power "to endure." By these more stringent criteria, which the situation dictates, Ike's inadequacy is apparent, for throughout section 4 his fundamental response is one of progressive flight. Rather than lead him to a more mature, pragmatic activity, his failures always lead him further away from meaningful action. He moves from direct action (arranging the payment of Fonsiba's inheritance), to quixotic action (relinquishing the land to Cass), to abject flight swiftly followed by fatalistic submission. In attempting to preserve his "moral" purity from contamination by circumstance he refuses, significantly, to act upon the very evils he opposes.

Rather than representing his actions in detail, however, Faulkner focuses the drama on Ike's attempt to explain to his cousin his decision to relinquish his inheritance—and, in effect, his responsibility. That artistic choice is a brilliant one because it centers the entire section in a representation of the basic causes determining

Ike's failure. As so often happens in Faulkner, the profusion of words is a substitute for deeds. What his actions alone might not indicate, Ike's "philosophizing" makes clear. The large amount of abstract quasi-philosophical and theological discussion in the commissary does not represent a wealth of reflection on Faulkner's part—as critics in search of "meanings" and spokesmen would have it—but rather the depth of confusion on Ike's part. As Aristotle argues, "thought" is strictly subordinate to character and action in a mimetic work. Faulkner uses "thought" brilliantly here to dramatize the essential defects in Ike's character. His rambling arguments betray pompous posturing, sentimentality, moral absolutism, and simple confusion—the very flaws of character manifested in the quixotic self-indulgence and lack of pragmatic flexibility that permeate his actions. Both will find their fitting complement, by simple inversion, in his subsequent fatalism.

After recording his early attempts at restitution, the discussion resumes. We desire that his experience enable Ike to bring matters to some clarification. Yet we expect and receive only further evidence of his confusion. He admits as much himself, significantly, at the very moment when he recalls the power of the wilderness. Rather than adapt its values to his situation he can only reflect, nostalgically, that everything "seemed to him simpler" when in nature.[21] That is, precisely, the tragic fact. Unable to bring the values of the wilderness to bear upon his situation, he can only desire a permanent return to the simplified world it provided. Ike's immersion in the eternal, natural order of the wilderness has made it impossible for him to understand his society or act significantly in it. By attempting a direct transfer of its values he becomes, ironically, more primitive with each failure.

After the debate ends in mutual misunderstanding, the final paragraphs trace Ike's tragedy in the ensuing years to its brief and foregone conclusion. In carpentry he achieves no more than a parodic "imitation of Christ," and ironically contributes, by that activity, to the destruction of the wilderness. The final scene, representing the pathetic outcome of his marriage, brings to a fitting end the pattern of mutual misunderstanding that has characterized all of section 4. Ike forms no bond of values with his wife. Consequently, her desire to possess all he has tried to relinquish triumphs in her seduction of him. He surrenders with the comforting fatalistic admission that "we were all born lost," thereby confirming a tragic loss of purpose devoid of recognition.

From this perspective section 5 may be seen as a fitting emotional, if not chronological, completion to the tragedy. In order to bring us to a proper estimation of the wilderness, it eulogizes the whole way of life that has been tragically represented in Ike. Despite Ike's failure, the lure of the wilderness remains. The corruption of Ike's society is so total that we have not ceased to desire that the values of the wilderness—which provide the only ethical frame of reference dramatized in the work—might relate to that society in some more responsible way. But the wilderness to which Ike returns in section 5 is a place that is already effectively dead. Having experienced his tragedy, we now see in the wilderness what he failed to see.

Faulkner emphasizes the pastness of the wilderness in a variety of ways. The railroad signals its coming extinction and drives the replica of Old Ben, a young bear, to near insanity in an absurd parody of the hunt. Only the graves remain—and Ike can return to them only for the moment. His nostalgic vision of the cyclic permanence of the wilderness is broken by the sound of Boon frantically hammering his rifle, equally incapable of adapting to a rapidly changing world. The man of the woods no longer knows how to act in them, and has already surrendered to the lust for possession that defines the encroaching society. Pounding his gun, with "the frantic abandon of a madman," in a fury to possess all the squirrels, and without looking up at the comrade who comes to join him, Boon shouts: "Get out of here! Don't touch them! Don't touch a one of them! They're mine!"

Ike in society betrayed the same frantic inability to comprehend historical change. His is the tragedy of a man living in the past. And that tragedy appears, in the retrospect of section 5, the mere aftermath of a way of life already dead. By his use of reversed chronology Faulkner gives a poignant inevitability to Ike's trag-edy—and offers us an extended ironic reflection upon it. It was all, in effect, over three years before the beginning and eight years before the end of its unraveling in section 4. Section 5 is a eulogistic *Dies Irae* for the wilderness and for Ike McCaslin, full of compas-sion for his failure but secure in the judgment of it. Thus it completes our emotional experience of "The Bear."

Kenneth Burke's Rhetorical Theory of Literature

Theory

For Kenneth Burke, literature is the most complex mode of rhetorical activity. The purpose of literature is to communicate a coherent framework of attitudes and motives to an audience by involving them in a symbolic action. The artist begins with a disruptive conflict within the social order and proceeds to transform that situation by dramatizing it. Our participation in that action engenders in us a new order of attitudes and motives. A work like Euripides' The Trojan Women, for example, "purges" the entire city of Athens of the destructive motives recently expressed in the sack of Melos and instills in its audience the new order of motives that is symbolized in its heroic action.[22]

To understand the revolution Burke works in the traditions of rhetorical criticism, we must rethink the concepts of content and form in dramatic terms. Communication, for Burke, is a far more complex affair than traditional rhetorical theory—"what oft was thought, but ne'er so well expressed"—is able to handle. For rather than simply presenting a body of abstract commonplaces or quasi-propositional themes that are enhanced but in no way essentially altered by the writer's verbal and mimetic power, communication is an inherently dramatic activity involving the basic social needs and functions of the psyche and transpiring primarily through our engagement in symbolic actions. In taking deliberative speech and the communication of a specific proposal as its model, traditional rhetorical theory understands communication in what is merely its simplest instance.[23]

Attitudes, motives, and frames of action rather than commonplaces, themes, or abstract ideas are the primary content of communication. The primary way in which they are formed, moreover, is through our response to those symbols (the cross, the flag) and dramatic actions (the passion of our Savior, the revolution of 1776) in which the social self seeks and finds identity. The term persuasion connotes a change in belief or intellectual position as a result of rhetorical argument. To signify the more dynamic social process from which persuasion arises and on which, finally, it depends, Burke replaces it with the term identification.[24] We mull over proposals, but we identify with symbols.

The rhetorician finds his true subject in the dynamic principles of social conduct which inhere in action rather than in thought; and because those primary attitudes and motives are inseparable from the mimetic forms in which they reside, literature becomes, for him, the paradigm of communication. Since there is no longer any way, either in social theory or in interpreting literature, to separate what is communicated from the way in which it is communicated, rhetoric must become part of a general theory of drama which will be based on a grammar of the motives which structure social action. Rather than summarizing an author's views on a number of discrete topics—Faulkner's attitude toward the Negro, his conception of nature, his view of the hero—which may be loosely held together, if at all, under the general category of his "vision," the rhetorician's primary task in interpreting literature is to demonstrate how the action of the literary work structures the motives that make up the social being of rhetorical man. Even in its most concrete forms, thematic criticism fails to apprehend the real locus of rhetorical activity in literature and will continue to do so as long as it continues to treat the literary action as if it were finally little more than a means of developing a body of propositions (however existential) or a "vision" which can be restated in abstract terms. The search for themes scarcely makes contact with the real rhetorical process, and R. S. Crane's alternative theory of emotional form doesn't take us much further. Crane focuses on action, to be sure, but his affective theory hardly begins to deal with the complex nature of our participation in a work's action and severely compromises the end to which that participation proceeds, for our involvement in literature is at base a process of identification which instills in us the attitudes and motives that shape social conduct.

To develop the categories needed to interpret that process Burke sets up the pentad of scene, agent, act, agency, and purpose, the five categories that constitute any action. He then establishes a number of ratios among those terms in order to express the different ways in which the terms can determine one another: scene, for example, being the container of agent in a determinism with agent performing the opposite function in a philosophy like existentialism. Burke's purpose in studying the pentad and its ratios is to formulate a logic of all the possibilities that make up the drama of social action.[25] As a grammar of the motives that shape communal living, the pentad simultaneously develops a theory of the social content of communication and of the dramatic forms through which communication proceeds. We must see it from both perspectives in order to understand the organic relationship Burke establishes between form and content and the consequent focus upon action which so notably distinguishes his theory and practice from that of traditional rhetorical critics.

As a philosophic project, the pentad enables Burke in *A Grammar of Motives* to reinterpret the major philosophic systems sociologically and ideologically by discovering the implicit view of motivation each contains. For example, Hobbes, standing at the beginning of the modern age, reduces everything to scene, while Marx, hoping for the reversal of that tendency, roots everything in the act of revolution. Corresponding to the five terms of the pentad there are five basic modes of philosophic thought—naturalism, idealism, realism, pragmatism, and mysticism. By basing their thought, in turn, on one term in the pentad, each of these philosophies provides a distinct focus on the nature of action. So understood, each contributes significantly to our understanding of social life as an ongoing drama. For philosophy is no more than ideology—and no less. Its final purpose is suasive: to make us identify with the theory of motives it propounds. Through the pentad Burke makes philosophy a moment in a broader social theory.

As a social theory, in turn, the pentad enables Burke to locate the basic sources of conflict that plague the social order. In a healthy society, by definition, the five loci of motivation reciprocally engender the common good. But the pattern for such an order, like Plato's ideal state, exists only in heaven. Conflict among motives is the primary fact of social life. Rather than a system of checks and balances, motives meet, most often, in a struggle for existence. Either in maintaining themselves like Spinoza's *conatus*, or in developing their inherent powers, the loci continually modify one another. Thus their relationship generates constant tensions and in many ways each locus strives to become absolute at the expense of a vibrant social order. Yet action is the substance in which they inhere and is constituted by the process of continuous, reciprocal transformation enacted by these its modes.[26] As a result, social life must be conceived as an ongoing drama, and the dynamic character of the motives that shape it make it an open-ended historical process which operates without theological sanction.[27]

To carry that realization into the historical present, Marx demonstrated that each advance in productive capacity—an agency that becomes scene—revolutionizes the entire social fabric: capitalism and human alienation are of a piece. While Marx placed his faith in the possibility of a revolutionary act that would transform that scene, our time witnesses the totalizing thrust of a technological agency inimical to change: it threatens to become a total scene which, sacrificing the human to the mechanical, will make any action that could alter its basic tendencies a priori impossible.[28] Its purpose, as Jacques Ellul demonstrates, is to reproduce itself with an ever-increasing reduction of everything to the single cult of efficiency.[29] The conflicts inherent in this situation determine many of the problems of the contemporary rhetorical artist. If he is to recover human possibilities, his task lies, not in Utopian flight from the situation, but in creating dramas in which the directions for historical reversal will be concretely established and engendered.[30]

Practice

"The Bear" presents one of the conservative artist's characteristic strategies when faced with this situation. Turning to a natural world of values still present in his rural society, Faulkner places those values in simple juxtaposition to the dehumanizing tendencies of modern life. It is a simple strategy, but Faulkner's purpose in using it is far from simple, as we shall discover by interpreting the work along the lines Burke sets down.

Faced with a disruptive historical situation, "The Bear" returns to nature in search of a new and restorative order of motives. But rather than impose those values upon his historical situation in a quixotic manner, Faulkner dramatizes the flaws endemic to such a project. The relationship between the work's two central symbolic actions—the hunt and Ike's refusal to accept his inheritance—is profoundly ironic: the naturalistic perspective Ike adopts proves futile as a principle of significant action in the historical scene to which it is opposed.

In dramatizing Ike's tragic failure to actualize the values he cherishes, Faulkner effects a complex transformation in our attitudes. In sections 1 through 3 he leads us to identify with Ike's aspiration to create from the values he finds in the wilderness a frame of acceptance[31] that will enable him to redeem his society. In witnessing his failure and recognizing its causes, that identification undergoes reversal in section 4. Structurally, sections 1 through 3 and section 4 present, in effect, a simple opposition of thesis and antithesis without the possibility of synthesis. Thus, purged of Ike's Utopian inclinations, section 5 gives us a new perspective on the wilderness, thereby forcing us to face our situation in a more forthright fashion. Once we adopt that perspective, the work's rhetorical process achieves completion.

To explain that process in depth we must focus on the grammatical structure of the work: to understand the process of identification through which our attitudes are transformed we have to locate with precision the motivational conflict on which the action of the work turns. In structuring "The Bear" Faulkner exploits a strategy of "essentializing simplification"[32] in order to bring two orders of motives—the wilderness and Ike's historical situation—into the most thoroughgoing, though contemplative, opposition possible. As I will now try to show, the whole work is based grammatically on what Burke terms the scene-agent ratio.[33] That ratio defines the ways in which an agent and his actions may be derived from his scene—from the givens of his environment, heredity, and place in history. As Burke points out, such a scenic grammar is logically determined by the relationship of container to thing-contained. In using such a logic Faulkner depicts his two scenes, nature and society, as the source and ground of the total motivational order each generates.

Faulkner employs this strategy for two sharply opposed, yet thoroughly connected, rhetorical reasons. Initially it enables him to create our identification with the universal ritual and mythic values that the wilderness contains; subsequently it forces us, by the same grammatical logic, to recognize the impossibility of imposing those values on a society which is just as encompassing, frustrates natural instincts, prevents heroic action, and reduces all motives to the lust for possession. Because it is scenically based, the opposition of the two orders precludes any meaningful contact.

From the beginning Faulkner forces us to adopt an ambivalent attitude toward the wilderness as a source of motives. The natural scene described in section 1 is a world of the past already "doomed." Yet that fact is purposely kept in the background, for Faulkner's primary intention in sections 1 through 3 is to create our identification with the wilderness. To catch us up in the movement of Ike's initiation, he presents the wilderness as the container of permanent moral possibilities. Significantly, Ike witnesses "his own birth" as an agent only when he relinquishes himself completely to that scene. In the central symbolic action of section 1, Ike (agent) sheds all the contaminating agencies (gun, watch, and compass) of his society in order to identify himself with the wilderness in a condition of total dependence so that it might fill him, through Old Ben, with a vision of purpose.

At the end of section 1, however, Ike has merely entered the presence of the bear. In the course of the subsequent yearly pursuits of the bear, he enters more deeply into the mystery and progresses from the partial to the total identification with the wilderness required for him to become its human embodiment in section 4.

Three events structure this development: (1) the yearly ceremonial hunts of Old Ben build up the ethical significance of the wilderness; (2) Ike purges himself of the remaining social attitudes that stand in the way of his total identification with that scene; and (3) his society is progressively excluded from the central act that will reveal its essence.

Ike's education thus proceeds through a growing exclusion from his society and an equally unquestioning immersion in the wilderness. From the rather contemplative mood of section 1—Ike's passive vision of the bear's sheer magnificence—the wilderness becomes for Ike a scene of primitive and elemental forces engaged in heroic ritual activity. When he realizes, by the end of section 2, that he should neither hate nor fear Lion, his sympathetic identification with "the wild, immortal" and "indomitable spirit" of the wilderness is complete. He places himself wholly at the disposal of the event which embodies the essence of the scene, the hunt, because he sees manifested in that event the virtues of courage, endurance, pride, and humility necessary for manhood.

We are largely one with him in this movement. When compared to the heroic action in progress, Ike's kinsmen always appear "puny and insignificant." The scenic hierarchy that structures the tale forces us to make such judgments because it creates a norm in which every character in the story is evaluated by the degree of his participation in the primitive mystique of the hunt. Sam identifies with it fully and is Ike's mentor and spiritual father. The instinctive love Boon has for Lion confers courage on him. General Compson and Major de Spain, who later sells the wilderness, stand midway: they salute the hunt but are unable to identify with it fully. Cass, Ike's guardian, is too preoccupied with his farm and his investments to grasp the importance of the event Ike insists on participating in.[34] The swampers and the townsmen only understand the hunt as a "yearly spectacle." And only the select, worthy few will witness its culminating mysteries.

Once these patterns of initiation and exclusion are firmly established, we are ready to participate, with Ike, in the imperatives he finds in the end of the hunt. By living out the harsh yet heroic rhythm of nature that has dignified them, Ben and Lion achieve fruition in the "lover-like embrace" of death. Sam, the man most in harmony with that event, sees that its significance stretches "further than the death of a bear and the dying of a dog" and takes upon himself the mystery of things by joining himself to the natural cycle which achieves in death its completion. As he hoped, Ike does not grieve. He accepts death as a necessary part of the heroic life he wishes to emulate. Though his understanding is not on a par with Sam's, he knows that Sam must die and, without protest, helps Sam fulfill his wish for a ritual death. Of greater importance, he is now ready to assume the burden of manhood that participation in these symbolic acts has conferred on him. Significantly, his first act affirming that more heroic way of life is the opposition to his cousin with which the section concludes. The wilderness, now embodied in the character of Ike, confronts what his formation by it has excluded; this, the true completion of Ike's education, is prelude, for him and for us, to the essential conflict of the work.

The unraveling of that conflict in thought and in action forms the substance of section 4. At its beginning Ike poses the central problem. He wishes, by bringing the values of the wilderness to bear upon his society, to take up the burden of guilt and restitution which is his heritage. The wilderness has provided the ethical perspective that enables him to understand his historical situation and should, as a principle of action, enable him to transform it. He seeks, in effect, to impose the values of one scene upon another.

That project is replete with potential reversals. As an agent Ike is essentially the walking embodiment of his scene. Yet he must bring its values to bear upon the alien world which has been so pointedly excluded from his formation. Should that scene demonstrate the same totalizing power over agents, the very values he embodies will find no reference point there.

In the debate with his cousin, Ike reveals his understanding—and its inherent limitations. To justify the nature of his choice and to define the goal of his activity, he employs, as we might expect, a scenic grammar. He portrays the wilderness and his society as comprehensive and exclusive orders of value. Southern society is without redeeming possibilities, the wilderness is a normative world of ultimate values. Invoking divine purpose to confirm his action, Ike places his success or failure in extreme and apocalyptic terms: to succeed he must, through direct action, totally transform his society.

Any action, however, requires, at the very least, an agency that corresponds to its purpose.[35] (Think, for example, of a concerned journalist in a society in which the press has been effectively silenced.) Earlier, to enter the wilderness, Ike had cast off the products of his society (gun, watch, and compass); now, ironically, he tries to transform that society by using the agency which is its animating motive—money. But action based on money inevitably generates its corruptions. Rather than transforming the scene, it perpetuates it. As a further irony, the very people Ike tries to aid, Fonsiba and her husband, are striving, at the expense of the natural dignity he finds in them, to become part of that economic order.

A scenic grammar is inexorable. Being exclusive down to their very agencies—money and ritual—the two worlds can come into no direct contact: yet without such contact dramatic transformation is impossible. For Ike, however, the choice must remain exclusive. After his initial failures, all he recognizes is that his actions must henceforth be wholly symbolic. Rather than modify his scenic grammar, he retreats more completely into it. But the renunciation of his possessions ironically propagates, rather than retards, the corruptions Ike would oppose: Cass gladly receives the gift and knows precisely what to do with it. Ike's stylized imitation of Christ, in turn, can have no positive effect on his world because it addresses no one in it. Rather than symbolic action leading "towards a better life"[36]—a frame of acceptance and creative action—it is a "frame of rejection" that confirms Ike in his loss of the power to act. It leaves him, in fact, powerless before the motives he once opposed. Ike ends a spent agent, engulfed by another agent, his wife, who embodies the lust for possession which characterizes Southern society. Rather than reaching a mystical fulfillment similar to the "marriage" of Ben and Lion, Ike's revolt culminates in fatalism, seduction, and the failure of love. Given the scenic basis of the conflict dramatized in section 4, things could end no other way. Any attempt to relate two scenes so opposed can only drive them further apart. Any agent formed solely by a scene cannot act meaningfully outside it.

For all of its technical convolution and historical detail, the rhetorical structure of section 4 is finally quite simple. From the exclusive opposition of two scenes we move to a direct action which naturally fails to bring them together. Subsequently, one can preserve the extreme opposition of the two scenes only by engaging in "purely" symbolic action. Since we are *in* the second scene, however, by the very logic of scenic thought it necessarily triumphs. Having no way of acting upon a scene, there is no way to withstand it. Through Ike's failure our attitude toward an excessive reliance on scene undergoes transformation: trust in it as a ground of motives has been subjected to a complete reversal. Thanks to Ike we now see the attitude he represents from a tragic rather than a romantic perspective, and thus are prepared to adopt a more responsible attitude toward historical existence.

Ike is denied that recognition. We are not. It forms the substance of section 5. Rather than a postlude tacked on to the work, section 5 is its true rhetorical conclusion. In it Faulkner develops the restorative awareness Ike's tragedy has prepared. From the pessimistic nadir on which section 4 concludes, we return to the scene which generated Ike's tragedy—but with a new awareness. After having identified with the wilderness in sections 1 through 3, we have experienced in section 4 the thoroughgoing failure of the agent who embodies its values. Realizing that his defeat resulted primarily from his extreme reliance on a scenic grammar, we are prepared to adopt a more complex attitude toward that very scene. Moving directly from section 3 to section 5, as in an earlier version of the story,[37] would have been grammatically proper since everything in the work is scenically based. But we would not have experienced the conflict imagistically enacted in section 5 with the clarity and breadth of context which the intervention of section 4 provides. The two scenes, formerly met in dubious battle, are now presented in pure and universal images that express the inevitable outcome of their conflict: the railroad that terrifies the young bear, the graves, the snake, and Boon frantically hammering his dismembered rifle. These images symbolically summarize the entire work.

Cleansed of Ike's illusions, we return to the wilderness in a reflective mood. We view the two scenes pictured there as fundamental contexts of human motivation and adopt a critical stance toward their opposition. We return to the scene prepared, in effect, to see the inherent limitations of the scenic grammar that has structured the work. To understand Ike's tragedy in its ultimate terms it is crucial that we return to the scene which gave it birth and lent it dignity. For Ike's tragedy is only a "moment" in a larger tragedy—the coming destruction of the wilderness. That tragedy— the disappearance of a whole way of life—must be the final focus.

Faulkner's use of reversed chronology addresses all of these problems. The world Ike tried to transfer to the present in section 4 was already effectively dead prior to the attempt. Yet it, not he, is the proper object of eulogy—and the tense appropriate is the past. The pastness of the wilderness, which Ike refused to recognize, is here presented as its defining quality. Major de Spain has sold the land to the lumber company. This is the last time Ike can return, and the railroad which takes him back is no longer "harmless." Witness its reduction of the infant bear to near madness: the hunt survives only in a ludicrous parody. Ike returns to a place of death. It is no longer a scene of heroic activity or a human abode, but a graveyard already fast disappearing. Its magnificance can be recaptured in memory alone, and then only for the moment. In the graves of Sam and Lion lie buried a whole world of mythic, ritual, and heroic values which preserve their immortality only in the purely physical cycle of the seasons, not in a vital symbolic action which could inform human conduct. The final eulogistic recognition is appropriately under the sign of death. Without premeditation, obscurely foreshadowing his own fate, Ike salutes the snake "evocative of all knowledge and an old weariness and of pariahhood and of death" in the "old tongue" taught him by Sam Fathers: " 'Chief,' he said: 'Grandfather.' " The final vision Ike is given— that of Boon's frantic self-division—parallels and foreshadows his own collapse at the end of section 4. Neither man can escape the possessiveness that defines their society.

Nor can the wilderness, and to complete the rhetorical action of "The Bear" Faulkner in section 5 depicts the wilderness as itself inherently historical and subject to the actions of man. It is no longer viable as a source of motives; only its sheer physical qualities escape the tyranny of human will. Tragically, it has become no more than the material for productive development by a society single-mindedly dedicated to the principle of plunder and greed. In section 4 nature proved tragically inadequate as a guide to action in the present; now we see it subjected to an eventual disappearance in that present. Nature is historically dead. Economics is the sole god of modern life.

It is from this perspective that Faulkner's "cultural primitivism" must be understood. The concluding section of "The Bear" both completes Faulkner's indictment of modern society and recognizes, though with great nostalgia, that the natural order it has so powerfully evoked for that purpose is a vanished world that can no longer inform conduct in the present. Faulkner shares Ike's horror of present history and instinctively turns toward the only other framework of motives his culture provides. But through Ike's failure he dramatizes the impossibility of a return to nature: total reliance on the formative power of scene leaves an agent like Ike the victim of a complete defeat by the forces of modern history. For Faulkner the disappearance of the possibilities Ike symbolizes is an unshakable historical fact. Ike is scapegoat, and through him "we are cleansed thanks to his overstating of our case."[38]

Whether history contains its own "dialectic" is another question, and one that the scenic grammar of "The Bear" has not enabled Faulkner to pose, for to discover transformative possibilities in history requires a radically different grammar of motives—one based on agent rather than scene and purposive activity rather than quixotic nostalgia. To develop it Faulkner would have to adopt a Marxist perspective strongly existential in its orientation:[39] since the oppressed in his society remain in a prehistorical condition of passive endurance, the organization of opposition must come from agents who would freely recognize their responsibility for undertaking revolutionary acts directed upon the reification and class character of that society, rather than agents enamored with the desire for return to an encompassing ahistorical scene.

That perspective, of course, is one that Faulkner was never able to attain. What he has developed—and it is a major achievement—is a critical awareness of the inherent limitations in a scenic grammar. Rather than a "frame of acceptance" and guide for creative activity in a disruptive historical situation, such a grammar can only serve, finally, as a rhetorical vehicle for maximizing its horror. Though Faulkner rightly persists in honoring naturally good characters, some of whom endure, the larger question toward which his works move is always that of how to prevail—in history.[40] "The Bear" forces us to recognize that nature cannot be our Vergil in that task. In Ike's tragedy and the coming destruction of the wilderness, man's persistent desire to find his identity in an order of natural motives—whether natural law, Rousseau's benign primitivism, mythic universals of the psyche, or simply those "little, nameless, unremembered acts of kindness and of love" that form the "best portion of a good man's life"—bows before the unshakable facts and harsh imperatives of history.

"The Bear" confesses a nostalgia for the past which becomes all the more powerful by reason of the irretrievable pastness of that past. A lesser artist would have "overcome" that recognition. Faulkner makes it the center of his rhetoric. Rather than providing a secure thematic message, a confident resolution of our problems, or a detailed program for action, "The Bear" attempts the far more difficult rhetorical task of destroying our illusions, maximizing our discontent, and delivering us over to a painful self-questioning. It is a rhetoric in the problem-posing rather than problem-solving mode. And since Faulkner endeavors not only to change our views but to transform our attitudes, his is a rhetoric which depends for its success on our engagement in a drama. A rhetorical criticism which goes to literary works seeking extractable themes will always fail to apprehend the nature and vitality of that more dynamic method of communication.

Dialectical Poetics

Theory

According to the dialectical view, which has gained ascendance since the Romantic period, literature is a special mode of knowing which alone, perhaps, gives us an adequate apprehension of concrete experience. Whereas other ways of thinking inevitably compromise life's complexities, literature preserves "the whole of things" in a nonreductive and concrete totality. The literary work is a concrete universal;[41] it seizes the fundamental principles of experience in the full complexity of their operation—and presents this awareness structurally as the immanent movement of its action. Literature strives, in effect, to establish a coincidence of itself with the real; thus the essence of literature lies in the cognitive relationship between reality and form.

So understood, literature, like philosophy, is a comprehensive and autonomous mode of ontological knowing.[42] Rather than a particular discipline with a particular object, it is directed toward "the whole of things": it represents the comprehensive principles of being which animate the "existential" dynamics of human life.[43] By constantly focusing on thought in its actualization, literature seizes reality not in the form of abstract ideas or contemplative thought, but in the very movement of its concrete development.

The essential task of dialectical poetics, accordingly, is to explore the cognitive power of art to apprehend reality, a logic which requires the dissolution of any distinction between idea and form. To attain that understanding the first requirement is a thorough-going liberation from rhetorical conceptions of content, form, and the "meaning" that results from their fusion. Through that critique it becomes possible to conceive of literature as a truly foundational mode of thought rather than merely as a means, however preeminent, of persuasion.[44]

For the dialectician art is not a way of giving preexistent concepts or commonplaces a persuasive verbal form, but rather an autono-

mous activity which generates ideas of a fundamentally different
and higher order. Whereas rhetorical criticism grants preexistent
content an independent status as the artist's starting point, dialectical critics strive to apprehend form itself as an original way of
knowing. There is a world of difference between the ideas that
enter into "The Grand Inquisitor" and what happens to those
thoughts in the course of *The Brothers Karamazov*. And the
mimetic process is where the literary idea, properly speaking,
comes into being. Commonplaces and concepts may form part of
the artist's materials, but in the artistic process they are transformed and lose independent status. Roughly stated, the artist tests
"ideas" by drawing out their consequences in and for human
existence. In stronger terms, mimesis is itself an original mode of
cognition which transcends, as it transforms, other orders of
conceptualization.

The literary idea is always too large and too concrete for our
concepts. We scarcely begin to approximate it when we talk
abstractly about an author's "vision" or his major existential
themes: if a theme is truly existential it is a way of acting, a project,
and has its being wholly in action. As a concrete universal, literary
thinking is best defined initially by the impossibility of translating
it into other modes of conceptualization. There is a characteristic
reply artists make when questioned whether anything from a
particular thematic statement to an entire philosophic system
expresses the "meaning" of their work: "If the subject of my work
could be expressed in such terms, I'd have had no reason to write
it." The reply contains the basic problem for a dialectical poetic.
The literary work *is* the substance of its "meaning"; nothing less
expresses its thought.

Artistic form, so conceived, provides an original access to
experience. The only thing prior to it, strictly speaking, is the
"splendid waste"—raw, nonverbal immediacy. From the ground
up, and solely through its unique cognitive powers, dialectical art
constitutes an autonomous order of ideas which are of a fundamentally new and unprecedented kind.

Linguistically, the task lies, with Heidegger, in "freeing language
from the tyranny of logic."[45] By extending language beyond its
ordinary conceptual limits, the poet rediscovers the lived world
(*Lebenswelt*) and achieves that primary awareness of Being which
philosophic, scientific, and rhetorical speech have continually
forgotten. In opposition to the rhetorician's view of language as the

vehicle of persuasion, the dialectician sees in poetic language the only way of articulating the primordial preconceptual awareness of existence uncovered in fundamental human moods.[46]

It is always hard to tell precisely what a particular dialectical critic includes under the category of poetic language. The New Critics and their followers conceive form in exclusively linguistic terms; they analogize all literature, accordingly, to the ambiguous, ironic, and paradoxical "statements" found in lyric poetry and, as a consequence, are unable to see narrative and dramatic works as anything more than structures of imagery.[47] For a critic such as Erich Auerbach, on the other hand, language and style are merely the most immediate manifestations of a writer's total mimetic awareness, for language most fully realizes itself in the apprehension of concrete historical existence—in, that is, the imitation of human action. Rather than the paradigmatic instance of artistic form, lyric poetry is perhaps merely the initial expression of a creative process which proceeds necessarily toward more complex mimetic structures.[48]

It is a long way, aesthetically and ontologically, from the lyric articulation of revelatory moods to the organization, in action, of fundamental human projects in the entire course of their development.[49] And a theory of poetic language alone will not take us there. To attain an adequate mimetic comprehension of experience it is necessary to go beyond the state of lyric contemplation, however intense. But how? In the final chapter of *Mimesis* Auerbach presents the conflict within twentieth-century narrative fiction between lyric contemplation of internal states and the projection of self in action as a fundamental crisis in our consciousness of the real. To understand that crisis correctly, we must see it as simultaneously aesthetic and ontological: in choosing the forms of artistic cognition, one also determines the reality that art may intend and comprehend.

Modeling their conception of artistic cognition in almost exclusively linguistic terms, the majority of dialectical critics have thus far contributed to the growth of the problem rather than its solution. If a literary work is finally only an instance of language, the lyric may provide the paradigm of artistic thought. A work such as "The Bear," however, offers a more complex reflection on the problem. By developing the conflict between lyric contemplation and narrative projection—and generating from it an overarching dialectic of transcendent awareness and historical time—Faulkner self-critically explores the cognitive powers and limitations of each artistic mode.

In so doing, "The Bear" presents a dialectic familiar to students of Plato, Lévi-Strauss, the Romantics, and the New Critics. Like Plato, Faulkner employs a comprehensive division between a lower realm (of opinion and social behavior) and a higher realm (of permanent eidetic truth); like Plato he proceeds to approximate everything encountered in experience to these two distinct realms of thought and being. The ultimate oppositions defining Faulkner's divided line are being and becoming, eternity and time, the unchanging and the contingent, the measureless and the quantifiable. Structurally, also, "The Bear" proceeds from opinion through argumentative thought and logical statement to image, ritual, and myth. The Platonic dialogues frequently culminate in a noetic insight that can only be shadowed forth in myths that transcend the antinomies of conceptual thought. In a similar fashion, section 5 of "The Bear" sets forth Faulkner's culminating "vision" in a dense, wholly symbolic structure of images that affirm opposites.

In substance, however, Faulkner's dialectic is radically different from Plato's. Plato enacts a continuous movement of hierarchical ascent to a noetic perspective which both transcends and corrects phenomena.[50] Faulkner's dialectic, in contrast, is strikingly discontinuous because the nature of his generating opposites prevents the establishment of any meaningful ontological relationship between them. Whereas the dialectic of Plato takes place wholly within philosophic thought and reflects a developed culture, Faulkner opposes a primitive precultural awareness to the dehumanizing and inherently positivistic attitudes that animate his society. In establishing a dialectic of nature and culture, he foreshadows Lévi-Strauss. But whereas Lévi-Strauss focuses on the transition from nature to culture—and knows that "you can't go home again"—Faulkner attempts the return and implicitly opposes Lévi-Strauss' belief that the antinomies of logical thought define the nature and limits of human understanding. Both dialectics, however, rest on insoluble oppositions: in their respective fates both Ike and Boon resemble the myth of Asdiwal, which Lévi-Strauss has analyzed brilliantly.[51]

In going beyond logical antinomies for his fundamental terms, Faulkner's dialectic is similar to those of both the Romantics and the New Critics. Like the Romantics he finds in the natural sublime (the wilderness, Ben, and Lion), the primitive (Sam), the childlike (Boon), and the aspirations of youth (Ike) a preconceptual awareness which he generally terms "the heart's truth" and "the heart's driving complexity." And like the Romantics he feels that only art and, paradigmatically, Keats' "Ode," which he echoes so pointedly throughout "The Bear," can grasp the transcendent. Yet beginning, like Rousseau, with a confidence in the educational power of nature and its revolutionary social impact, he proceeds to record the failure of an effort so inspired to have any effect upon the social milieu it opposes. And unlike most Romantics he finds that the essential reasons for that failure lie within nature, the norm which the Romantic opposes to history. Society is not the only villain; there is something rotten within the natural.

Along with the New Critics, Faulkner seeks in ritual, myth, symbol, and the paradoxical language of lyric poetry exemplars of an awareness that is vanishing from modern culture. With them he rests his dialectic on a thoroughgoing opposition of poetry and science, and like them he locates in this opposition the central problems of modern culture. Poetry alone can save us because it frees us from the positivistic reduction of language to statements of fact, and restores us to a human dignity which transcends the scientific reduction of everything human to calculation and mechanical behavior. But while Faulkner relies on moments of lyric contemplation of nature for the embodiment of such a consciousness, he also dramatizes the inability to locate that perspective in a world of narrative movement. By continually reflecting on the discrepancy between these two modes of artistic cognition, "The Bear" constitutes both the apotheosis and the overcoming of the many dialectical traditions it employs.[52]

Practice

The work's dialectical structure is complex but clear. Sections 1 through 3 take us from historical time and the conceptual constraints of Ike's society to a timeless realm of mythic and ritual values that can achieve lyric expression only in images and symbols. From Ike's partial understanding of that world the action descends to conceptual statement in section 4: his tragic effort to bring his vision into the cave. Ironically the section takes the form of a debate and focuses on his attempt to explain his actions in terms that will be intelligible to his society. But he fails to realize the ideal, both in conceptualization and in action. On the basis of that failure section 5 resumes the upward path of vision and embodies an awareness beyond Ike's powers. But that final vision is far from comforting. In returning once again to image and lyric contemplation, section 5 discovers inherent in the very substance of the wilderness the primary cause of its tragic discontinuity with Ike's world. In its dense structure of images, section 5 reveals the wilderness both in its grandeur and its exclusiveness. In so doing it is both a culminating vision (analogous to Plato's use of myth and symbol) and a reversal. For, as we shall see, its image-structure simultaneously celebrates and negates the kind of dialectical knowing epitomized by Keats' "Ode on a Grecian Urn" and championed in so many contemporary dialectical theories of literature.

Given the scope of his concerns, it is amazing how fluidly Faulkner's dialectic evolves. The key is Ike, who stands "betwixt and between" and bears the contradictions of that dialectic as the immediate reality of his existence. Through his development in section 1, the dialectic first coalesces in the ambiguous tension that will define it. With the ease of the young, Ike moves from the society of men to the primeval world of nature. Remaining a member of his community, he holds the promise of a future mediation of those opposites. In harmony with the movement of his aspirations, section 1 appears to enact a continuous hierarchical ascent from a decadent social world to a mythic order that promises renewal. Yet Ike's ascent develops by exclusion and suggests discontinuity.

The opening description of the wilderness functions to lift us from ordinary frames of social and conceptual reference into a symbolic realm. Rather than intensifying the empirical qualities of the wilderness, that description lifts us out of time, place, and the perspective of "little puny humans" in order to initiate us into a world of unchanging mythic and ritual verities. The wilderness is a polysemous symbolic landscape: literally outside human coordinates of time and place as well as of thought and will, it is morally Ike's birthplace and anagogically an embodiment of the absolute perspective he strives to achieve. Rather than serving to enhance an action that can be interpreted naturalistically, the symbolic terms describing the wilderness indicate that to enter Faulkner's dialectic we must cast off ordinary ways of thinking.

The bear emerges "out of an old dead time" as the "epitome and apotheosis of the old wild life"; "little puny humans," unable to understand that life "swarmed and hacked at [it] in a fury of abhorrence and fear like pygmies about the ankles of a drowsing elephant;—the old bear, solitary, indomitable, and alone; widowed childless and absolved of mortality—old Priam reft of his old wife and outlived all his sons." Ike's initiation, and ours, proceeds through a progressive shedding of that decadent way of life. By discarding the gun, he casts off the manipulative laws of hunter and hunted that men have tried to impose on the wilderness. The technical means men use to maintain their supremacy in the wilderness are shields that prevent understanding. But ridding oneself of such constraints is only a beginning—one must "choose" to relinquish oneself "completely" to "the markless wilderness," for only to an "untainted ... child ... alone and lost" will nature reveal itself. By casting off the remaining devices of human control—watch and compass—Ike becomes worthy of that experience—one that necessarily takes place outside human space and beyond human time. Even Sam Fathers' directions are of no use: Ike wanders, lost, in circles that refuse to bisect. Beyond measure and direction the wilderness coalesces, and one with it in the resulting totality stands the mysterious presence of the bear. (One recalls Eliade's *Cosmos and History*, the Mt. Snowdon experience in Wordsworth's *Prelude*, and Book 6 of Plato's *Republic*.) Its paws arise "as though they were being shaped out of thin air." The bear does "not emerge, appear; it was just there ... looking at him" and just as mysteriously it sinks back into the wilderness "without motion." Ike intuits their oneness in a dimensionless, immediate totality that is beyond all human coordinates.

Significantly, his experience is a silent, purely lyric moment of contemplation. The relationship it may have to human under-standing—and human action—is purposely left ambiguous. Only Sam and Ike are properly attuned to the wilderness. But Sam is asocial and remains silent or gnomic. Ike alone retains the possi-bility of "human" comprehension. But his "birth" is also a death, of human coordinates. Throughout section 1 Faulkner stresses the activity of the wilderness and the passivity of men. Ike's major action lies in placing himself wholly at its disposal, and it stands objectively beyond human will. When it gives itself to him, at the end of section 1, the vision he receives transcends both thought and language. The wilderness can be recognized only in a moment of nonverbal contemplation. The dialectic of nature and society that section 1 establishes is fraught with contradictions that suggest potentially tragic discontinuities.

Ike's awareness, at the end of section 1, is analogous to that of the man just emerged from the cave who is blinded by the light of the sun. He has undergone the abrupt Socratic reversal required of the apprentice to dialectic. But liberated from illusion, he is ironically left speechless. From the moment he first entered the wilderness he sensed that "he had experienced it all before, and not merely in dreams." He has now come into direct contact with the experience that ran in his memory "from the long time before it even became his memory." But rather than a culminating awareness, he achieves in section 1 no more than a first dim approach to the wilderness. The precariousness of his grasp is underscored in the first lines of section 2. "So he should have hated and feared Lion"—for the wilderness is not primarily a place for quiescent contemplation but is, above all, the place of the hunt.

To grasp the mystery of the wilderness Ike must enter that ritual. It, too, transpires in a realm beyond the terms of social, historical man—and the representatives of Ike's society are pointedly excluded from partaking in its apotheosis. The virtues manifested there—courage, humility, pride, endurance, and spirit—are of a wholly different order than their human equivalents. They can be earned only by sympathetic participation in that ritual and they arise through unreflective spontaneous activity. Ike, for instance, only finds courage when, disdaining his chance to shoot Ben, he rushes under him to save the fyce. Though the terms are the same, the virtues found in the ritual of the hunt transcend ordinary human behavior. Initiation in them requires Ike's further willed suspension of his society's attitudes as well as the overcoming of his own desires.

The hunt culminates in a "lover-like embrace" supremely violent yet supremely just and sublime. The terms of statuary describing it again recall Keats' "Ode" and bring together for a brief moment—in death—the paradoxes which, as we shall see, express the essence of the wilderness. But the full significance of the event is deliberately withheld. Only Sam Fathers enters fully into the mystery by his own willed death. He alone "has the profound look which saw further than them or the hunt, further than the death of a bear and the dying of a dog." But he speaks only in "the ancient tongue," and his development in the story is one of progressive withdrawal from the community of men. In section 1 he moves from the town to the camp, in section 2 from the camp to a little hut "on the bayou a quarter-mile away"; now he passes into the natural cycle itself through his silent death. He is as free from the dialectical tension dramatized in the work as the most inveterate townsman.

Ike alone suffers the dialectic as a contradiction, as a dynamic tension upon which he must act. But even though his participation in the ritual is absolute, excluding judgment—his understanding is far from articulate. Dimly aware that what has occurred is beyond his comprehension—and perhaps beyond any merely human comprehension—he does know that it has brought him to a fundamental choice. The opposition to his cousin, to a world unable to understand ritual, is the necessary consequence of his unquestioning participation in those primitive rites. That opposition alone completes his "novitiate to the true wilderness," and with it section 3 concludes. However incomplete and fleeting his awareness, he must now try to direct it upon its antithesis. To make the confrontation imperative, he will bring his "vision" into the cave and earn a place for it in the very language of that imprisonment. Should he fail to redeem the time, he will at the least attain an explicit consciousness of the values to which one must adhere. It is, as we shall see, an attempt doomed to failure. Rather than a maieutic art for uplifting its opposite, his vision proves ineffable— and, as a principle of action, merely drives the opposites further apart. Rather than an ascent of thought from image to idea, the relationship between sections 1 through 3 and section 4 is ironic and finally tragic.

In taking the form of a debate, section 4 reveals through irony and indirection the inadequacy of "reason" to articulate the experience of the wilderness. And it does so with a vengeance. Mere confusion results from Ike's attempt to conceptualize his experience. The endless, self-contradictory, inconclusive twists and turns that characterize the debate embody a terrible discrepancy between Ike's experience in the wilderness and the terms and limits of conceptual knowledge.

To compound the irony, it is possible to regard section 4 as a high point in the work's dialectical movement, for Ike employs a method of reasoning characterizing a classical mode of dialectical thought.[53] He sets up a comprehensive opposition between two orders of being, knowledge, and value and proceeds to assimilate everything encountered in experience to one or the other side of that comprehensive dichotomy. For him "the whole of things" may be subsumed under two exhaustive "ideas"—the wilderness and the land. To the land he attributes, in an endless repetition throughout

time the continuing degradation of nature and of man. Its *logos*:
the principle of possession in unchecked extension. Under the
wilderness, in turn, he subsumes "the heart's truth" and all natural
virtues in a timeless ritual order. Drawing out their extensions
merely drives the opposites further apart. Rather than a prelude to
their Platonic resolution by creative transformation of the lower
world from above, Ike's act of articulation is prologue to an
unavoidable tragedy. The two realms Ike opposes can, by definition, come into no meaningful contact. His failure in action is the
necessary result of the dialectical mode of understanding he adopts.
Unlike Romantic expressions of that dialectic, Faulkner concedes
the lower world unremitting predominance in its realm. Beauty and
truth, as it were, go down with Ike to a total defeat; the section
ends pessimistically, forecasting the doom of everything its dialectic has established as normative.

Ike's defeat is not a final end however. It is only so in time. The
reversed chronology that sets off the final section from his tragedy
signals its timelessness—and paradoxically, its subjection to time.
We must see everything in section 5 from this double perspective in
order to apprehend in its image-structure the necessarily paradoxical resolution it gives to the dialectic worked out in "The
Bear." After the downward path of section 4 we again assume the
upward way of lyric contemplation—but with a crucial difference
and with results staggering to any further reliance upon lyric
knowing as a principle of dialectical thought.

In two ways section 4 prepares us to understand section 5.
Having witnessed the failure of conceptual explanation in section 4,
we are ready to return to a more sophisticated mode of thought.
Given Ike's failure, we recognize that the preservation of the
wilderness as an ideal requires that we see it in a far more complex
manner. We will rely for that apprehension on the same mode—
lyric contemplation. But if the reascent is to move toward a
reconciling awareness, we must achieve in that mode of artistic
cognition a new level of paradoxical affirmation.

After experiencing the ravages of time in section 4—the entire
history of the South—we are slowly moved back into a timeless
realm through the same techniques of symbolic description
employed in section 1. Now we return to the timeless, with the
marks of time omnipresent. We apprehend the wilderness in terms
of its coming extinction: Major de Spain has sold it to a lumber
company and even before its imminent destruction his colleagues
wish to lease the hunting camp. The railroad which takes us back

"had been harmless once" but is so no more. Earlier it reduced a half-grown bear to a parody of Old Ben. Now it threatens the entire wilderness with extinction. Yet as the railroad returns us, we move beyond all that it symbolizes.[54] It is "absorbed by the *brooding* and inattentive wilderness without even an echo."[55] Its speed and force are reduced to a "frantic and toylike *illusion*." Once "the wilderness soared, musing, inattentive, myriad, eternal, green; older than any mill-shed, longer than any spurline" it is as if the railroad "had not been."

Once home again Ike is liberated again from time. In an interlude he recaptures the day when Sam anointed him with the hot blood of his first buck.[56] Faulkner's unbroken description of the seasons "in their ordered immortal sequence" underscores the eternity of that past. *"Memory* at least does last" and moments of glory are there preserved.

As Ike moves toward the graves, the images of eternity, patrimony, memory, love, and death come together in a culminating and paradoxical vision of the wilderness which is Faulkner's analogue of Keats' "Ode on a Grecian Urn." In its "ordered immortal sequence" the wilderness embodies "the deathless and immemorial phases of the mother" who is Ike's true "mistress and his wife." "His spirit's father," Sam, is in death one with it more than ever. It is a sacred timeless place in which opposites are canceled, preserved, and uplifted; for here death and life are inextricably one, beyond time. The wilderness is a "place where dissolution itself was a seething turmoil of ejaculation, tumescence conception and birth, and death did not even exist." The graves are "healed already into the wilderness' concordant generality," and with the rhythm of the seasons everything is "translated into the myriad life." Nature's cycle of life in death is the mother of beauty—and receives all back into itself. One with that rhythm, Ben and Lion achieved fulfillment in the "lover-like embrace" of death; it was to that rhythm that Sam Fathers responded. Attuned to it, Ike sees Sam and Lion and Ben *"free* in earth" to renew eternally the sacred rite of the hunt, but with "no heart to be driven and outraged, no flesh to be mauled and bled—"

But this pantheistic vision of nature ("myriad yet undiffused of every myriad part, leaf and twig and particle, air and sun and rain and dew and night, acorn and oak and leaf and acorn again, dark and dawn and dark and dawn again in their *immutable* progression and being myriad, *one*") in which the hunt, preeminently expressive of its cruel yet just cycle, may be projected beyond the grave, is broken, as it must be, *by that dash*. For it is also a cycle of death in life, and the snake is its paradoxical apex. The snake, "evocative of all knowledge and an old weariness and of pariah-hood and of death," reveals that death does not exist in the wilderness only because death rules. It is doubly proper that Ike salute the snake in "the old tongue," for the snake symbolizes not only the wilderness' but Ike's patrimony—

Unlike Keats' urn, the ultimate reach of Faulkner's lyric dialectic is a vision of death. And to complete his larger dialectical design, even that vision must be disrupted. The moment of silent lyric contemplating of a truth outside of time must be submitted to time's ravages. For the "truth" eternally alive in that natural order is historically dead. One can ascend to it only for the moment— and there is no way to bring the vision back into time. One necessarily passes from it into division and confusion. Ike's final "vision," appropriately, is of Boon overcome by the spirit of the time with its *logos* expressed in the final lines of the work: "Get out of here! Don't touch them! Don't touch a one of them! They're mine!" From a realm in which mine and thine did not exist to one in which it is everything, there can be no passage. Boon and Ike, the still living figures who shared in the ritual deaths at the end of section 3, suffer a parallel fate. Boon, who inarticulately parti-cipated, suffers an immediate reversal. Ike, who attempted com-prehension and action, has his fate drawn out, ironically, in time.

Reference to the wilderness itself, however, is the deepest function of Faulkner's reversed chronology. It makes emphatic the tragic inadequacy that defines the very substance of the wilderness. Since the experience had there endures outside time, we pass beyond concern for Ike into a timeless realm. But doing so only underscores the precariousness of that movement and of the desire that animates it, for the wilderness has no bearing on the world to which Ike opposes it. Being outside of time and recognizable only in the moment of vision, it finally is irrelevant to the ordering of human life. Had he comprehended that, Ike would not have made the futile attempts recorded in section 4. Having experienced his failure, we now see its cause inherent in the wilderness itself. Discontinuity with its opposite forms the true substance of the wilderness. The moment outside of time is precisely, tragically, a "brief *unsubstanced* glory which inherently of itself cannot last."

Thoughout section 5 Faulkner draws us in contradictory direc-tions, insisting that we see the wilderness from the double perspective of the permanent human desires it fulfills and the inherent limitations it contains.[57] The dialectic of nature and society—here bodied forth in a dense structure of converging image and language patterns—proves tragically discontinuous. There is no way to bridge the Plotinian gulf between nature's timeless One and historical time.

With this realization the work completes and destroys itself, for discontinuity is the death of a dialectic that would remain in the world. Rather than evolving a "vision of the whole" grounded in a dynamic principle that gives a hierarchical direction to experience, a discontinuous dialectic ends in the disjunction of two utterly opposed realms—one, normative and removed from experience, the other, decadent and unredeemable. Such an opposition is by definition self-defeating. When it is impossible to find the normative principle of a dialectic immanent in experience, the norm itself progressively becomes more and more abstract, reified, and "spiritualistically" removed from a world it faces with increasing disgust. As the gap between its norm and its world widens, such a dialectic has no option but to become a hectic flight into an intense inane.

It was to prevent such flight from the world that Aristotle, perhaps unjustly, criticized Plato's theory of forms. For similar reasons Kant located the illusory tendencies of pure reason in the desire for transcendence. In a sense Faulkner goes further than both, for he discovers the artistic principle that underlies the dialectic of transcendence and reveals its innate cognitive limitations. This, the self-reflexive relationship between its substance and its artistry, is the essence of "The Bear." Like all dialectical works it is ultimately about itself: a reflective apperception of the cognitive power, and the cognitive limitations, of its own artistry is the final reference to which everything in the work proceeds. "The Bear" explores the conflict between the lyric and the narrative modes of artistic cognition in order to discover the inherent limitations of a dialectic shaped solely by the former. To that end Faulkner gives the lyric mode full sway. The narrative mimesis of experience is represented primarily as a departure from lyric vision: its own cognitive powers are not directly explored. Merely as a term of contrast, however, the narrative mode reveals the striking inadequacies within the lyric principle, for lyric awareness proves powerless to establish itself in the narrative frame in which it is contained. When faced with realities of historical experience that cannot be resolved into states of lyric contemplation, the only possibilities it offers are confusion, flight, and final submission. The discontinuity that Faulkner establishes between moments of lyric contemplation and voids in the work's narrative movement proves as extreme as the discontinuity between nature and society and is, in fact, its basis.

Nature coalesces in moments of lyric contemplation which, while they discern a transconceptual awareness of the ultimate, prove incapable of transference to a historical world demanding narrative development. Lyric knowing articulates a transcendent perspective which reconciles opposites in a wholly meditative state of contemplation. But Faulkner shows that there is no way to move from such "oceanic moods" of cosmological completeness to a concrete projection of self in action.[58] The narrative movement of the work in section 4 is a falling off, both in intensity and in direction, precisely because there is no way to bring the lyric principle into the real world. While it is the definitive power for expressing the paradoxes that converge in an absolute awareness, lyric art is paralyzed—in thought and in action—when confronted with the bare givens of historical existence. While it restores us to a permanent world of ritual and myth, it finds no way of reentering the cave. Being essentially no more than a nostalgia for the vanished past, it necessarily becomes a principle of flight from the anguished temporality of existential projection in the present.[59] The ordering of experience it offers flourishes only in a setting somehow immune to time and human conflict because lyricism rests on an aesthetic desire to consecrate experience under the sign of sacred play[60]—the noblest and most recalcitrant expression of man's persistent desire to escape time. Unchecked, it betrays a debilitating aesthetic retreat from being-in-the-world.[61]

Contemplating natural and ritualistic experiences frozen in statuary, Keats' "Ode" moves beyond historical time and the limitations of conceptual thought to a paradoxical awareness of opposites reconciled in beauty. "The Bear," too, is replete with nostalgia for a natural world in which the forms of an eternal awareness are an immediate reality. But it is a cold pastoral, and within the lyric mode alone its limitations do not emerge clearly. By juxtaposing the lyric principle with a world that demands narrative projection, however, Faulkner makes the lyric heights of his work become fraught with all that they exclude. In section 5, preeminently, he insists that we see in this contradiction the essence of the wilderness: in its apotheosis, the wilderness reveals all that it is not. The work's ultimate dialectical reach is thus held before the reality of a historical reversal that it is powerless to check, understand, or meaningfully encounter.

"The Bear" enacts the contemporary crisis in dialectical art, and signals what should be the end of the lyric principle as the basis for dialectical knowing. Lyric thinking can achieve no more than "a brief *unsubstanced* glory that inherently and *of itself* cannot last." Its only relationship to a world of narrative movement is contiguity. Its lure is overpowering but self-destructive: precarious creature of the mood and the moment, it generates paralysis before the world without discovering any projective possibilities in experience. By dramatizing that awareness, "The Bear" celebrates lyric art while revealing its tragic inadequacy before realities that can no longer be suppressed. In the act of reflecting on itself, the work criticizes itself and calls for a new mode of dialectical artistry which would immerse itself in the narration of present history and would reject any stance that tried to transcend that horizon: Such a dialectic would focus on the actions of a subject existing in the world; existential possibilities, uncovered solely within the world, would be submitted to the world for actualization. It would, in short, discover a dialectic implicit in culture—and would assay in action the reconciliation of human inwardness and concrete existence. Hegel and the early Heidegger, among others, provide the terms for initiating such a dialectic. But we leave "The Bear" with little notion of how to move toward it. In Hegelian terms, "The Bear" cancels itself without lifting itself up—and thus preserves itself in the very inadequacy which it has made so explicitly apparent. The power of the work resides in its profound critique of the lyric principle. Its limitation lies in having explored that principle to such exclusion. It is a great act of negation and opens, for reflection, a significant void—

Toward the Text

Possible Theoretical Responses

Heidegger argues that a discipline is mature only insofar as it is capable of experiencing a crisis in its basic concepts.[62] Our experiment, if successful, has brought us to such a pass, but it is admittedly not a situation critics are likely to endure without resistance. For why tolerate such ambiguous and frustrating results when there are so many available means of escape?

Let us consider two predictable responses. One could engage the three interpretations theoretically in a debate over the "true" nature of literature, or one might regard them as complementary perspectives in an evolving eclectic attempt to discuss the manifold aspects, qualities, and general effects that any literary work presents.

The first option entails some variation of Platonism. Literature is hypostatized as an existent universal the one true nature of which must be discovered. Given the nature of poetic language or creative imagination, the underlying dynamics of history or depth psychology, or the principles inherent in any act of mimesis, there is only one kind of thing all artists necessarily do or try to do. In opposition to such reifications I have begun with the simple assumption that there is no such thing as literature, only literary works, and have justified that assumption by presenting three coherent and interpretively powerful theories of literary form. Unless we deliberately trivialize two of those theories, I see no way of reducing that plurality.

The second option offers a resolution only to those willing to abandon the concept of form. Each theory, deprived of that status, may be regarded as useful for the partial insights it provides: a literary work has no essence but is rather the multiplicity of things our diverse concepts enable us to make it. Following W. K. Wimsatt's frank eclecticism, one could argue that any literary work is somehow "a tensional union of making with seeing and saying."[63] By neglecting the question of structure, one could then show that each interpretation focuses on one of the general effects or qualities that may be found in any literary work. If one keeps terms like *emotion, communication,* and *idea* sufficiently imprecise, it is not difficult to do so. If they refer to nothing more than local qualities or general effects, each critic may find all three vaguely present in his total experience of any literary work.

Emotion, communication, and idea have concerned us, however, only insofar as they are synthesizing principles of structure. If we understand each concept in that highly developed form, whatever ambiguities *emotion, communication,* and *idea* may retain as terms recede before the precise concepts they have come to signify.

Formally Relating the Interpretations

Preserving the formal status of each theory removes any possibility of eclectic combination. But is there a further possibility? Could one recognize the holistic structure that each interpretation reveals, yet establish a dynamic, formal relationship among them, a relationship which would lead toward a grand theoretical synthesis of the three positions? Let us consider this possibility concretely.

Read in succession, the interpretations appear to enact a process of Hegelian *Aufhebung*: the first interpretation is preserved and deepened in the second, and both, implied throughout the third, achieve in it their true significance. In an order of increasing complexity, the three interpretations thus appear to progressively approximate the substance of the work. Or is that possibility merely a result of our procedure? Since dialectic is a theory of unified sensibility that allows no sharp separating of emotion, communication, and thought, our developing awareness of the idea being evolved in "The Bear" may be seen as a function of our total involvement in it. If we read the three interpretations successively or diachronically, this conclusion appears to hold.

But looking backward we get other results. Crane would contend that the "elements of thought" focused on in the second and third interpretations have been improperly abstracted from the work's action. The markedly rhetorical character of the work functions to increase our emotional involvement in its action, and "thought" likewise achieves its proper function in serving that purpose. Burke, in turn, would see our emotional involvement as only one constituent of the work's rhetoric, and he would see the drive for a transcendent perspective, which is given a subsistent status in the third interpretation, as no more than part of the rhetorical process—a "rhetoric of religion"[64] which strives, and more significantly fails, to find a place for the divine in the order of human motives. To be understood properly, emotion and thought must be integrated into the controlling rhetorical purpose of the work. As in the conflict of philosophic systems, each theory remains, in the words of Richard McKeon, "an architectonic reorganization of what is sound . . . and a cathartic exposure of what is absurd"[65] in competing views.

Once again, mere combination provides no solution to a substantive problem; it merely sacrifices the whole question. Like the Socratic problem of virtue and the many virtues, the problem of relating the three interpretations cannot be solved by an indeterminate commingling, but requires instead that we establish a precise relationship of logical subordination among them. In supposing that all three structures may be present in any literary work, one simply makes that problem explicit. And Socrates' problem is finally simpler that ours: for the virtues remain distinct and the problem of relating them is solved once it is seen that one among them—justice—is the art of keeping the others properly proportioned; it is not one virtue among many, but rather the form or architectonic principle that animates the virtuous life, making it an organized totality. Each of our theories, however, claims that prerogative.

Were the three interpretations discrete or partial, it would be possible to search for the larger form which synthesizes them. If a given structure accounts for only part of the work, that fact already indicates the necessity of subordinating it to a larger structure, and this is the foregone conclusion implied in the way that most discussions of critical "approaches" are conducted.[66] Following it one could give a mythic reading of "The Bear" followed by Freudian, structuralist, Marxist, and "formalist" readings. By then showing how each of those frameworks merely enables one to describe selected materials and isolated structures, the discrimination of these and as many other approaches as one cares to distinguish does no more than bring one to the problem with which we began—that of their formal relationship and the nature of "The Bear" as an artistic whole. It creates the need for an apprehension of form without giving us any way of satisfying that need.

In contrast, the three interpretations we have developed are not discrete or partial, nor are they combinable in any simple or ad hoc manner. Each articulates the structure of the whole. Each can incorporate "insights" gained in the others, but only by finding a subordinate position for them. One can, it seems, relate the three interpretations meaningfully only by adhering to one of them. But in doing so, each theory tenaciously reserves for itself a privileged status.

The more ambitious notion that as a whole any work brings all three structures into some determinate relationship remains a promising avenue of inquiry, and with many works the problem of logical subordination may not prove as extreme as it did in "The Bear." But we can only begin dealing with that problem once we accept it as a problem—and to do so we must move toward a new conception of critical pluralism.

Radical Pluralism

For critics to come into conflict they must attempt the same task and must actually talk about the same things. A careful scrutiny of most critical controversies shows, however, that most discussions of literature are not opposed, but simply different. Employing vague general terms such as *art, structure, form, experience, meaning,* and so on, one critic discusses the psychological state of the artist, another the historical conditions reflected in the work, a third the audience for whom the work was intended; some critics concentrate on enumerating conventions or the "formal qualities" of the work, others turn their attention to the mythic universals, existential themes, or deep structures of linguistic signification revealed in literature. And so it goes. The safest initial definition one can give of criticism is that it consists of the multiplicity of distinct approaches (or languages) that are developed to handle the many different "aspects" of the literary work.

The pluralism of R. S. Crane derives from this situation. It is a pluralism which sets out to discriminate the many distinct questions one can ask about literature and the many distinct approaches one can develop in answering them. It is a sound and modest program, and appears descriptive rather than prescriptive. But with one troubling addition: Crane contends that there is one language of criticism, that derived from Aristotle, which enables us to understand mimetic works as artistic wholes. An approach based on that language has a theoretical and logical primacy and, in a loose and unspecified way, other approaches, if legitimate, stand in a definite relationship of subordination to it. Leaving the immense problems contained in this claim aside for the moment, Crane's pluralism looks like an eminently sensible, descriptive, and useful program, the apparent intent of which is to resolve unnecessary disputes among critics by distinguishing the variety of distinct "things" we talk about while using the same common and inherently ambiguous terms. Once one makes such elementary distinctions, most of the "conflicts of interpretation" disappear.

But what are we to make of the problem that our three interpretations have dramatized in giving us a situation where different critics are in conflict because they do, in fact, ask the same questions yet answer them in fundamentally different ways? That situation is also an undeniable characteristic of the critical scene, and all the distinctions in the world won't explain it away. And what about the many different questions critics ask? Do those questions arise at random or is there an implicit order to them, an order which suggests a definite, though still unrecognized, relationship among the many "aspects" of literature? The further we push our inquiries into the "languages" of criticism the more we come upon the fact of necessary relations among the questions critics ask yet fundamental conflicts in the answers they give—which is the situation *The Act of Interpretation* addresses.

The inquiry is founded on the belief that there is a single order of questions implicit in critical study yet a plurality of distinct and legitimate ways of answering those questions. The pluralism I am developing accordingly stands in sharp contrast to Crane's. It first began to take shape, in fact, out of a dissatisfaction with the notions of "aspects" and "approaches" that play such a big part in Crane's program. In reflecting on those concepts I kept asking myself, "Aspects of what?" "Approaches to what?" How can we know that some quality is an aspect of something unless we already, in some way, know what that something is? Approaches are approaches to something, and we can only distinguish and/or relate them by in some way knowing the object to which they refer.

If, following Crane, we resolve these problems by claiming that there is one theory or language of criticism appropriate to the literary work as an artistic whole yet a multiplicity of other languages appropriate to the consideration of other artistic and "nonartistic aspects" of literature, we must admit that the distinction is a theoretical rather than descriptive one. The understanding of other approaches and the assignment of them to various artistic or nonartistic aspects of the literary work derives, in fact, from the particular theory of art we endorse. Classification and division imply definition: a purely descriptive catalogue of critical approaches is not merely trivial, it is impossible.

Had we followed Crane's program it would, of course, have been comparatively easy to bring the conflict of interpretations to a foregone and comforting resolution. We could have argued, for example, that dialectical critics concern themselves solely with poetic language and image patterns; having no way of understanding action, they necessarily spatialize the work and resolve it into its least component—language. Rhetorical critics, in turn, simply reduce the work to a bundle of abstract themes. Following these models—by giving an abstract rhetoric of themes in the second interpretation and tracing image patterns alone in the third—it would have been comparatively easy to show that both interpretations fail to apprehend how the materials they wrest from the work function within it.[67] By converting opposed theories of form into species of qualitative criticism, one may thus resolve the dilemmas that their fundamental and thoroughgoing conflicts have produced.

Once one has thereby cornered the market on mimetic works, it is possible to concede, in a moment of "pluralistic openness," that there are also didactic works for which another kind of theory is needed,[68] for we know, by the fact that we respond emotionally to it as an "imitated action," that "The Bear" is not one of these. And at this point one could begin ticking off the other "clearly mimetic" works such as *Hamlet, King Lear,* and *The Brothers Karamazov* which the follower of Crane claims as his particular province.

The fact of the matter, however, is that all three interpretations focus on action—on the form of the work's plot, to use Crane's term. One may profitably regard them, indeed, as three distinct versions of Aristotle's *Poetics.* The ambiguity of that great text resides in the fact that Aristotle simultaneously establishes the general categories of dramatic analysis (plot, character, thought, diction, spectacle, and melody) and propounds a single theory of the kind of synthesizing principle that informs imitative art.[69]

Crane's strongest claim for his theory of mimesis lies in the respect it pays to our immediate emotional response to the representation of "characters about whom we are made to care." He is justly proud to concur with the response of "generations" of "ordinary" readers who have not found it necessary to sacrifice that enjoyment to the search for deep or obscure meanings. Pleasure is its own justification and one may join Elder Olson in wondering "what swine they have lain with" who contemn it as a sufficient end for art. Crane has made such beliefs the basis for a rigorous theoretical explanation of how emotional response serves as the index of a work's artistic structure.

But is emotion the only principle of structure capable of shaping character and action in a mimetic work? Perhaps Faulkner's art gains in significance what it sacrifices in the power so to please. It is possible to imitate human action for the sake of initiating social change by transforming the attitudes and motives that inform our conduct, and it is also possible to conceive of imitation as a distinct principle of cognition essential to man's attempt to grasp an existential world which eludes other modes of thought.

At the same time, there is no a priori reason to regard either of these theories as the single purpose all artists must follow. The fact that we intuitively respond to any imitation[70] may not provide proof for the validity of Crane's approach; our need to find great significance in literary works hardly provides conclusive evidence for either of the other theories. At the risk of failing to attain such ends, Faulkner could quite possibly have been concerned with the kind of artistic purpose that Crane reveres. Who is to say, and on what grounds other than disguised theoretical preference?

If by critical pluralism we mean the resolution of unnecessary or frustrating disputes among critics by pointing out to each the distinct things they discuss under vague terms such as *art* and *form*, there is, perhaps, no solution other than Crane's open to us. Being unable to tolerate any fundamental conflicts in interpretation, one is forced to resolve critical debates by granting legitimacy to opposed frameworks—within the bounds of their inherent limitations.[71] But such a pluralism is in some ways an instance of the very dogmatism that Crane so frequently and persuasively attacks, for it depends on a benign neglect of what our experiment has discovered to be the substantive problems of interpretation. If by critical pluralism we mean the recognition of fundamentally different artistic purposes, then Crane's solution clearly will not do. What we need instead is a pluralism which will accept the existence of opposed, coherent, and equally valid theories of artistic purpose without feeling the necessity of abandoning the concept of form or of covertly diminishing that plurality.[72]

The New Interpretive Situation

Yet hasn't that pluralism exacerbated the problems of interpretation, taking us beyond the bounds of any foreseeable resolution? Since it makes explicit the problems inherent in interpretation, it may be regarded as an act which makes it possible for interpretation to become self-critical in principle. But knowing those problems and providing a solution to them are two very different things. We have seen in detail that the same initial observations provide evidence for fundamentally different inferences. "Percepts without concepts" may be "blind," but when there are a plurality of competing formal theories there seems to be no way to resolve the conflict of interpretations on the basis of "internal evidence" alone.

The other half of Kant's maxim—"Concepts without percepts are *empty*"—is also of little help. For if anything our concepts are too full. However abstract each theory may have appeared in its initial formulation, each legitimized itself in the act of interpretation. In Kant's terms, each hypothesis was "given in experience" and each presented us with a coherent experience of "The Bear."

Having deliberately bracketed the question of historical evidence throughout this inquiry, I have no intention of invoking it now as a *deus ex machina.*[73] Faced with the dilemmas we have developed, the desire to turn to history for a "factual"solution is quite natural. But I see no reason to assume that context will prove any less ambiguous than text. How does one go about constructing the historical evidence in favor of one concept of an artist's purpose rather than others? Historical documents are not self-explanatory, and in their interpretation we confront, at one remove from the text, the same problems we discovered there. History is as much a construct as is anything else, and the only way we can derive a coherent hypothesis of artistic purpose from historical data is by bringing a theory of form to bear upon that data.

Poets are notoriously poor as critics of their work because they generally have little understanding of the kind of rigorous statement of artistic purpose interpretation requires. Faulkner's Nobel Prize Address is a stirring document, yet as a statement of artistic intent it is inherently ambiguous. The same holds for historical knowledge about Faulkner's milieu and the kind of information provided by the study of genre and conventions.[74] No matter how well we know the givens of a writer's period, it is always possible that he will use them in a radically new way. Before we become historians we must be theorists. If we turn to history naively it can tell us nothing, for without prior concepts of form there is no way we can construct historical hypotheses in any meaningful way. But if our theoretical overture to historical investigation is abbreviated—as it is in E. D. Hirsch, who apparently assumes that all literature is rhetorical discourse and then uses historical evidence as a means of establishing the generic type of "meaning-intent" instanced in a particular text[75]—we merely posit a privileged theory of form outside the text rather than within it. To put ourselves in a position to deal with the question of historical evidence in a self-critical manner, we need to bring a plurality of distinct artistic hypotheses to that study. In providing such a plurality the present chapter may be taken as a prolegomenon to the study of historical evidence. If we use it as a way into the study of backgrounds, sources, statements of artistic intention, and so on, there is nothing to prevent historical data from becoming a significant stage in the testing of hypotheses. But the place of historical investigation in the critical enterprise is and must be strictly secondary because the constitution of historical evidence is a derivative act dependent on the theoretical concepts which first make it possible.

An endorsement of the hermeneutic circle likewise offers no way out of our dilemmas.[76] As it is used by Heidegger and Gadamer, that concept articulates the important insight that object and method can never be separated because the horizon of our total understanding—our existential and historical situation—is what shapes any act of interpretation. But we have uncovered not one, but three instances of that circle. Understood in its broadest implications, however, the hermeneutic circle reveals the next step a reflection on the critical process must take. The differences among critics are, finally, not merely aesthetic, but result from the opposed methodological and ontological assumptions that underlie distinct critical theories. At present I shall only introduce the basic directions for such an inquiry.

The thought of R. S. Crane rests on a problematic method[77] which assumes a plurality of distinct human activities and attempts to discover the principles proper to each. As in Aristotle, philosophic and scientific thought, ethical conduct and political theory, rhetorical discourse and poetic art are distinct subjects which propose distinct ends and operate by distinct principles. To preserve all of those differences Crane locates the integrity of imitative art in the emotional forms that distinguish poetry from thought and persuasion. Burke, in contrast, employs an operational method[78] in order to develop a general theory of communication. Language makes man a social animal and all linguistic activities (from philosophy to advertising) are directed to the sharing of communal values. The rhetorical process is the constant that underlies thought, shapes social living, and determines the artist's task: having conceived society as a drama, Burke finds literature the most effective instance of genuine communication. For the dialectical thinker, both of the former modes of thought appear reductive. His goal is to grasp the whole of things, the interdisciplinary unity of knowledge, experience, and being, by discovering in thought a principle of "absolute dialectical unrest" capable of eventually reconciling radical human inwardness and concrete human existence.[79] The existential reflexivity of consciousness cannot be reduced to the Burkean givens of social behavior, nor can consciousness find rest in the separations and antinomies of Aristotelian reason. Beginning with the radical existential complexity of man, the dialectician seeks to discover those concrete structures of thought in which a totalizing apprehension of lived experience achieves expression. He finds the literary work, accordingly, one of the primary instances of concrete thinking.

Are such thoroughgoing differences in method and ontology possible, or is there ultimately only one way in which all men necessarily view the world, think clearly, and create works of art? Of greater importance, could we solve our present problems by shifting to such a metahermeneutic inquiry? The discovery that elaborate ontological assumptions underlie not only critical theory but shape the most minute perceptions critics achieve in practice would extend our a priori knowledge of criticism in many valuable directions, as will become apparent when we take up these questions in subsequent chapters. What I want to emphasize here is that such an inquiry should not necessarily be regarded (as it usually is) as a way to solve or eliminate our problems.

Even if we posit, though only as an unrealizable ideal, a grand philosophic synthesis and a single philosophic truth, there is no reason to assume that the discovery of such a system would resolve the problems we have uncovered. For there is no reason to assume, either a priori or on historical grounds, that there is only one thing that all human beings—in this case as artists—do or must try to do. Even if we wish, following Hegel, to see all of culture as the striving through time toward a single truth, we must also, with Hegel, recognize a rift between that movement and the actual diversity of human choices. Culture is, indeed, preeminently the realm not of accidental but of fundamental difference.[80]

Multiple Working Formal Hypotheses

Generally one may assume with Kant that an inquiry, such as ours, into the principles which make a discipline possible as a rigorous science is nothing to fear. Yet our inquiry has run up against seemingly insoluble dilemmas. Having established what, following Kant, one might term "a probable sufficiency of formal hypotheses *a priori*,"[81] we found no way in interpretation to choose among those hypotheses. Within the terms of the present experiment one can go no further.

Yet isn't it possible—on the basis of that experiment—to adopt a new approach to the problem? Each of the interpretations we have developed reveals how a formal theory operates when unchecked. By their mere juxtaposition, however, the seductive force of each position is mediated by the seductive force of equally legitimate views. With all that is implied in that realization made an explicit canon of interpretive method, it should be possible to examine each interpretation in a different spirit.

R. S. Crane argues that literary history can become a rigorous discipline only by adopting what he calls the method of multiple working hypotheses. When confronted with different possible explanations for a historical occurrence, the rationale of self-critical historiography is not which interpretation we find easiest to apply or most congenial to our inclinations, but which hypothesis, among many, is hardest to eliminate.[82] If we brought that logic to the act of interpretation, we might reach a new understanding of our texts, and a new conclusion of our experiment.

Procedurally, we would take up each interpretation anew, this time with a search for "negative evidence." We would focus, that is, on the recalcitrant, on those things in the text which resist our concepts. Indeed, the fact that things in the text do resist our concepts would become significant in a completely new way. The fact that a given theory can accommodate and explain all the "data" in the text if we just exercise our "interpretive powers" sufficiently would no longer strike us as quite so impressive: the discovery of interpretive difficulties would become instead the occasion for considering the possibility that the approach we are using may not be appropriate to the text under examination. After using this procedure to gain a self-critical stance toward each interpretation, we would then scrutinize each interpretation further by comparing its account in detail with other possible accounts of the work. This operation would provide us with a number of fresh skeptical reflections on each interpretation.

In basing itself on these two general procedures, the act of interpretation would begin with the critic experiencing in his mind—both positively and negatively—each of the interpretations we have constructed. Rather than covertly favoring one of them or seeking for a way to combine them eclectically, the critic who followed such procedures would seek to found criticism in an act of self-criticism. If he reached a decision in favor of one interpretation or sought to establish a genuine relationship among interpretations, the critic who followed such procedures would do so not on the basis of truth in theory or ingenuity in practice, but as the result of a thoroughly self-critical attempt to understand each theory of form he employs in its weakness as well as in its near hypnotic strength.

Such an experiment, of course, would only speak to an audience which had experienced the present essay as its own crisis and had attained through it the Keatsian capacity to endure "doubts and uncertainties without any *irritable* reaching after truth." If the problems we have uncovered are the substantive problems endemic to our activity, the first thing we must learn to do is to sustain them as problems.

Before we can have any hope of solving them we must also gain a deeper understanding of how and why they came to exist in the first place. To the dismay of some, we will discover that those reasons are not contained in critical theory alone but involve us in some of the fundamental questions of philosophy. But this is the subject of subsequent chapters.

Thus "phenomenology" means ... to let that
which shows itself be seen from itself in the very
way in which it shows itself from itself ... here
we are expressing nothing else than the maxim
formulated above: "To the things themselves!"

Heidegger, *Being and Time*

How you turn things upside down,
as if the potter ranked no higher than the clay!
Shall the thing made say of its maker, "He did not
    make me"?
Shall the pot say of the potter, "He has no skill"?

Isaiah 29:16

2 The Text, the Disciplines, and the Artistic Agent

Contemporary Criticism and the Disappearance of Man

In literary criticism ours is supposedly the age of close textual analysis. And it goes without saying that we are all humanists, engaged in wresting from literature the values our time so desperately needs. Given the currency of these commonplaces it would be distressing if we discovered that our grasp of the text is fitful at best, and that our humanism masks a fundamental indifference to that which makes human beings distinctive, their freedom.

Two fundamental issues were present throughout chapter 1, determining its basic procedures as well as its ruling concepts. First, the problem of focusing interpretation on an understanding of the text as an artistic whole. Second, the notion that the individual artistic agent is the source and cause of form.

For obvious reasons, most critics prefer to keep the two issues separate. The first looks like an eminently pragmatic and ad hoc decision. Deciding to center criticism in close analysis of the text rather than in historical or biographical studies apparently poses no major theoretical problems, and having made that decision one should simply be able to get on with one's business. The second issue, on the other hand, entails complex philosophic questions about the nature of the human agent, the fundamental causes of human action, and the possibility of human freedom—and most of us feel competent to resolve such questions only through arbitrary assumptions of sentiment, humanistic or otherwise.

Much as we would like to keep them separate, we shall discover that the two issues are necessarily connected. Their connection is so intimate, in fact, that until we confront the philosophic issue the text will continue to elude us no matter how minute, exhaustive, or conceptually sophisticated our attention to it. Having lost the artistic agent, one is forced to sacrifice the text. As we shall see, the continued failure of contemporary critics to preserve the text as a phenomenon, despite meticulous attention to it, is the direct and

unavoidable consequence of their failure to develop any meaningful conception of the artistic agent—as well as the readiness in some
quarters to locate the origin and shaping principles of art in some
agency other than the human artist.

One of the dominant facts of our time is the widespread
displacement of the conscious, purposive agent from the origin and
determination of his acts. Not surprisingly, a development of such
magnitude has its analogues in literary criticism. As artist, too, our
acts are apparently determined by history, the family romance, and
the forces of our society; our products are shaped by language, the
universal and unchanging structures of the human mind, and the
permanent myths and needs of the collective unconscious. The
individual artist is an occasion, never a cause. Although critics
continue to employ the terms of human agency, as convenient and
perhaps unavoidable metaphors, most of the approaches fashionable in literary studies today actually require the sacrifice of both
the artist and his art. For once the human agent has been deprived
of the power to determine the nature of his products, the "true" text
must be found in materials, elements, and underlying forces rather
than in the phenomenon.

Both reductions are at work, rather innocently to be sure, in the
tendency of most historical critics to reduce the literary work to its
conventions and generic properties and to solve all interpretive
problems by referring to the givens of a writer's period, as if the
artist really does little more than express the "mind" of his "age."
They are present as well in the attempt of the New Critics to define
literature by means of language alone and to interpret all literary
works as instances of the ambiguous and paradoxical nature of all
poetic discourse, as if each poet and his poems served merely as a
further instance of that hypostatized universal. In the first case,
history or genre, and in the second, language, is the true cause of
form. In both approaches literature may be understood without
explicit reference to the artist as agent. And these examples are
merely the tip of the iceberg.[1]

Assuming that art is at base an expression of the unconscious,
traditional Freudian critics reduce the text to underlying, latent
forces which are by definition beyond conscious awareness and
artistic control. Following a method similar to the one Freud
developed for the interpretation of dreams,[2] criticism may discount
a work's manifest "content" and structure in order to concentrate
on the import of isolated, and often apparently unimportant

elements, images, and episodes. Having identified the pregnant moments in the work and wrested them from their apparent context, the critic proceeds to order them anew by subsuming them under the unconscious conflict they manifest. One thus arrives at the true text only after discounting the phenomenon as a phenomenon: and that procedure is justified because the fundamental forces at work in art do not, by definition, realize themselves in the manifest structure of the work. The unconscious expresses itself covertly and discontinuously. The concrete whole before us is only the apparent work of art and the artistic functions that words, images, and episodes play in its development are likewise only apparent. What's really going on in art takes place beneath the surface. To get at it one must do violence to the phenomenon *qua* phenomenon.

The same assumption reigns in most variants of mythic criticism, though under a more traditional humanistic guise. In an effort simply to identify archetypes, early myth critics concentrated on isolated figures, images, and quasi-symbolic episodes. By abstracting those elements from the text and subsuming them under the categories provided by the study of myth and primitive religion, it was possible to regard art as essentially an expression of the collective unconscious and the permanent ritual and mythic needs of the psyche.[3] Subsequently, critics like Joseph Campbell and Northrop Frye attempted to account for the structure of entire actions in mythic terms. But once again at the expense of the phenomenon. After positing his monomyth, for example, Joseph Campbell shrewdly selects just those episodes in particular texts which conform to that abstract pattern, discounting as accidental whatever cannot be assimilated to it.[4] Northrop Frye's system may be larger and subtler but it is not essentially different. In fact Frye makes a guiding principle of mythic criticism what we take to be its characteristic defect. More than once he argues that if we just "stand back far enough" from the text before us even the most naturalistic fictions will reveal themselves as essentially myths, albeit displaced ones. Applying the method, Frye finds, for example, that *Tom Sawyer* is really a representation of the myth of Theseus in the Cretan labyrinth—the true significance and power of the tale lies in that fact.[5] It is a staggering discovery. Having reduced the complex action of the work to a bare "plot summary"[6] and having no way of interpreting that action except by subsuming it under abstract mythic categories, Frye has advanced mythic criticism from isolated elements and episodes to the total object of representation without taking us any closer to the concreteness of the phenomenon. In principle he has no way to get there. The "plot" of the most naturalistic literary work can finally be no more than a displaced myth for Frye because what may be represented in literature has already been fully determined by the universal and unchanging patterns of experience (or basic plots) that constitute collective mind. All the artist really commands is the way or manner in which he gives these universal patterns "a local habitation and a name."

To complete the circle of his thought Frye argues that the major developments in psychology and anthropology (on which he relies for the substantive categories of interpretation) have at last put us in a position to systematize the study of literature by bringing the whole field of apparently random events under the sway of a single "scientific" hypothesis.[7] Literature expresses the religious and essentially ahistorical needs and beliefs of the collective unconscious. That universal agent, fitted prior to experience (or at a relatively early stage in history) with the storehouse of archetypes and myths which in a quasi-Kantian sense make experience possible, thus exhausting the possibilities of literary mimesis, is the true source of form, the particular artist being the mere occasion for the continued manifestation of that universal agent. The artist may contribute accidentals, giving the archetype his "personal" and "historical" signature, but the essence of what art represents and the essential needs it fulfills have already been determined by that universal and essentially unchanging intelligence which moves through time in its awesome cycles of dispersal and return. To substantiate such a hypothesis, criticism becomes an attempt to show how the "history" of literature moves in a broad circle away from, then back to, a pure representation of its basic myths. But the universality of the system has been purchased at the cost of the phenomenon and of any meaningful principle of artistic individuation, let alone the possibility of man's existential and historical integrity. If, to be saved, humanity must be saved in "minute particulars," we need not fear the imminence of the Apocalypse. Not only is that day far off. It is, in principle, unattainable.

In structuralism and its offshoots, contempt for the phenomenon becomes explicit. To apply the interpretive method developed by Lévi-Strauss one must resolve the temporal or diachronic structure of a plot into its episodes and arrange those fragments into abstract synchronic patterns. Interpretation proper then proceeds to make those patterns intelligible by ordering them around a logical or linguistic antinomy.[8] In the process the concrete work of art is resolved into an underlying conceptual dilemma or "deep structure" which can, by definition, have nothing to do with an immanent principle of mimetic development working itself out in the phenomenon and continuous with it. "Structure" in literature is discontinuous and nonphenomenal. Fixed and insurmountable logical and linguistic antinomies underlie and determine what is represented in any tale. The artist may *translate* these conceptual dilemmas into narrative terms, or present them in a quasi-narrative guise, but there is no way he may use mimesis to enact their transformation, for literature is finally impersonal. Like all other modes of signification, concrete literary structures really do no more than reveal, with mathematical precision, the abstract and abiding antinomies which supposedly constitute "the unchanged and unchanging" nature of "the human mind."[9] In Lévi-Strauss, as earlier in A. O. Lovejoy, all human creations instance the recurrent efforts of that hypostatized agent to surmount—then to reaffirm—the principle of contradiction. Since that effort defines the nature of mind and exhausts its powers of operation, literature can be no more than another of the ways it plays that game. As Paul Ricoeur has noted, structuralism is an abstract and purely formalistic variation on the neo-Kantian theory of mind,[10] and thus it is no accident that history and individuation remain unintelligible, even abhorrent, to the structuralist.

And so it goes. Historians of ideas search for unit-ideas or commonplaces into which philosophic and literary texts may be resolved irrespective of what the particular thinker or artist under investigation may have been doing with those materials. Followers of the New Critics continue to isolate linguistic and imagistic patterns and then combine them into structures of purely formal self-reference apart from any real concern for the specific contexts in which those patterns function or their relationship to the larger wholes they serve to develop.[11] In most of what goes under the name of "thematic criticism," the concrete structure of events represented in a literary work is accorded no more than loose passing attention. After positing a theme or body of themes, most thematic critics simply shuffle events at will, the sole problem being to bring whatever one chooses to consider under the abstract sway of an englobing theme or "vision."

The general tendency to lose sight of a work's concrete action while searching for themes continues to exert its force even in recent developments in thematic criticism that could have been far more concrete given their existential backgrounds and aims.[12] Assuming the single-minded fascination of Dostoyevsky, Proust, Cervantes, Stendhal (and apparently all other writers) with the triangular structure of human desire, René Girard proceeds to select and rearrange whatever "events" in their works best serve to illustrate that formula, consigning the rest to silence.[13] Thus, despite a powerful existential orientation, the discontinuity between theme and action persists. The work of the "critics of consciousness" is handicapped by a similar procedure. Rather than account for the phenomenological integrity and concrete structure of particular works, critics like George Poulet and the early J. Hillis Miller set up general categories such as the representation of time, space, history, art, and, above all, the nature of human consciousness, and then proceed to construct a given writer's *Weltanschauung* or "sense of reality" by extracting from his works whatever details will serve to flesh out those categories, without bothering to consider how the structures thereby uncovered function in particular works.[14] The approach, like Girard's, is in many ways an advance, since here at least criticism is concerned with the "consciousness" of particular artists. But the understanding of that consciousness remains abstract. It is a consciousness that realizes itself above and beyond the structure of particular works, rather than in them. We find it in a writer's *Werke*, rather than his works, for it is not, finally, an immanent principle of structure capable of realizing itself in particular works in a continuous way but a curiously disembodied awareness that manifests itself in the phenomenon only from time to time.

If the interpretive methods discussed above are fairly representative we must, I think, conclude that loss of the phenomenon rather than its recovery has been the primary direction of modern criticism. Whether the categories used in interpretation are purely aesthetic categories of "form," abstract categories of "content," or some indeterminate combination of the two, that which is supposedly closest to us, the text, has become that which is furthest away. Interpretation must be "deep" because the "essence" of the literary work does not lie in the integrity of the phenomenon, but in the underlying forces, elements, and "structures" that are at work beneath the surface; and the basic reason we seek form there is because for most of us the artistic agent is not, except accidentally, the determining cause of his products.

In stressing that fact I am not suggesting that we ignore the significant insights into "human nature" that recent developments in psychology, anthropology, sociology, philosophy, and linguistics have put at our disposal. On the contrary, I will later argue that criticism needs a far deeper grounding in those disciplines than has thus far been attained. The real problem is not whether to employ such disciplines, but how; and to solve it we must regain an understanding of form as an immanent principle of purpose continuous with the literary work's phenomenal structure rather than continuing to regard it as merely a container powerless to do anything more than present in a stylistically ingratiating way contents and materials which other disciplines alone enable us to explain. With respect to the way in which critics presently turn to other disciplines for their bearings, the directive implicit in the recovery of such a concept of form is clear and unequivocal: it is not enough simply to know a number of disciplines; we must take the concepts we derive from other disciplines and reconstitute them by establishing their strict subordination to form understood as a principle endowed with the power to transform those materials, giving them what Aristotle termed "an end or purpose which they would not by nature assume."

Much of what is questionable in modern criticism derives from our reluctance to move in such a direction. Having no more than a minimal conception of "form," critics are forced to rely almost totally on other disciplines for the substantive categories and principles of interpretation. As long as critics continue, for instance, to regard the artist *qua* artist as a medium who simply selects and arranges in some casual or ill-defined way materials which psychology, anthropology, or some other discipline alone enable us to understand, those materials *qua* materials will remain the true substance of art. If "form" has no greater force, the artist can, by definition, do no more than present us with universal forces and/or historical givens that remain intelligible independent of his activity. Try as he may he remains the slave of whatever general law he happens to instance.

Making form a truly purposive principle would lead to a fundamentally different procedure. We would turn to other disciplines not in order to discover the substantive categories of interpretation but, rather, to gain a preliminary knowledge of the complex human materials art strives to order. Moreover, no matter how broad that inquiry it would provide no more than a beginning, for the essential problem is to find a principled way to relate the concepts derived from other disciplines to principles of artistic determination which those disciplines do not and cannot provide.

Let me develop the problem narratively. A friend of mine, who calls himself a Freudian critic, has been working for the past few years toward a view of Elizabethan drama as what he calls a ritual or symbolic structuring of universal psychic needs. Due to the decline of religion and the sense of cultural loss and disorientation attendant upon that event, the Elizabethan artist took upon himself the task of making whole again the torn psyche of his time. According to this theory, the masterworks of Elizabethan drama reintegrate the psyche and fulfill the communal and religious needs of man by enacting a dramatic purgation of the disruptive psychological forces that had been set loose with the breakdown of values that occurred at that time.

There is much that I quarrel with in this theory, but in terms of the present problem I find it quite significant, especially since my friend has been concerned to distinguish works such as *Titus Andronicus* and *Timon of Athens*, which break down structurally because Shakespeare fails to master the unconscious conflicts present in them, from works such as *King Lear* and *The Tempest*, where essentially the same materials have been given a successful— indeed cathartic and restorative—artistic form. Works of the first sort are, as it were, case studies in neurotic conflict unable to become art—frustration made manifest in all its overpowering and uncontrollable horror. Works in the second group are products of a fundamentally different order: the same psychological conflicts are present but they have been mastered, and that mastery is a direct result of Shakespeare's art. Works in the first group fail precisely because the Freudian or unconscious materials present in them have not been brought under artistic control, just as works in the second group succeed because something fundamentally new has come into being as a result of the artistic process.

My friend is able to have both perceptions because the artistic concepts he employs, rather than the categories of Freud, are what shape his critical activity. From the beginning he has always been more than a Freudian. The act of interpretation focuses for him on questions of artistic structure and artistic unity—on whether a work coheres as an artistic whole or, having failed to attain that status, breaks down into its Freudian components.

Most Freudian critics have no need for such a distinction nor any way of making it. The business of criticism is taken up instead with the effort to identify Freudian materials and then to wrest them from their artistic context. And on strict Freudian principles there is no way or reason to avoid such procedures. The "true" text is necessarily the hidden one. To arrive at it we must reduce the phenomenon, discounting as unessential whatever in it fails to conform to the unconscious neurotic complex we posit as its true source. It is no accident that traditional Freudian critics concentrate on isolated words, images, and episodes, frequently, in fact, on what appear to be the least important moments in a work. For if the unconscious is the determining agency at work in art, interpretation must, by definition, concern itself with the latent import of selected parts and isolated elements. Given the constitution of the Freudian psyche, there is no way the unconscious can serve as the informing principle of a work's phenomenal structure. Essentially fixed in the neurotic conflicts and infantile wishes that define it, the unconscious stands outside the possibility of control by the conscious mind, artistic or otherwise. The only way it can gain expression is by overcoming the attempts of the conscious mind, as censor, to repress it. Since it is a product of the conscious mind, the phenomenal or apparent structure of the literary work can, by definition, be no more than disguise and pretext, an effort to flee from or repress the unconscious. In principle the unconscious is indifferent to that structure and must remain so. The unconscious is that archaic part of the psyche which, like Schopenhauer's will, simply craves expression and refuses to submit to any principle of ordering. Its appearance in the work of art, accordingly, can only be sporadic and the parts and elements in which it is most present must necessarily stand in opposition to the artistic structure of the work. At best the work of art is the uneasy truce in a battle waged between two irreconcilable forces. In "interpreting" that tug of war, the doctrinaire Freudian necessarily splits the literary work in two.[15]

As in the analysis of dream and fantasy, it is possible to note a general movement in the literary work toward and then away from those points at which the unconscious achieves expression. Following this method a traditional Freudian can in a loose sense account for structure. But the movement thereby studied is unessential to what is really important—the manifestation of the unconscious— and may be discarded once the critic locates those points in the work where its neurotic component rises momentarily to the surface. Having gone this far the critic may, if he wishes, interpret the unessential parts of the work as efforts by the conscious mind to disguise from itself or escape the unconscious forces seeking expression. Viewing the bulk of what goes on in a literary work as a rationalization, perhaps best explained once it is explained away, the critic can thereby give the illusion that he is accounting for the entire phenomenon, and it is worth noting that such a procedure offers a neat explanation of many troubling issues, such as the existential nature of Hamlet's soliloquies: they become no more than rationalizations meant to conceal his "true" problems. Rather than trying to make sense of the concrete development of Hamlet's reflections, one posits a hidden motive of which he is unconscious, thereby reducing the phenomenon to more manageable proportions. That procedure characterizes the method in general. Lacking any rigorous concepts of artistic synthesis and artistic structure, there is no way to avoid resolving the work of art into the necessarily fragmented expression of the unconscious psychological state of the artist.

My friend's method is radically different. Interpretation begins for him with an artistic examination of the entire work, and it is only on the basis of that examination that he is able to decide whether he is faced with a strictly Freudian situation, where reduction is appropriate, or whether he is presented with something of a fundamentally different order. He is able to make that distinction because he has from the beginning subordinated his Freudian concepts to a theory of form which explicitly guarantees the power of art to transform its materials. The particular theory he employs is derived from a Burkean interpretation of Aristotle's *Poetics*. Briefly, he holds that mimetic art takes the deep communal and personal needs of the psyche and through their aesthetic containment gives structure to psychic conflicts which would otherwise prove destructive. Beginning with a deep unresolved conflict in the psyche, the literary work constructs an action which produces the catharsis of that tension and the restoration of psychic equilibrium, thereby offering both the artist and his audience a means of psychic reintegration. Of utmost importance for the present argument, the achievement of that purpose depends on the concrete movement of the literary work and resides therein. While Freud helps my friend identify the psychic materials of art, it is Burke and Aristotle who enable him to discover how the artist orders those materials. It is they, not Freud, who lead him to the text and keep his attention focused there; they, not Freud, who enable him to assert the power of the individual artistic agent to determine the nature of his product precisely insofar as it is and remains a phenomenon.

In discussion my friend and I have agreed on the need for a genuine synthesis of artistic and interdisciplinary concepts while quarreling rather consistently over particulars. Granted, we need to develop a broad philosophic understanding of the fundamental human problems with which art deals—and common sense alone won't take us far enough. But why go to Freud rather than to Binswanger or Marx, Hegel or Heidegger, or even Jung for that knowledge? Why not all of them? Or different ones in different cases? Does Freud offer the one universally valid theory of human motivation, or are we perhaps just beginning to develop the broad directions for a philosophic anthropology?[16] Granted, we need to base criticism on a rigorous theory of form. But why a Burkean version of Aristotle rather than a Cranian or dialectical one? Is Burke's theory of artistic purpose the only viable one, or have we perhaps scarcely begun to consider that question in a complex and nondogmatic manner?

As one can imagine, the consideration of these questions leads into a number of complex philosophic issues. The battles waged between psychologists, anthropologists, sociologists, and philosophers for dominion over the "science" of man are not likely to be resolved. Nor are critics likely to agree on a single theory of form—and chapter 1 shows why they should not. Reflection on the general theoretical orientation to which the discussion of my friend's project has brought us offers something that may be of greater importance, however, at least for our activity as critics. Criticism requires more than a correct understanding of the deep needs and/or structures of the psyche, the universal forces of history, or the fundamental problems of human existence. No matter how thoroughly we pursue those questions, their development is only part of our task and not our primary problem. To preserve the integrity of art, criticism must begin with an inquiry into the principles of form. Not only is that question logically primary; its answer alone enables us to use the concepts we derive from cognate disciplines in a nonreductive manner. If we try to get by with extra-artistic concepts alone, we will inevitably resolve the work of art into its materials. Even a comprehensive philosophic anthropology that would synthesize Freud, Jung, Marx, Hegel,

Heidegger and others in a theory of the hierarchy of possible integrations that constitute the experiential route to authentic freedom would not give us all that we need, for there would remain the problem of locating that freedom as cause in the realm of artistic activity. The theory of forms alone enables us to perform that task.

Although it has been neglected for quite some time now, there is such a thing as the philosophy of art and its principles are the object of autonomous theoretical inquiry. The autonomy of our "science," if we wish to call it that, does not depend solely or even primarily on new developments in psychology or anthropology, as Northrop Frye contends, but on a recovery and deepening of our understanding of form. Because that science remains a possibility for future developments in criticism, it is even possible to imagine a day when criticism might make a vital contribution to the very disciplines upon which at present critics depend in a somewhat unreflective manner. By rediscovering in art the existence of free purposive activity determined by the individual agent and concretely realized in his products, criticism could become an active participant in the present dialogue concerning the nature of man, rather than, as it now is, a marginal discipline which is considered only after the real questions have already been addressed and the underlying causes of human behavior already established. It could, in fact, become an original source of philosophic reflection on the nature of man which could lead other disciplines to reconsider possibilities in the realm of human action that most of them have chosen to eliminate.

If we want to move in that direction, most of the concepts of "form" floating around will be of little use to us. As long as we continue to locate "form" in isolated aesthetic qualities, to define it by means of language and technique alone, or to regard "structure" as no more than a mechanical principle of selection and arrangement, there is no way the artist can achieve a determining power over his materials. The weakness of such concepts of form is, in fact, one of the primary reasons why so many critics have turned to other disciplines for their ruling concepts, thereby reinforcing the bifurcation of "form" and "content" that continues to be the "deep structure" controlling contemporary criticism, generating the contradictions it regards as alternatives.

Most of the schemes used to distinguish and classify critical "approaches" mirror and reinforce that bifurcation. Again and again in the classification of critical methods one runs up against a purely "formalistic" understanding of literature contrasted with the variety of approaches to "content" which the use of different inter-disciplinary concepts makes possible. In such schemes "formal criticism" is usually defined as a purely aesthetic attention to those self-referential qualities in literature that may be discovered by bracketing all considerations of "content." Opposed to it, one finds an equally abstract concept of "content" based on a suspension of aesthetic concerns. From time to time, tired of "formalism," critics go "beyond" it by shifting attention to "content," in the process becoming Marxists, Freudians, existentialists, structuralists, or simply students of relevance and "meaning." In a "synthesizing spirit" some even try on occasion to combine the two approaches, usually by simply putting them alongside one another and doing each in turn. It really doesn't make much difference which of these alternatives one chooses, however, because the dichotomy con-trolling the entire enterprise makes it a priori impossible to establish any dynamic relationship between the two terms. As long as we continue to base the distinction and classification of critical approaches on such an opposition, a questionable division of labor is inevitable, for we have yet to discover a means of synthesizing form and content in a single critical act.

The adequacy of such a scheme of classification as a description of the present critical scene is not in question here. It is of great value, in fact, precisely because it so accurately reflects that scene and its controlling contradiction. We miss the distinctive value of a critical method such as my friend's, however, when we try to force it into such a framework. His method is not just another example of "Freudian" criticism or an uneasy marriage of Freudianism and "formalism," and to understand it (and efforts like it) we need to scuttle popular classifications of critical "approaches" and begin again, this time basing the description of critical methods on a philosophic foundation of problems and principles rather than on vague general terms and a dichotomy which cannot withstand conceptual scrutiny. (I return to this problem in chapter 3.)

Considered from another point of view, the impossibility of fitting my friend's method into the traditional scheme is a clear index of the defects in the many critical practices to which that scheme does apply. If we are genuinely in search of form, we do not at one moment find ourselves "formalists" and at another Freudians, Marxists, Jungians, or whatever. Genuine criticism abhors a divi-sion of labor: the criticism of forms is not one approach among many, but the architectonic of all critical inquiries; and it is now apparent that rather than a secure achievement of the past, no longer *au courant*, now that we have moved on to questions of "structure," or "meaning," or *differance*, the criticism of forms remains the task of the future.

I have tried to show that our inability to understand art as a purposive activity determined by the individual artistic agent in his freedom to adopt projects of his own choosing and our failure to preserve the integrity of the literary work as a phenomenon are of a piece. It is not the most powerful argument that can be made for the possibility of human freedom, but it is the one that speaks most directly to the business of literary criticism insofar as the text is and remains our primary concern. Should we accept the challenge implicit in that argument and attempt to put the artistic agent at the center of criticism, we should have no illusions that the decision will in any way simplify our tasks. On the contrary. If, as a phenomenon, art is the result of the free activity of individual human beings—rather than the product of some universal agency— we have found another and perhaps the most powerful reason why criticism must endure a plurality of formal theories no matter how great the resultant problems.

In art, as in life, human beings act for many different reasons. This truth of common sense is worth remembering because there are many kinds of reductionism, some motivated by the highest idealism. Indeed, one of the arguments frequently advanced for a single theory of form and a single framework for understanding all human activities holds that freedom resides in the attainment of authenticity: all men face the same existential situation and are measured by the degree of their engagement and the adequacy of their project. Earlier I argued against a reductive criticism that tries to explain all activities by positing a single underlying and un- conscious motive regulating human behavior; I now want to comment briefly on a teleological criticism that explains the diversity of human phenomena by positing a single overarching goal in which all activities necessarily participate.[17]

The order of freedom as well as the activity of one who has achieved existential authenticity or what Hegel calls absolute knowledge is one thing; quite another is the equally self-determined activity of one who tries to actualize the comic pleasure in a work like *A Midsummer Night's Dream* or the rhetorical freedom of one who tries to demonstrate the absurdity of war in a work like

Catch-22. While from the perspective of a comprehensive dialectical philosophy only men of the first sort are truly free—since freedom resides in comprehensive knowledge and significant action—the conception of human agency I am arguing for is of a less exalted and more descriptive order. When used as a principle of explanation in the study of culture and art, freedom is a concept that must be used in a number of different ways. Although I am inclined with Plato, Spinoza, Hegel, and Heidegger to argue the ultimate status of dialectical freedom and to see all other activities as in some way derivative and inauthentic, the quest for such freedom is as difficult as it is rare and must be conceived as an ethical call rather than a descriptive concept; its application is to the exceptional man rather than to all artists or to human activity in general. Art presents us with much that is trivial in the human, much of what Kenneth Burke calls the barnyard, as well as some of man's most significant efforts to attain an authentic (and perhaps inherently tragic) apprehension of reality. I doubt if artists like Sidney or Marlowe, Dryden or Goldsmith, Dickens or Updike offer much to one moved by the complex of problems in which thinkers like Spinoza, Hegel, and Heidegger situate the possibility of freedom. We do such artists wrong—and unwittingly reveal the paltry understanding we have of such problems—when we make them bear such burdens, for the question that concerns us as interpreters of literature is not one of ultimate freedom but of artistic freedom. In that latter and frequently inauthentic realm there are in principle as many different kinds of freedom as there are distinct modes of artistic purpose.

A Logic of Recovery

Let me now renew the project of chapter 1. In the use of interdisciplinary concepts we face an epistemological problem analogous to the one we encountered in the war of competing formal theories. Here, as there, most of us fall under the hypnotic spell of favored concepts. In an effort to demonstrate their explanatory power, rather than to test them, we make the search for supporting evidence our preeminent concern. We seek out those materials in the text that can be most readily assimilated to our concepts and proceed to build up our interpretation from the "positive evidence" thereby established. Noting the presence in "The Bear" of mythic patterns associated with "the birth of the hero," the Jungian assigns constitute significance to that "fact."

Others follow the same general procedure. The Freudian concentrates, quite naturally, on Ike's search for a surrogate father and the paralysis attendant upon the ego-ideal with which he identifies; the Marxist upon historical setting and the economic and social contradictions with which the tale is replete; the existentialist on Ike's failure to appropriate the anguished responsibility for his existence which he keeps running up against. And so it goes. Under their spell, and unchecked by other possibilities, we use our concepts as dogmas of interpretation rather than as hypotheses of inquiry. Everyone wants to give his approach a chance, to see if it "works." To that end we are always on the lookout for that "evidence" which is so clear we need only point to it to give our interpretation the stamp of self-explanatory fact.

If we want to use the interdisciplinary conceptual frameworks available to us in a self-critical manner, we have to adopt a radically different procedure. In outline it is similar to the method of multiple working hypotheses developed in chapter 1. First, we want to be in a position to consider a number of possibilities: eventually we may in fact need to construct a probable sufficiency of interdisciplinary concepts a priori, analogous to the pluralism of formal theories developed in chapter 1. Though Freud, Jung, Marx, and the existential tradition[18] most likely do not satisfy that demand, for our purposes here they are sufficient.

The distinctive value of those four frameworks, in contrast to others that come to mind (Lévi-Strauss, common sense, the Judeo-Christian ethic),[19] lies in the fact that in their different ways each attempts to develop the broad outlines of a philosophic anthropology capable of revealing the basic structures that shape the concrete drama of human existence. That is, each attempts to articulate the driving forces of human character that make our lived relationship to the world issue in conflicts which give birth to a sequence of events. Each thus offers a coherent explanation of the "materials of human experience" that go to make up the structure of action we find in "mimetic" works such as "The Bear." Each gives us a way to explain the process of change in the state and situation of characters which results from the actions in which they become engaged when striving to realize their basic needs and to deal with their essential problems.

The simple act of positing a plurality of such frameworks is a significant step toward a self-critical program. While before the explanatory power of each framework held full sway, now their limitations come into focus. Mediated by one another each reveals its characteristic blindness as well as its strength. The different "data" each chooses to highlight as well as the differing ways each explains the same "data" become objects of explicit attention. Exclusiveness and precarious selectivity become embarrassments rather than habits. Although they increase our problems, these perceptions are salutary. They show us, once again, that more is involved in interpretation than a direct appeal to unambiguous "facts," and they remind us that if our responsibility is to the work as a whole we must constantly remain on guard against the tendency to construct its interpretation from selected insights and privileged data.

In applying the method of multiple working hypotheses to these perceptions, the criticism of each framework, rather than its confirmation, becomes the central concern. In this phase of the inquiry primary importance must be given to those materials in the text which resist our concepts—and we must seek out that "data" no matter how much the attempt goes against our inclinations and beliefs. There is no way to prove that a hypothesis is true unless there are ways in which we might discover it to be false. Following that basic rule of critical reasoning, we must take each hypothesis and try to disprove it.

No matter how comprehensive it is potentially, any framework initially focuses the attention on the "data" most amenable to its concepts. We now reverse the procedure. Attention is brought to bear on those parts of the work we tended to skim over in our initial readings. Naturally one can always find ways to assimilate the data thus uncovered. Either by incorporation or by reduction, any hypothesis can be made to handle the most intractable materials. Our attitude by now, however, should be of a different order. The goal is not to explain away troubling data, but rather to discover that there is such data, perhaps a great deal of it. Depending on how much evidence of this sort we find, or how striking that evidence appears, we may decide to eliminate a given hypothesis as most likely of little bearing on an understanding of the materials of human experience being shaped in the work under investigation. We may, on the other hand, find no compelling evidence against a given hypothesis. But we shall have looked for it. That fact itself creates a probability for the given hypothesis which we could not have had otherwise.

The general requirement that one account for the entire text, and not just selected parts, plays an important role in this phase of the inquiry. To be taken seriously, any hypothesis must actually preserve all of the "data," if not in the simplest fashion, at least in the one that proves least reductive. With a mimetic work such as "The Bear" this demand means no more and no less than that the hypothesis must explain those materials that are continuous with the structure of the work's entire action rather than those which are local or of passing importance.

Let us suppose that a given hypothesis survives these tests. That alone is not enough to confirm it. Other hypotheses must be given a hearing and the results compared. As we know from chapter 1, alternative explanations of the same phenomena are possible. More than one hypothesis may prove comprehensive, and there are important philosophic reasons for keeping this possibility in mind: human action is frequently overdetermined. In art as in life, there is no reason why an agent might not act at one and the same time from a variety of political, psychoanalytic, and existential motives. Since that is so, apparently opposed hypotheses may render equally coherent—and perhaps complementary—accounts of the total action represented in a given literary work. Even those which fail to survive the test of comprehensiveness may call our attention to important dimensions of the action which more successful hypotheses have failed to take into account and need to incorporate.

In some cases we may be able to eliminate all hypotheses save one. Sartre's *Nausea* for the existentialist, Dreiser's *An American Tragedy* for the Marxist, Lawrence's *The Rainbow* for the Freudian, and Hesse's *Siddhartha* for the Jungian provide convenient examples of this possibility. More complex outcomes are likely, however, and we need to attain a flexibility based on principles to deal with the three possibilities I will now discuss.

First, there are texts where only one framework accounts for the whole action while others call attention to materials that enter importantly into its constitution. The problem with such texts is not to eliminate the latter frameworks but to integrate them within the framework that proves comprehensive by demonstrating their subsidiary yet vital function within it. Thinking along such lines, Sartre argues in *Saint Genet* (convincingly I think) that while one must not discount the Freudian and Marxist forces present in Genet's life and work, the existential framework of explanation alone accounts for the integrity of his activity. The same relationship is established in Sartre's *Les Chemins de la Liberté*, but a different (and rather reductive) use of the three frameworks is at work in Moravia's *The Conformist*, where Freudian principles dominate; and a third possibility is instanced in Malraux's *Man's Fate* where a Marxist perspective contains and gives direction to profound Freudian and existential motives.

Second, there are texts where different frameworks apply to selected materials in the work yet none accounts for the structure of the entire action. The problem in such cases is to discover that structure and thereby establish the precise function each framework has in its constitution. Joyce has always been for me the prime example of this interpretive problem; whether the fact indicates his profundity or his eclecticism I leave to others. The encyclopedic impulse is clearly evident in a work like *Ulysses*, where almost every theory of man and culture imaginable is given its hour upon the stage at different points in the action with the synthesis of perspectives possibly left an open question. In interpreting such a work the methodological problem is to find a way to use a multiplicity of frameworks for the partial insights each provides without commiting oneself philosophically to any one of them. None apparently provided the philosophic basis for Joyce's representation of human experience, which is precisely what remains to be discovered.

Third, there are texts where more than one framework, and possibly all the ones we have mentioned, account for the structure of the entire action. For methodological reasons this is the most important case to consider and to move directly to the most complex interpretive problem: what if, after testing all the hypotheses available to us, we found ourselves faced with a situation analogous to that we confronted when we applied three theories of form to "The Bear," a situation, that is, in which a plurality of different—and philosophically opposed—theories of human activity rendered coherent accounts of the materials that constitute the structure of a work's entire action. Such is, I think, the kind of problem we face in interpreting *Hamlet, King Lear,* and the novels of Mann, Dostoyevsky, and Proust. (As we shall see below, "The Bear" is a less difficult case yet entails somewhat similar interpretive problems.)

To overcome both eclecticism and reductionism the problem in dealing with such works is to establish a determinate relationship among equally comprehensive frameworks of explanation. To solve that problem one has to discover which framework among them proves architectonic and, in Hegel's terms, cancels, preserves, and uplifts the others; that is, which framework not only permits but requires the total experiential development of the other frameworks yet rigorously subordinates them, thereby achieving in the structure of its action a concrete realization of the hierarchy of integrations it makes possible. A work like *The Magic Mountain*, for example, is simultaneously and throughout Jungian, Freudian, Marxist, and existential because Mann has grasped the concrete experiential nexus of those four frameworks (that is, indeed, the subject of his book) and has succeeded in constructing the kind of action in which all four frameworks are constantly held together in ongoing dynamic interaction—the *bildungsroman* of a character who strives to make understanding "the whole of things" the concrete condition of his choice or project. In interpreting such works, the task we face is strictly analogous to the concept and method of logical subordination developed in chapter 1.[20] But since none of the frameworks we are using, with the possible exception of the existential, enables one to establish such a relationship at the level of first principles, the interpretive act has become immensely difficult, even daring, for our problem is now a genuinely philosophic one: to overcome on philosophic grounds the conceptual limitations which led each of the frameworks to set up their frequently unnecessary oppositions in the first place. Until we think that problem through at the level of principles—at the level of a philosophic anthropology—we will most likely end up with an eclecticism of frameworks rather than a principled integration of them.[21]

Initially, as in chapter 1, we may have regarded our basic problem as one of ruling out all hypotheses save one. In the frequently dubious battles of Marxists, Freudians, Jungians, and existentialists for exclusive dominion in the study of man, that is the way the problem is usually handled. Such a solution, however, only applies to the first of the four kinds of works we have discussed. In the other cases the problem is to perform the far more difficult task of establishing determinate relationships among competing frameworks; and I focused on three different ways this can be done to indicate that the problem cannot be solved in the abstract but must always be developed with respect to the particular text under examination. The possibilities, in fact, are potentially unlimited. But the general logic for reaching a decision is clear, even though it requires both the utmost degree of self-criticism in the testing of conceptual frameworks and the utmost degree of flexibility in dealing with the different possible outcomes of that inquiry.

One application of that general logic was implicit in the examination of "The Bear." Prior to its interpretation, a self-critical hearing was given to the four frameworks of explanation we've been discussing. From that preliminary examination I concluded that Freudian and existential concepts played a relatively minor part in the action Faulkner was constructing while there was much in the text to which Marxist and Jungian concepts applied. It is possible in fact to apply either of these frameworks to the structure of the entire action.[22] Yet neither alone proves sufficient. There is a coherent structure of Jungian myth in the tale. If one focuses on it alone one can assimilate the work to "the myth of the birth of the hero." But to do so one has to discount the coherent and equally comprehensive historical-social structure of the work's action. And vice versa: for a reason not apparent at this stage of the inquiry Faulkner has brought together two opposed frameworks of thought in "The Bear." The critic's problem is not to eliminate one of those frameworks, but to discover their determinate relationship in that text.

As I worked on that problem it became evident to me that although Faulkner makes great use of Jungian materials and structures in "The Bear"—and calls explicit attention to their importance at crucial points in the action—they do not have for him the universal and constitutive experiential significance they have for Jung and for most myth-critics. On the contrary, Faulkner places the "quest for myth" in a historical context precisely in order to make its inherent limitations become apparent. He uses Jungian structures to characterize Ike and to define the ahistorical nature of his quest. But the mythic pathos thus evoked proves woefully inadequate when confronted with the world of historical and social responsibility to which Faulkner refers it.

Preliminary to the act of interpretation proper, critics might reach such a broad general agreement concerning Faulkner's materials and the conceptual frameworks useful in explaining them, an agreement analogous to the stage of preliminary observation discussed in chapter 1, pages 8–9. It is, I think, a considerable advance beyond the reductive and exclusive ways in which such concepts are usually employed. Even so it provides no more than a beginning.

The essential act is what each theory of form does with that knowledge; and as chapter 1 makes clear, the differences are striking. To cite just one example: Crane interprets Faulkner's use of Jungian materials as one of the devices used to create and magnify our desires and expectations for Ike; Burke views the same structures thematically as part of the work's attitudinal content; the dialectician sees myth as the ultimate cognitive issue of one of the two modes of knowing dramatized in the work. Each theory, in short, uses interdisciplinary concepts differently because each entails a fundamentally different understanding of what we have termed "the materials of human experience" that constitute the object of representation in mimetic works such as "The Bear." For Crane they are simply that—matter to be given form. Materials *qua* materials have no predetermined significance; their selection and arrangement is controlled, rather, by the particular emotional form the artist wishes to confer upon them. For Burke, on the other hand, matter is content. The materials of human experience an artist chooses to represent are determined by the preexistent conflict in the order of human motivation he wishes to dramatize and the attitudes he wishes to communicate. For the dialectician, finally, our apprehension of the world is initially constituted by the forms of artistic cognition. Applied directly to unmediated experience, form is an original way of knowing which itself generates the "materials of human experience" which make up the substance or world represented in a literary work. For distinct theoretical reasons, each theory necessarily uses common interdisciplinary concepts in fundamentally different ways.

Moreover, for theoretical reasons proper to it alone, each theory has already chosen to emphasize some interdisciplinary concepts and to subordinate or eliminate others. Given his theory of form, it is no accident that Burke relies heavily upon Marx, Freud, and Mead in order to establish the inherently social contents of communication, while the dialectician, working from a far more radical conception of experience and the cognitive power of art, sees the givens of social life as moments in a broader anthropology of the existential subject and turns to thinkers such as Hegel and Heidegger in an effort to get beyond the limitations of sociological thought. Nor is it accidental that Crane makes relatively little use of interdisciplinary concepts, relying instead on "common sense" for his understanding of a writer's materials. As Crane sees it, the inherent significance of a writer's materials is not finally what is most important; what really counts is the universal principles of emotional response he strives to impose upon those materials.

These differences are not merely important, they are essential and outweigh all previous considerations. Left to itself, each theory would quite naturally and necessarily dispense with the detailed procedures we have developed for testing the relevance of different interdisciplinary frameworks to particular texts, for on philosophic grounds each theory has already determined a priori which inter-disciplinary concepts are appropriate to the study of literature. That fact does not invalidate our argument, but it does indicate one of the inherent difficulties of establishing and maintaining it in a truly pluralistic fashion.

It also indicates what must be the next stage of the inquiry. We have seen that each theory entails a determinate relationship to specific cognate disciplines, but we are not yet in a position to understand why this is and must be so because we have still not cast our net widely enough. Thus far we have considered critical theory by and large as if it were a product of autonomous speculation carried out independent of prior philosophic assumptions and concepts. I have adopted this procedure, somewhat against my own inclinations, as a concession to the desire of critics to conduct their business with a minimum of abstract theorizing, especially theorizing of the sort that takes us into issues best left to philosophy. We have reached a point, however, where the consideration of critical theory by itself has taken us as far as it can and has left us with a number of disturbing questions. How can a critic decide to commit himself to a particular selection and use of interdisciplinary concepts, determined by a particular theory of form, when the philosophic bases for both decisions remain unclear if not opaque? Or, to take the other side of the coin, how can we justify a pluralism of formal theories and a pluralism in the selection and use of interdisciplinary concepts when the philosophic bases of that pluralism remain tacit at best? Is criticism content to let the principles that structure it remain a mystery, or is it possible to open the entire field to philosophic scrutiny? To understand how and why critics interpret literature in different ways and are attracted to different disciplines we must confront the troubling realization that the ways we think about literature are shaped by the general philosophic and methodological principles we bring to that study. Elaborate and controversial philosophic assumptions, concepts, and principles of reasoning underlie each of the theories we have considered. If we want to attain an in-depth understanding of critical theory, we must make an inquiry into the philosophic foundations of criticism our next concern.

There is no way such an inquiry can avoid generating further controversy. It will, in fact, reopen all of the questions we have considered thus far. For although there may be complex reasons why Crane, Burke, and the dialectician think about literature in the different ways that they do, the substantive questions is, Can their thought stand up under philosophic scrutiny or does pluralism rest on a fallacy of misplaced concreteness? Until the philosophic bases of each theory are established, pluralism remains open to the charge of being no more than an appeal to flexibility and common sense—which are fine things but hardly first principles, since the fact of the matter about human affairs may be contrary to the beliefs of ordinary reason. Whatever artists may think they are doing, once we understand the "deep structures" of language, culture, and the human mind we may discover that all creation and signification are of a piece. However complex and inherently plural literature may appear to a phenomenological or historical view concerned to distinguish the many fundamentally different kinds of products we group under the abstract designation literature, there may be ultimately only one kind of thing that all artists necessarily do or try to do. The structuralism associated with Lévi-Strauss is the latest, but by no means the only, instance of this argument; one might regard it in fact as the implicit teleology in much of modern thought. Its implications for the possibility of a pluralism of literary theories are clear and direct: given the way in which we all necessarily think and, by extension, create, only one of the three theories we have considered justifies itself before the bar of philosophic scrutiny. Pluralism may be a prephilosophic position destined to disappear once we get to first principles. Thus the question becomes, are there many legitimate ways of thinking or, ultimately, only one? In the deep structures that control all its activities (art included), is the human mind "essentially unchanged and unchanging," as Lévi-Strauss would have it, or is "The Human Mind" perhaps the ultimate Platonic myth? Whether we like it or not, opposed theories of literature are implicated in a larger philosophic debate concerning the nature of thought, the principles of valid discourse, and the reference of both to reality. Are those realities ultimately one, or might they, too, be radically plural? Once again adopting the spirit of Wittgenstein, let us look and see.

I was thus led to infer that the ground of our opinions is far more custom and example than any certain knowledge. . . . By these considerations I was induced to seek some other method. . . . never to accept anything for true which I did not clearly know to be such; that is to say, carefully to avoid precipitancy and prejudice, and to comprise nothing more in my judgment than what was presented to my mind so clearly and distinctly as to exclude all ground of doubt.

Descartes, *Discourse on Method*

To be radical is to go to the root of the matter. For man, however, the root is man himself.

Marx

3 Critical Theory and Philosophic Method

What Is Critical Discourse?

Perception is never unmediated. As we saw in studying "The Bear," our most minute perceptions are theory-bound. The problem is not to cleanse oneself of concepts, but to discover one's concepts—and then inquire as deeply as one can into their grounds. Having seen that what we do with the text in interpretation is determined by the concepts of form we bring to it, we should not be surprised to discover that those concepts, in turn, have complex antecedents. It could be argued, in fact, that rather than an area of autonomous and essentially imaginative speculation, critical discourse is a branch of philosophy and rests on principles and assumptions which have intricate philosophic roots. To understand a critical theory it is not enough to state or summarize what a critic says, we have to discover why he says it, and to do that we must begin with an inquiry into the principles that organize a critical discourse as a whole, giving a systematic character or logical coherence to the problems a critic raises and the kinds of explanations he gives. Our failure to develop this question in a rigorous way may be one of the major sources of our problems. Ironically, we argue about the nature of literature without having a very clear notion of what it means to talk about it or of what critics of various persuasions are doing when they advance opposed conceptions of its nature.

In many ways we confront the same problems when we try to understand one another that we faced when we attempted to understand the literary work, the task now being to formulate, in philosophic terms, the methodological principles which shape the distinct modes of critical discourse. In addressing that problem it is probably prudent to make a sharp break with the way critical discourse is usually discussed. When one of our most respected critics calls "hard work" a distinct critical method and proceeds to distinguish a plethora of other "methods" along similarly vague lines, it is evident that the concept of method is not being thought through in a very complex manner.[1] When we turn to specialists in the history and philosophy of criticism, we don't really find a significant advance. Most scholarly discussions of critical theory and the history of criticism treat critical discourse as if it were little more than a collection of isolated doctrines or commonplaces: art is an imitation of nature, the purpose of poetry is to instruct and delight, the imagination is an esemplastic power, the true poet possesses a unified sensibility. Apparently one need not spend much time worrying about the reasons why critics developed such doctrines, the philosophic presuppositions on which those doctrines depend, or the particular problems they were designed to solve. Summarizing doctrines appears to be enough. What we want to derive from the history of criticism is a collection of clear and distinct statements which we can accept or reject as they stand, leaving the philosphic bases of critical discourse to the philosophers.

Viewed in this way critical discourse becomes the commonplace book of each critic's sensibility, a bundle of unrelated assertions which arise willy-nilly out of pure aesthetic speculation. Following a procedure similar to Mortimer Adler's "system" of "great ideas," we ransack the house of criticism for isolated statements and doctrines which we then proceed to arrange around a number of discrete critical topics and ambiguous terms. What do the Greeks mean by imitation and how, after Croce, can anyone take such a view seriously? What do Longinus, Edmund Burke, Kant, Schopenhauer, and Santayana mean by the sublime? What is Coleridge's view of imagination, of language, of organic form? What is the objective correlative, the concrete universal? The dominant concern is almost always with *what* critics say rather than *why*: the logic and the unity of critical discourse escape us.

As a result the history of criticism becomes, even in a scholar as eminent as Wellek, an atomistic collection of commonplaces held together by severely abstract and subsumptive conceptions of the critical mind or "sensibility" of distinct ages. Having no way to account for the shaping principles of particular critical theories, it is necessary to hypostatize "the mind of the Age" in order to give the study of criticism whatever unity it can possess. Semantic, topical, and doctrinal constants alone hold together Wellek's understanding of critical discourse, making it impossible for him to account for genuine conceptual and methodological differences. Thus he asserts, in a recent revision of his now standard article on trends in modern criticism, that there is little "formal" criticism today because the term is seldom used, much "structural" criticism because we find the term everywhere.[2] Criticism presents a succession of ruling doctrines or schools; its real unity is sociological—the consensus of the profession. And in all such histories the latest dogma rules the day: the history of criticism becomes the heroic march toward the sensibility or mind of whatever twentieth-century critic happens to be writing its history.[3]

A closer scrutiny of almost any moment in the history of criticism calls such procedures into question. Neither the terms nor the doctrines contained in a critical discourse have any isolable or autonomous meaning. Nor do the different periods of critical speculation constitute internally unified epochs in the evolution of aesthetic mind. Aristotle and Plato, for example, both regard poetry as an "imitation" to be sure. But Aristotle uses the term univocally in order to establish a particular science of productive art which is independent of the problems of ethics and metaphysics, whereas Plato uses the term analogically in order to integrate poetry into a comprehensive dialectic of being and becoming.[4] The problems Aristotle develops in the *Poetics* follow from his decision to elaborate distinct principles and methods for the treatment of different subjects. The problems Plato encounters in the *Republic*, on the other hand, grow out of his effort to develop universal categories to which all things and all activities, including poetry, may be assimilated. Thus despite a similarity of terms, statements, and incidental doctrines (that is, poetry imitates nature), Plato and Aristotle in fact think of mimesis in radically different ways because distinct ontological and methodological principles shape their "opposed" conceptions of its nature and value. To understand the specific meaning of the terms and doctrines found in either theory—or in any critical discourse for that matter—we must turn from popular conceptions of critical discourse to the study of philosophic and methodological principles.

As usual R. S. Crane provides a valuable starting point. He argues that any discourse is composed of a particularly formulated subject matter or problem and a particular method or mode of reasoning about it.[5] The relationship of the two constituents is one of matter to form. Any discourse can be characterized by the relationship between the specific problem with which it deals and its method; that is, the assumptions a critic makes, the logic implicit in the way he employs terms and develops inferences, and the precise meaning he thereby gives to common and ambiguous topics and theses (such as imitation) in the process of evolving a specific body of doctrines. The method or mode of reasoning a given thinker employs is the formal cause which determines the coherence and direction of his discourse as well as the meaning of everything contained in it. Because that is so, until we attain a rigorous conception of method we are unlikely to gain anything more than a rudimentary understanding of what is going on in any critical discourse.

Thus R. S. Crane and so far so good. Unfortunately the theory of methods Crane develops doesn't take us much further than the old adage that all men are either Platonists or Aristotelians. He distinguishes inductive and deductive approaches, empirical and a priori procedures, and along these lines opposes his own method of inquiry to the dialectical methods of hypostatization he finds rampant in modern criticism. One gets the frequent impression, in fact, that the entire examination is designed to show that there is something necessarily sound in the former and something inherently suspect in the latter. Indeed, Crane gives a far from adequate or unbiased account of the internal logic of dialectical thought, taking as a paradigm of the method what are some of its most questionable instances. Be that as it may, the larger defect in Crane's theory of methods is its failure to account for the full range of discursive possibilities. It fails as a taxonomy. If one wants to describe the history of philosophic debate or to distinguish the methods of contemporary thinkers such as Russell, Wittgenstein, Dewey, Heidegger, and Lévi-Strauss, Crane's system is of little use. Nor would Crane's system enable one to account for the distinct theories of form developed in chapter 1. To understand such differences we need a richer, more philosophic, and, I might add, more pluralistic understanding of method, based on a broader inquiry into the distinct modes of human thought.

The Modes of Thought

In an attempt to describe the basic differences in principles and method that have characterized the history of philosophic debate, Richard McKeon has developed an elaborate schematism of philosophic semantics and the modes of philosophic inquiry. That project—which is of great complexity and importance, and which I will make no attempt to trace in detail here—is based on the distinction of four modes of thought.[6]

Before turning to a detailed consideration of the four modes, a few words are in order concerning the relationship between Mc-Keon's thought and my use of it in this chapter. If method is one of the primary concerns of twentieth-century thought, McKeon's work deserves far more consideration than it has thus far received; one of my purposes in this chapter is to offer a coherent if somewhat simplified exposition of McKeon's complex and challenging investigations. McKeon would be the first to point out, however, that one always interprets the thought of another in terms of one's own principles and problems: every interpretation is in a sense a reinterpretation, and this is especially true when we approach another thinker not in a purely "scholarly" spirit but with our own thought at the center of that act.

For these reasons it would be a mistake to identify any of the concepts developed in the following discussion with the thought of Richard McKeon or with positions McKeon would be likely to endorse on the problems we are considering. In a strict sense, only the initial definitions on pages 93–94 are straight McKeon; the detailed description of each mode is my responsibility, as is the contemporary and at times controversial direction given to those descriptions, especially on pages 110–17.[7]

For my purposes, the most important fact about McKeon's vast schematism is that it is generated out of a repeated distinction of four basic modes of human thought. Mode of thought may be defined as the shaping principle which gives coherence to the totality of methodological operations which constitute a discourse. It determines the beginnings or principles upon which a thinker bases his activity, the procedures through which he organizes his discourse, and the characteristic interpretations he thereby provides of phenomena. It thus accounts for the particular problems a thinker poses and the way he employs terms to give specific meaning to the themes and commonplaces of his time in constructing a body of doctrines.

In general terms, the modes may be defined as follows: *Dialectic* is a method of assimilation to a model whereby comprehensive truths are approximated or embodied. *Operational* thought is a method of discrimination and postulation whereby arbitrary formulations are interpreted in order to distinguish the different legitimate perspectives on a topic. The *problematic* is a method of inquiry which separates questions into the distinct disciplines in which particular problems are determined and solved. *Logistic* thought is a method of composition in which irreducible least parts are put together by means of invariable laws.

As McKeon explains them, the modes are exclusive, exhaustive, and irreducible, thus providing the ultimate foundations for philosophic pluralism. Naturally one can use any one mode to eliminate the others: the history of philosophy turns, in fact, on such efforts. The only way to eliminate or incorporate competing frameworks, however, is by adhering to one of the modes. It appears that the only way to avoid pluralism is by appealing to a principle which is somehow beyond human thought.

The Dialectical Thinker

The Mode

The goal of dialectic is to demonstrate that "the Whole is all there is" by discovering "the essential connections that bind all things together."[8] In ordering thought toward such an end, the dialectician endeavors to assimilate everything encountered in experience to a comprehensive model. To evolve such an understanding every dialectic sets up an exhaustive and ultimately evaluative opposition between a lower realm (becoming, *doxa* and *pistis*, consciousness, science), where division and confusion reign, and a higher realm (being, *dianoia* and *noesis*, self-consciousness, poetry), where everything converges in the march toward a single understanding of reality in which the good, the true, and the beautiful are inseparable and freedom and knowledge are ultimately one.

Because experience can only be understood as a whole, dialectical thought requires the rejection of separate substances, clear and distinct ideas, and univocal terms. Terms must be used analogically in order to bind together realities initially thought separate; thus in the course of every dialectic its central terms—such as eros and imitation in Plato, imagination in Coleridge, consciousness in Hegel—necessarily wind through curious shifts, doublings, and expansions in their basic meanings as the dialectical process advances toward a completion in which all reality becomes intelligible in terms of comprehensive categories of thought such as eros, self-consciousness, and will to power. To grasp their place in the whole, all things, all thoughts, all modes of discourse, and all the actions of men must be assimilated to such universal ideals or notions which establish internal relations among experiences initially regarded as distinct and separate. Dialectic is inherently idealistic and every dialectic establishes a graded hierarchy of ascent (as in Plato's divided line or Hegel's phenomenology of self-consciousness) to a single, unconditioned principle (such as the Good or Absolute Knowledge) which is implicit from the beginning of experience and directs the entire process. All activities participate in the quest to attain it. The scientist, the philosopher, the man of action, and the poet are thus engaged in directly comparable efforts, with one and all judged by their adequacy to the whole of things. As a result there is no way to separate logic, metaphysics, and epistemology, to bracket ethics, politics, or poetics for future consideration, or to keep the pursuit of any problem from running up against the same fundamental questions. As Socrates demonstrates, one cannot ask one question without implicitly asking all questions. Since all human activities are engaged in a common effort, all disciplines meet in the single discipline of dialectic. Plato's inquiry into the nature of justice—personal and political—necessarily becomes an ontological inquiry into the nature of knowledge and being; and it is within that framework alone that it is possible for a thinker like Plato to achieve an adequate understanding of poetry.

Dialectic is thus the method of interdisciplinary thought; all its procedures are based on the insight that all problems and questions are necessarily interrelated. To demonstrate that fact Hegel, in *The Phenomenology of Mind*, constructs a comprehensive drama in which all the attitudes that consciousness can take toward the world are referred to a single problem which Hegel finds at the center of all human strivings—the problem of reconciling inwardness and existence, systematic thought and concrete life. That problem is present at the origin of consciousness in the dialectic implicit in desire which leads man to reject creaturely comfort and seek recognition as a free human being; its development generates the struggle of master and slave (the origin of politics) and animates the sequence of necessary stages through which the unhappy consciousness passes in its quest for world-historical freedom, thus giving birth to the ever-widening drama of personal, social, artistic, and religious activity recorded in the *Phenomenology*. By tracing that process Hegel is able to apprehend human activities as a series of approximations to that comprehensive understanding of man as Being-in-the-World which he terms Absolute Knowledge. The essence of all human activities lies in their contribution to that goal; to understand any activity, one must establish its determinate place in that total framework.

To attain such an understanding of experience, Hegel argues that dialectic really requires no more than a strict adherence to the Socratic discipline of self-questioning: the rejection of all unexamined presuppositions, including the axioms of common sense, and the willingness to subject all experiences to a reflective process that is defined by the concepts of contradiction and determinate negation. The perception of contradiction is the lifeblood of dialectic as a process, its source of motion. Theaetetus thinks knowledge consists in immediate and fleeting sensations, Thrasymachus holds that justice lies in power, Euthyphro goes to prosecute his father unaware that he carries the ultimate problems of knowledge and conduct with him. Thanks to Socrates the contradictions in those views become apparent. Their negation, in turn, is a determinate process because it generates a new awareness. On it the process of reflective questioning is repeated. As that process develops, questions initially thought separate come together and an understanding of the comprehensive internal relations among all things begins to emerge. Begin with immediate experience: dialectic remains the inescapable discipline because everything we say and do implicates us in fundamental questions and the search for a principle which can sustain itself before the bar of reflection. The simplest assertion is fraught with implications which, if traced by a sufficiently reflective consciousness, bring us before the unity of experience and the necessary connections among all things—and it is in this sense that dialectic can claim to be the only philosophy which is grounded in the recognition of reflection as a distinct philosophic principle.

The burden of dialectic in fact is to carry the reflective process to its fullest experiential development. Genuine dialectic has never been in the business of collecting contradictions and then arranging them into mechanical triads, nor does it make contradiction into an abstract fetish. Although such conceptions of dialectic still have a popular currency, they miss the basic import of even a maxim like Blake's "without contraries is no progression," for the concern of dialectic is with the dynamic progression of contradictions, not their random collection. The fundamental task of dialectic is to discover the fundamental contradictions in which all human efforts necessarily participate (inwardness and existence, eros and thanatos, ethics and aesthetics) and then to trace the ever-expanding realities and relations that emerge from their clash. As a structuring of thought dialectic must be defined, accordingly, as a drama of dynamic yet systematic ascent which grows out of the self-movement of contradictions and proceeds toward a comprehensive understanding of experience which cancels, preserves, and uplifts (*Aufhebung*) the entire process by establishing a single order of thought in which the identity of knowledge and being is assured. Apart from such a formulation, none of the procedures which characterize dialectical thought make any sense. Dialectic is necessarily circular and organic; in dialectic, as discourse and as ontology, "the whole is all there is."

Its Application to Literature

The treatment of literature within this mode of thought ranges from Plato's condemnation of mimetic poetry for its violation of reason to the many efforts of post-Romantic critics to see poetry, in opposition to science, as the model of concrete knowing. The two views are not as far apart as they initially appear, for in both cases the same basic assumption with respect to the purpose of poetry controls the estimation of its nature and value: all that is needed to get the poets back into the Republic—and the abstract philosophers out—is a change in the object of knowledge. Like all other activities, poetry is one of the ways we apprehend reality; it is burdened, like other ways of knowing, with a comprehensive task. Socrates speaks of the "quarrel between philosophy and poetry" as already ancient. It is also contemporary—but the dialectical framework of the debate has shifted rather dramatically. While Plato used reason as the model of truth and judged the impassioned and vague nature of poetic perception, utterance, and mimesis accordingly, since the Romantic period imagination and the ambiguous, ironic, and paradoxical resources of poetic language have been exalted for their ability to give us an understanding of concrete experience which transcends the limitations of scientific, logical, and rhetorical thought. Plato's dialectic aspires to the rational understanding of transcendent realities that are beyond change, whereas ours is a dialectic in and of the world, in and of the cave. In such a dialectic, poetic knowing is prized above other ways of thinking because it brings the whole "soul" of man into activity, giving us an apprehension of lived experience which preserves "the whole of things" in an irreducible and concrete totality.

In developing a dialectical poetic of the latter sort, the basic problem is to comprehend the forms of literary creation as original modes of access to experience capable of giving us an understanding of the world which other ways of knowing fail to provide.

The possibility of literature as a distinct mode of thinking emerges, in fact, as a direct result of a realization of the limitations of logical, propositional, and categorical thought: witness, as examples, Coleridge's attempt to extricate the spirit of Kant's philosophy from its letter and the effort of the New Critics to construct a cognitive opposition of poetic language and the languages of scientific and philosophic discourse. In making the forms of artistic creation original modes of cognition, however, the dialectical critic necessarily lays an immense task on them: applied directly to immediate experience, literary form must prove capable of generating a comprehensive ordering of experience.

To earn that possibility it is absolutely essential at the start to achieve a liberation from the conceptions of form and content handed down by the rhetorical tradition. For the dialectician, the mimetic, technical, and linguistic dynamics of literary form are not merely ways of presenting a preexistent content or body of themes; they must be comprehended, instead, as distinct cognitive principles which first bring into being that concrete awareness of the world which constitutes both the substance and the structure of the literary work as concrete universal. Embodied in the action of the literary work, and inseparable from that action, the ordering of reality which form makes possible is the locus of the literary "idea." By applying the forms of artistic cognition directly to experience, literature attempts to work out a concrete world view by constructing a concrete world. The various modes of artistic cognition must be defined and evaluated in terms of their adequacy to that task.

Thus we attain the dialectical theory of form developed on pages 35–39 and the attempt in applying that theory to see the two modes of artistic cognition dramatized in "The Bear" in terms of the apprehension of reality each makes possible.

Operational Thought

The Mode

In an operational philosophy man is the maker and measure of all things. Thought is inherently social and at base ideological. It grows out of the process of social interaction and reflects the economic and class conflicts that make up the structure of social life. Even in perception, interest is primary: things are *pragmata*, they exist for our use, and what works best is good. The true sources and principles of thought lie in the world of communal action, for thought expresses the beliefs and values we share in common as a result of acting together to realize our interests. Philosophy arises out of the "scramble" of motives, attitudes, and ways of acting that shape rhetorical man. It is one of the ways we communicate—and insofar as man is a social being, communication constitutes his essence. *Doxa* and *pistis* are, ultimately, all that there is.

With that scramble as his primary object, the operationalist rejects the dialectician's search for ultimate norms of thought and conduct and tries instead to describe the different perspectives that may be taken on the issues that concern us. The primary characteristic of intellectual life is ambiguity. Since the principles of thought are found in social life, all distinctions are initially arbitrary and all terms and concepts inherently ambiguous. The same terms and concepts—democracy, freedom, duty, the right of peoples to self-determination—assume a number of different meanings and are used to support a number of opposed programs of action. As a social force, thought reflects the conflicts of social life. We use our ideas as fists to annihilate our opponents. Philosophic discourse is not above the battle: one interprets another philosophy in terms of one's own philosophy and in so doing inevitably distorts it. Accordingly, the first task of operational thought is semantic—until we understand the sources and pitfalls of ambiguity we cannot begin to communicate in a responsible manner.

And communication is all we have. There is no way to transcend the conflict of viewpoints and ascend beyond the social process to some ultimate dialectical perspective. That desire is a natural outgrowth of social tensions and a force at work in society, especially when a social order is falling apart. But the second-best state is all we have: all views are legitimized by the interests they express and we have no choice but to enter the fray. As Kenneth Burke contends, the scramble, the barnyard, the tangle of human motives met in dubious battle is our subject matter; *Ad bellum purificandum* the highest goal of thought. But to purify war we need to develop a comprehensive framework that will enable us to distinguish the various meanings common terms, concepts, and statements assume in serving the various causes for which they are enlisted.

To understand the complexity of the communicative process and to enable us to communicate in a noninvidious fashion, the operationalist therefore makes discrimination and postulation the basic moments of his thought. In the first moment he attempts to resolve the ambiguities that frustrate discourse by clarifying the different views that may be taken on a given topic. In the second he attempts to reconcile those viewpoints as warranted statements by constructing an overarching framework in which they become contributing perspectives.

Thus operational thought is by definition a systematic study of the principles, assumptions, and methods which enable men to develop conflicting views on the topics that concern them. As a philosophy of communication, its goal, as in Richard McKeon, is to clarify the ambiguities of philosophic debate by tracing conflicting doctrines and dogmas back to the distinct principles of thought and discourse which make them possible. As a concrete sociology of communication, its goal, as in Kenneth Burke, is to construct a grammar of the distinct, equally legitimate, and irreducible motives, attitudes, and modes of action which inform thought and shape the social process.

Since knowledge is something men make in pursuing their interests, communication also provides the end of operational thought. There is no way to transcend the world of rhetoric; the task, instead, is to improve it or at least to prevent its becoming the war of each against all. Like the dialectical, the operational is a universal method applicable to all questions and topics, but within that similarity there is a fundamental difference. Rejecting the dialectician's attempt to construct a hierarchy of approximations to a single englobing truth which transcends and corrects the phenomenal world of opinion, the operationalist attempts to construct a comprehensive philosophy of communication that will distinguish the many legitimate modes of human discourse and that will trace them back to the equally legitimate interests which they serve. Beginning with ambiguity and proceeding through discrimination and postulation to clarify the inevitable sources of ambiguity, the operationalist seeks to effect the communication of different perspectives on common topics. His goal is not to short-circuit debate but to contribute to its continuance and improvement. Operational thought might in fact be regarded as a methodization of the democratic process, since it gives us a principled understanding of the ways in which we differ as well as the ultimate court of appeal for the prosecution of those differences. Purifying war, the operational thinker has no option but to let the battle continue, hoping that, through his aid, the scramble will become the movement "toward a better life."

Its Application to Literature

Since all human activities arise out of the social process and are ultimately directed upon it, everything man thinks and does partakes in his effort, through communication, to influence the values and beliefs necessary to maintain and improve the life of the community. Following these general principles, the operationalist conceives literature as a mode of discourse; it is, in fact, one of the most important and powerful ways in which we communicate and both the rhetorician and the sociologist neglect it at their peril. The purpose of literature is to structure social life by presenting a preexistent content in the form that is most appropriate to it in light of the audience a writer is trying to reach. *Form* and *content* are the basic terms in operational criticism and both are defined rhetorically. Content consists in the preexistent ideas the artist wishes to communicate, ranging from abstract themes and commonplaces (that is, the proper study of mankind is man; war is absurd) to the more complex attitudes and motives which make up the concrete dynamics of the social process—ritual needs, psychological complexes, our response to symbols of authority and victimization. Form, in turn, consists in the resources of style, technique, and imitation (or symbolic action) which are used to present content in a persuasive way: the dynamics of form range from the power of weighted language to make commonplace ideas powerful, as in Pope's "what oft was thought but ne'er so well expressed," to the use of complex actions to dramatize a theme or body of interrelated themes, thereby effecting a complex transformation in our attitudes and ways of acting. The modes of rhetorical discourse in literature thus include everything from explicitly didactic works such as Pope's "An Essay on Man," Eliot's "Four Quartets," and the use of fable, parable, and allegory for moral instruction to the development of complex mimetic structures which concretely embody the very motivational and attitudinal forces which shape the self as a rhetorical being.

Because the purpose of rhetoric is to effect the communication of socially beneficial attitudes, a full understanding of rhetorical art requires a complex sociological theory: a grammar or systematic description of the attitudes, motives, and ways of acting which constitute the dynamics of the social process thus offers the deepest and most adequate understanding one can gain of the content of art. Because literary modes of presentation are likewise selected with a view to the audience and function best when they give direct expression to the basic forces of social life, the most important and powerful modes of rhetorical discourse will also be found in the mimetic rather than the didactic—that is, in the principles which enable artists to represent, in complex symbolic actions, the social forces which, in their interaction, make up the ongoing drama of social life. At this ultimate stage in the development of rhetorical art, form and content are organically one: a grammar of motives is, by definition, a discovery of the principles which structure symbolic actions.

Thus Kenneth Burke and the rhetorical theory of form outlined on pages 23–27.

Problematic Thought

The Mode

Problematic thought is disciplinary. There are many different kinds of things, many different activities, many distinct sciences. Because "the world is full of a number of things," the methods of thought must be many. There is no one method applicable to all questions, nor does everything in experience relate to some comprehensive dialectical scheme. Human beings face many distinct problems and act for many distinct purposes. The goal of problematic thought is to make the distinctions necessary to account for these differences. It is a method of inquiry which attempts to formulate the distinct methodological principles and procedures necessary to deal with the many different objects reality presents to thought.

Developing this method enabled Aristotle to distinguish the activities of thinking, doing, and making which are the subject matters in turn of the speculative, practical, and productive arts. *Speculative inquiry* formulates the principles of strict logical demonstration required for understanding the causes of natural phenomena and natural processes. *Practical inquiry* is concerned with the actions of men and formulates the principles of moral self-determination, political organization, and rhetorical persuasion that are at work in the various affairs of men, principles which are at best quasi-logical. *Productive science* inquires into the principles of making that enable artists to take preexistent materials and give them a form which they would not by nature assume. Physics, ethics, and poetics are distinct disciplines having distinct objects and resting on distinct methodological procedures. There are no "essential connections" binding them together dialectically into one order of being nor is there one logic applicable to all of them. Instead, the task of logic as the organon of inquiry is to formulate the distinct principles of reasoning required to understand different subjects: the principles of strict demonstration applicable to the science of nature are not the same as the principles of pragmatic reasoning through which men seek happiness nor are either, in turn, the same as the principles of making they use to create works of art. By the same token, history is not a translation of pure logic into temporal terms, a speculative dance of abstract concepts. To understand the causes of historical events one must develop a logic of probability which takes into account all the factors that enter into events, making history an affair that is overdetermined in a potentially unlimited number of ways. Although it is a sham art when taken as a substitute for the science of politics, rhetoric, in turn, is worthy of separate study because it instructs us in the principles of persuasion that reign for the most part in the sphere of human affairs. Rhetoric totally oversteps its bounds, however, when it attempts, operationally, to reduce scientific knowledge to a matter of opinion; and needless to say the a priori methods of mathematical thought are not open to debate. Each method is proper to its own sphere, to the particular problem it tries to solve and the particular phenomena with which it deals. The only way to achieve precision in understanding the many distinct objects of thought is to keep questions separate by establishing independent "sciences" or inquiries, each with their own first principles and distinct methodological procedures. In contrast to the universality of the dialectical and operational modes of thought, which are applicable to all problems and subjects, the problematic thinker thus develops a plurality of distinct methods for the treatment of a number of different problems and phenomena.

Because its objects and purposes are many, human thought is itself inherently plural. The ways we think when we inquire into the causes of natural processes differ from the ways we think when we deliberate over moral questions, imitate human actions in the medium of language, or endeavor to persuade our fellowmen to join us in a common action. And there is no hierarchy at work here. Pure logic may be intrinsically excellent and inherently satisfying to our aesthetic or contemplative sense, but we also live in the world and the many distinct problems we face there require other ways of reasoning.

By the same rationale, the conclusions reached in distinct inquiries are not directly comparable. What science tells us about the nature of the physical world, how we know, and the principles required for strict demonstration or proof are not directly applicable to the world of human action or the realm of art. Likewise, what practical inquiry teaches us about the social bases of human action is of little relevance to scientific inquiry into the nature of things. The objective validity of scientific knowledge is independent of the social situation and private disposition of the scientist.

Thus the problematic thinker rejects the operationalist's reduction of thought and discourse to the actional and arbitrary principles of social life as well as the dialectician's search for an ideal and hierarchical correspondence between the discursive order, the order of thought, and the order of things. Problematically, the integrity of each discipline rests on a strict separation of its problems from other problems just as the coherence of each discourse depends on a univocal use of terms. Terms may be initially ambiguous, but the words common to all discourse take on precise meaning within the specific context in which they are used. It is a Platonizing error to use common terms such as *knowledge*, *being*, *reality*, *imitation*, and *poetry* analogically in order to collapse distinct disciplines into a single hierarchy of being, as if every term had to have one and only one true meaning. Knowledge is many rather than one; the meaning we assign to common terms in distinct disciplines must be flexible and specific enough to preserve the substantial reality of the many distinct things we wish to know. One of the primary tasks of metaphysics, in fact, is to explain the many different ways in which the term *being* must be used in order to establish the possibility of a number of separate sciences.

Its Application to Literature

It is possible, of course, to consider the same object in a variety of disciplines. But it is essential when doing so to distinguish the substantial and accidental properties of the thing and to separate the understanding of a thing's nature, which is achieved through a scientific explanation of its causes, from the many "aspects" of the thing which emerge when we discount its nature and place it in a variety of other contexts. These distinctions are crucial for a proper understanding of poetry. The proper task of poetic science is to formulate the principles of productive activity which go into the construction of mimetic works. For the problematic thinker poetry is not a speculative activity directly comparable to science and philosophy as it is for the dialectician, nor is it a practical activity designed to communicate rhetorical truths to an audience. The "ancient quarrel between philosophy and poetry" need never have arisen: a careful analysis of the productive principles that shape poetic activity reveals that the purpose of mimetic art is neither to think, instruct, persuade, nor communicate.

Aristotle's application of the four causes to tragedy is still a classic example of the method. The material cause of tragedy is language; its efficient cause the dramatic manner of representation. The formal cause is plot: the imitation of a human action in a particular temporal synthesis of materials of plot, character, and thought logically subordinated to one another in that order, so that thought functions for the sake of representing character and both are shaped by the primacy of action. The final cause of tragedy is catharsis: that particular emotional *dynamis* or power which, conferred upon the experiential materials which constitute the plot or object of imitation, gives the work its particular power to move us. So understood, emotional form provides the first principle of artistic reasoning in mimetic art for both the artist and the critic. The primary fact about mimetic poetry is that it represents actions in which agents, as a result of their character, become "happy or the reverse"; our emotional involvement in "the fate of characters about whom we are made to care" is thus the ongoing principle of structure which accounts for the unity of such works as well as the principle determining the continuous interest we take in experiencing them. Everything that enters into the construction of mimetic works functions for the sake of realizing and maximizing an emotional *dynamis*; thus our response is the starting point which enables us to reconstruct the problems the artist encountered in embodying that pleasure—and that is the essential task of interpretation.

Naturally one can discuss a literary work in a variety of nonartistic contexts. Aristotle, in fact, uses the poets to illustrate rhetorical techniques in the *Rhetoric* and discusses the educational value of music in the *Politics*. It is one thing, however, to discuss the nature of poetry—and the artistic function of its components in constituting that nature—and quite another to discuss those "aspects" of poetry we may discern once we isolate its parts and understand them apart from their function. The use of quotations from Homer to illustrate general propositions or rhetorical tropes and the understanding of the same "statements" in their dramatic context are quite different things. The first procedure is quite legitimate for purposes of rhetorical illustration or moral instruction, but disastrous if taken as an artistic understanding of the function that "thought" and language play in a literary work or the general purpose that controls mimetic art. Contrary to the ruling assumption of most modern critics, literature by and large is not a mode of discourse and has little to do with the concerns of rhetoric, the social sciences, or philosophy. A consideration of poetry in light of its end, as opposed to a focus on isolated qualities or abstract themes, reveals emotion, rather than meaning, to be the primary cause of poetic structure.

Hence R. S. Crane and the theory of emotional form presented on pages 14–15.

Logistic Thought

The Mode

Logistic thought is the methodology of reduction. For the logistic thinker every complex may be resolved into its elements and the mechanical laws determining their combination. A whole is no more than the sum of its least parts, and they are independently intelligible. Thought and discourse, likewise, are processes of composition in which least parts are put together into complexes by invariable and, at base, associational laws. While the dialectician rejects least parts and separate substances and strives to apprehend the essential connections that bind all things together in an irreducible ontological whole, the logistic thinker rejects the possibility of a comprehensive scheme of internal relations and seeks instead to isolate entities and break them down into their component parts.

Since reality presents us with many different complexes, the logician, like the problematic thinker, sets up distinct areas of inquiry. In treating any object, however, he employs a uniform method. Whatever one's subject, to understand anything one must resolve the complex into its least parts and formulate the laws governing their combination. Thus, the world of things, the processes of thought, and the activities of men may all be treated as natural phenomena engaged in natural processes and obeying natural laws. In each case the complex is finally no more than the deterministic relations that maintain among its simple components. Substance is a fiction. Sensations, impressions, and invariable laws of association make up the structure of experience; ideas are mere copies of impressions; and thought is inherently positivistic and mechanical. Metaphysical concepts are not so much false as they are nonsensical; in philosophy the solution of the problem lies, indeed, in the disappearance of the problem. Scientific understanding requires exact methods of analysis. Man is no more than a creature of behavior determined by the mechanisms of stimulus and response, pleasure and pain; character no more than a product of unconscious, biological, and environmental forces; and conduct no more than the inevitable issue of prior determinations.

Although the logistic method is most often associated with the rise of modern science and the scientific study of nature, its extension has always been much broader. Heraclitus and Democritus applied it to all questions. Machiavelli and Hobbes used it to study the natures of man and the state. Descartes hoped to work out a mathematical ethics on logistic principles. Its use as a historical method ranges from Thucydides' narration of the natural laws which determine the construction and decomposition of empires to A. O. Lovejoy's attempt to resolve the history of philosophic thought into the combination and dissolution of unit-ideas which are mechanically glued together then broken apart in a never-ceasing attempt to surmount the principle of contradiction. Recently, Lévi-Strauss has attempted to explain "the unchanged and unchanging ... structure of the human mind" and its cultural products in logistic terms. His "structuralist" method resolves distinct modes of discourse such as myth, science, philosophy, and literature (as well as the rituals and customs of social life) into their elements and arranges those elements spatially into discontinuous synchronic patterns. He then proceeds to argue that those patterns only make sense once we see that fixed logical antinomies—such as nature and culture, the one and the many, identity and difference—underlie and determine all processes of signification. As in Lovejoy, thought is discontinuous and self-contradictory; all complex structures of thought may be resolved into their elements and the invariable laws of composition and decomposition that determine the relationship of those elements.

In many quarters logistic thought has, of course, become the law and the prophets and the morning-prayer of modern man; the other modes of thought are commonly viewed as metaphoric failures to attain the kind of analytic precision it makes possible. As McKeon suggests on occasion, ours is a logistic age. The phenomena or substances which appear to us to be most real are actually no more than epiphenomenal; the experiences we most want to talk about we must learn to consign to silence. In all matters under the sun what is really going on is determined by the elements and forces at work beneath the surface.

Its Applications to Literature

Rather than offering us a fourth theory of form, logistic thought presents the antithesis of that concept. The very concepts of a whole which is greater than the sum of its parts, of structure as the continuous manifestation of a synthesizing purpose, and of the irreducibility of the phenomenon are ideas foreign to the logistic mode of thought. Creation, like thought, is fitful at best; the absence of conscious purpose the cardinal fact of human behavior. All the talk about function, structure, and purpose introduce unwarranted, indeed mythical, notions which disguise the fact that making (artistic or otherwise) is no more than a mechanical process of selecting and arranging independently intelligible least parts into loosely unified complexes.

In the discussion of art the logistic thinker is concerned, accordingly, with local qualities rather than artistic wholes. As Santayana notes, "no one criticizes a sunset" and in the experience of it all the elements that enter into the logistics of pleasure are present, the meeting of inner needs and outer qualities which make some perceptions immediately and inherently satisfying.[9] Pleasure is one aspect of experience and art is its temple. The aesthetic transaction arises out of the interaction between the pleasurable qualities in things and the psychic needs in the "mind" of the observer which are responsive to such stimuli. The artist's task is to create, out of the expressive resources of language, appropriate responses to the aesthetic dimensions of experience. When he succeeds he incarnates in his art an immediately infective embodiment of the natural conditions of human aesthetic response.

Naturally such heightened states can only be achieved from time to time. Logistic thinkers concentrate on style, imagery, and isolated events rather than on total structures because they regard the aesthetic as a special state of mind which by its very nature is fleeting. It might be realized organically in a fairly short poem, but in longer works structure is no more than a loose principle of arrangement and one can expect to find many arid stretches between the moments of impassioned utterance in which general aesthetic qualities such as sublimity and beauty make an appearance.

Because literary experience resides in the interaction between the aesthetic needs and powers of the audience (such as sensitivity, taste, the sense of beauty) and the aesthetic qualities of the object (such as style, decorum, wit, expressiveness), it is quite proper to regard the literary work as no more than the sum total of local "commotions" and emotions it occasions. Thus despite a similarity of terms, the logistic and the problematic conceptions of pleasure as the end of art are radically different. In the problematic approach, the emotional forms proper to art, such as tragic catharsis, are understood as unifying principles of structure, objectively existent in the work as a whole, and present there as the potential cause of an experience which is not subject to the vagaries of private or subjective response. For the logistic thinker, in contrast, pleasure is immediate, local, and most likely full of mnemonic irrelevancies; the pleasure art produces arises out of the momentary responses of a stimulated subjectivity to the immediately pleasurable qualities of isolated parts and components. The artistic whole is no more than the "sum" of such experiences; objectivity in aesthetic experience is a myth. As Santayana put it, "Beauty is pleasure regarded as the quality of a thing."

Since they regard it as little more than the line upon which the pegs of pregnant utterance are hung, logistic thinkers generally pay but passing attention to the action represented in complex literary works. Recently, however, Lévi-Strauss has developed a logistic method for analyzing the actions or "plots" of narrative and dramatic structures. The particular logistic framework in which Lévi-Strauss places literature is somewhat different from the one discussed above. Rather than a special realm of aesthetic expression, literature is yet another mode of discourse, caught up like all others in the dilemmas of signification. And discourse for Lévi-Strauss is logistic rather than operational. Thus the materials of human experience which go to make up the "plots" of mimetic works are really no more than fragments or elements of signification selected and arranged to "dramatize," or translate into narrative and quasi-temporal terms, an underlying logical formula. Beginning with a plot summary—and, significantly, with what R. S. Crane calls plot matter in contrast to plot form—Lévi-Strauss' method resolves the concrete literary action into synchronic elements and the fixed laws underlying their logistic combination.[10] While it is a significant advance in logistic criticism, it necessarily stops short of the concern with artistic wholeness which distinguishes the dialectical, operational, and problematic theories of form.

So much for systematic criticism in the logistic mode. If logistic criticism appears at loose ends in the scheme I am constructing, that is, of course, the point; which does not mean one should underestimate the attractiveness or prevalence of logistic procedures. We are all logistic critics in a loose sense insofar as criticism remains a casual affair in which we discuss one discrete topic after another with little or no consideration of how those topics might be related.

Reality, Knowledge, Experience, and Man in the Four Modes

In logistic thought experience is a process in which sensations and impressions are put together into complexes. The physical world is primary, and mind is regarded as an essentially passive medium. Beginning with the object, the logistic thinker constructs the subject. Perception consists in combining impressions by means of the minimal principles of association mind brings to experience. Since both the physical world and our perception of it are ultimately resoluble into their elements, concepts such as substance and form are no more than fictions; by the same token, the sequences of ideas which constitute understanding, such as cause and effect, are products of custom and actually signify no more than the priority and habitual connection of perceptions. Reason, in making such concepts constitutive, is a faculty of illusion which refers vague terms to nonexistent relations.

Logistic thought is resolutely antimetaphysical and proceeds toward the naturalization of consciousness and the reduction of human conduct to the pleasure-pain mechanism. Man is a thing among things, a product of external relations beyond his control. Physical science is the architectonic discipline, and everything must eventually be resolved into matters of fact.

For the problematic thinker, in contrast, experience arises out of the interaction of subject and object, sensation and understanding; that primary relationship cannot be dissolved nor can its terms be analyzed separately. Mind is an instrument rather than a medium and constructs phenomena by bringing a priori principles and categories to bear upon the manifold of sensation. Kant's *Critique* is a classical example of problematic epistemology, both in its rejection of Hume's logistic reductions and in its equally strong critique of dialectical attempts to extend knowledge beyond the limits of possible experience. While a priori concepts and our innate rational powers enable us to have a scientific experience of the world, they also limit knowledge to the field of possible experiences. Reason, in its dialectical employment, tries to go beyond those limits in order to ascend from the conditioned to the unconditioned and a knowledge of the whole of things. But while that desire is natural, reason is a faculty of illusion if taken as a principle of scientific inquiry into nature. The value of reason lies in the ethical, historical, and aesthetic spheres of human activity where our desire for the comprehensive has an ethical and teleological value or may be granted a free play.

Problematically, experience is divided into distinct realms which are distinguished in a multiplicity of ways in terms of the distinct objects of knowing, powers of the knower, and purposes of human activity. As Aristotle argued, discursive being and real being are distinct and it is a Platonizing error to search for an ideal correspondence between them. Reality is plural and thought is disciplinary. There is no such thing as "the unity of knowledge" if by that notion we mean one set of concepts and procedures applicable to all subjects and one hierarchical order of being in which all things participate. Language may be inherently ambiguous, but words as terms take on specific meaning within the particular context in which they are used. Whatever its object, inquiry depends on a univocal use of terms and a scientific explanation of causes. Thus each separate inquiry remains constant unto its own principles and ends while the object remains constant over against a plurality of discussions of its substantial and accidental properties.

For the problematic thinker, consequently, man is many things. To understand him we must study the many different contexts in which he exists and acts. As a part of nature, man is an object of physical determination; as a social being, he is a subject of politics and ethics; as a thinker, he is a metaphysical being who endeavors to know the causes of natural phenomena and who finds happiness in the contemplation of things that are ends in themselves; as an artist, he is a maker; and as an aesthetic being, he takes delight in works of art, especially in responding emotionally to dramatic representations of the "fate of characters about whom" he "is made to care." As a man among men he is persuader and persuaded, and frequently gives himself over to all the idols of tribe, theater, and marketplace. Man is all these things and it is a mistake to collapse the distinct contexts in which he thinks and acts or to set up a philosophic anthropology (or phenomenology of spirit) which posits a single problem and goal at the base of all human activities. For essentially man is a problem solver. He faces many distinct problems, proposes many different tasks for himself, and a correct understanding of his "nature" requires that we regard him anew in considering each of the distinct disciplines he develops in his response to the manyness of being.

While both logistic and problematic thinkers begin with the physical world and use their knowledge of it to establish the principles and analogies needed to understand other phenomena— either by reduction or by disciplinary distinction—operational thought begins with the world of human affairs. For the operationalist, experience is essentially a process of social interaction. Knowing the physical world is a relatively secondary matter, and even then interest is the true mother of knowledge. Science itself is a social and historical event and must be understood within that context. As Thomas Kuhns and Jürgen Habermas have argued, scientific knowledge is a group product:[11] the search for value-free objective methods is itself an ideology; and the interests that determine what we will know are ultimately political. The goal of all knowledge is *praxis*. To understand why we think and act in the ways that we do, all activities and beliefs must be referred to the social contexts out of which they arise. Knowledge is primarily an affair of opinions and derives from the customs, values, and beliefs that either bind men together in a viable social order or give birth to the contradictions and injustices that drive them apart.

The primacy of social interaction defines operational man. Consciousness is a social process, the self a social product. We are shaped by the ways in which we communicate, and all our actions are ultimately directed toward bettering the structures of communal living which constitute the ground and horizon of our existence. The same reference holds ontologically: reality is a social and historical process rather than a body of subsistent entities or naturalistic processes independent of human will. Things exist for the sake of human possibilities. The true nature of each thing lies in the discovery of its use, and through labor man transforms the physical world. As Marx demonstrated, nature is a social category caught up in the relations of production and class conflict that define the dynamics of historical development.

The dialectician sees operational thought as a bold beginning which does not go far enough.[12] Man is the only true starting point, but man is first and foremost an ontological being; the fundamental questions of metaphysics contain the key to the innermost meaning of his existence. The being of man lies in his "to be," in the act of existence in which his being becomes an issue for him. Man is absolute dialectical unrest, a source of radical instability who refers every experience to the ceaseless debate with himself over the meaning of his being. For the dialectician, once the dynamic of radical existential reflection has been tapped it has a comprehensive experiential force. Through the process of existent-reflection, man discovers that the effort to work out the meaning of his existence implies the need to order all of his projects into a hierarchy determined by their adequacy to a single goal—the reconciliation of inwardness and existence, thought and life, in a concrete historical world that will be adequate to the deepest needs of the human subject.

Like the operationalist, the dialectician finds scientific objectivity a derivate mode of knowing inadequate to the needs and situation of man and, like the operationalist, the dialectician situates thought in a world of social engagement and opinion. The dynamic of existential reflection which dialectic introduces into that world, however, transcends and transforms the social givens upon which operational thought is based, and refers the actional principles of social life to a far deeper and more concrete source of principles and values. The drive for self-consciousness, which serves as the ground principle of dialectical thought, introduces an unsettling *telos* into the whole of experience and remains a permanent source of instability at the center of any social order. Political *praxis* is thus grounded in existential imperatives rather than in the need for creaturely comforts or communal identity. Moreover, since man's basic needs—freedom, recognition, self-consciousness, a comprehensive project—are simultaneously political and existential there can be no question of choosing between the two realms (as in Kierkegaard and much of Christian existentialism) or of opposing them (as in the doctrinaire Marxism of the later Lukács). The conflict of inwardness and existence cannot be solved by a choice but requires a concrete synthesis—and since the absence of that synthesis is the dominant fact of our time, living the widening rift between the political and human orders *as a conflict* and finding in that conflict the innermost meaning of one's existence has today become the acid test of "the dialectical nature," for, as Plato put it long ago, "he who can view things in their connection is a dialectician; he who cannot, is not" (*Republic* 7. 537c).

In a reversal that stands Kant's critique of dialectic on its head, post-Hegelian dialectical thought thus conceives experience as a process of comprehensive ontological transformation in which subject labors to transform all that is other than it in order to bring reality into correspondence with the values and ideals man projects. Pure reason is caught up in practical-aesthetic reason and "the whole of things" becomes a historical task rather than a subsistent cosmological totality. As a result, scientific, interpersonal, and political activity as well as man's richest aesthetic, religious, and philosophic speculations become directly comparable ways in which he strives to work out the basic ontological problems of his existence. As participants in a single grand phenomenology of spirit, self, or self-consciousness, all activities are understood and judged in terms of the contribution they make to the comprehensive task of bringing into existence a world adequate to the being of the concretely existent subject.

Thus dialectic cancels, preserves, and uplifts the other modes of human thought. The basic instincts and naturalistic determinations of logistic thought are caught up through Hegelian desire in the dialectic of self-consciousness.[13] The various disciplines distinguished by the problematic thinker are referred in and through the development of that drama to the one order of problems to which all human activities contribute in a definite if generally unrecognized hierarchy. With the drive for recognition and authentic freedom at the core of man's communal and historical existence, the operational self is referred to a principle of existential self-reference which is always implicitly beyond the merely social. Although it advances the most awesome speculative concepts, dialectic is the enemy of all abstraction; no mode of thought strives more ardently to begin and end with concrete, immediate experience. If the other modes of thought fail to stick with the concrete, it is because they have not begun with the concrete subject; that subject restored, they become moments preserved in a dialectical economy structured by the only principle which is actually self-grounding—the experiential self-mediation of consciousness.

The other modes of thought, however, make characteristic

responses to their dialectical reinterpretation. The logistic thinker sees the existential subject of dialectical thought as a speculative construct which, like freedom and dignity, needs to be dispensed with if we are to achieve a scientific resolution of our problems: in its unwarranted insistence on ascribing an autonomous principle of reflection to the "subject," dialectical thought stands in the way of a "positive" understanding and betterment of the human condition. The problematic thinker, in turn, views the existential drama on which dialectical thought is based as only one of the many situations man faces, and categorically rejects its claim to lie at the base of all human activities: existential man, in fact, appears to be the exception rather than the rule and common sense provides a sounder, more tempered guide to human nature and conduct.[14] The operationalist, finally, sees the existential subject of dialectical thought as the manifestation of a cultural malaise, the expression of a particular historical crisis—and the failure to see that crisis for what it is. Once again it appears that "any philosophy" is "at once an architectonic reorganization of what is sound in the statements of" competing "philosophers and a cathartic exposure of what is absurd." The continued debate of competing modes of thought is the irreducible ground-phenomenon of intellectual life.

The Hermeneutic Orientations Implicit in the Modes

In the preceding section I constructed a dialectic of the modes in order to show how thought and experience can begin in difference yet proceed to comprehensive unity.[15] At the same time, I maintained the difference of the modes and gave ample reasons for stopping at any of the three way stations on the road to dialectic. The other modes of thought may be moments within dialectic but they are also coherent philosophies independent of it. In seeing the different ways in which the modes view one another and can be related to one another, the discussion reveals the different ways in which pluralism may be established and dissolved. My purpose in doing so has been to offer readers of every possible persuasion what Coleridge termed "aids to reflection." The reasons why a given way of thinking appeals to a particular reader and others do not—as well as the impulse to separate modes or to relate them— are not purely logical questions but touch on complex issues that reach deeply into the recesses of each person's life and character and have a definite connection to the project or fundamental choice on which each of us, whether knowingly or not, stakes the meaning and value of his existence. The choice of one's mode of thought is grounded in one's fundamental way of intending the world and of being in the world. It is the conceptual manifestation of one's project. To attain self-knowledge and the possibility of self-criticism each of us has to know, in depth and from as many angles as we can, the reasons why a given way of thinking carries conviction for us, as well as the reasons why other ways of thinking strike us as fundamentally unsound, even abhorrent. The purpose of the preceding discussion has been to make us aware of this dimension of the problem: I have highlighted the concepts of reality, knowledge, experience, and man that each mode generates in order to reveal the philosophic anthropology implicit in each mode. By particularizing the modes in terms of the basic way each intends and experiences the world, it is now possible for us to see that *the relationship of the human subject to himself and his understanding of what it means to be a human being is the ultimate basis of any act of interpretation.*[16] That relationship—which implies the need for a psychological, sociological, and ethical interrogation of the modes—is the ground principle that shapes each critic's procedures from the inception of his inquiries. It is the implicit rationale to which each critic refers throughout his study of literature and determines both the questions he asks and the kind of answers he gives. Of greatest importance, it is the implicit world view from which each critic derives the principles of explanation and verification he employs to resolve a "conflict of interpretations" whenever one arises. Without an understanding of the modes of thought on which they are based and the philosophic anthropologies implicit in those modes, there is no way we can begin to test competing hypotheses or to see why, when faced with a real conflict of interpretations and genuinely open to the possibility of different solutions, one critic will solve the problem in one way and another "equally flexible" critic will solve it in another. It is quite possible that each of us is in effect condemned to his mode and the covert rationale and testing procedure implicit in it.

The possibility of employing the method of multiple working hypotheses in a truly pluralistic and self-critical fashion depends on an explicit understanding of the hermeneutic orientation implicit in each mode, and that depends, in turn, on each critic undertaking a radical self-examination directed toward a complete, transparent, and thoroughly self-critical understanding of the existential reasons why he intends the world and reasons one way rather than others.

Rather than having one unchanged and unchanging way of reasoning we all must follow, it appears that in understanding and interpreting poetry each of us has already made or is faced with a fundamental choice. Are we now in a position to make that choice—as a direct result of the understanding we now have of the different ways in which we think and the existential orientations implicit in those modes? Or do we face an even more difficult situation in which we must reject an exclusive choice because we find all these ways of thinking necessary for an adequate understanding of man and his works in all their irreducible plurality?

In discussing the modes of thought I have had three general problems in mind.

1. To formulate the philosophic and methodological principles that shape the distinct modes of critical theory, thereby enabling us to understand critical discourse and the history of criticism in a far more rigorous way than has heretofore been the case. Understandably, most of us would prefer to set reasonable limits to our inquiries, separate the problems that most concern us from the rest of reality, and leave the questions of philosophy to philosophers. Such decisions, however, are not simple matters, but require principles. Separating the disciplines is as much a problem as is bringing them together. Interdisciplinary thought may in fact be the only viable starting point because the experience of relations may be prior to the construction of difference. In the *Lebenswelt*, if not in the groves of academe, the separation of questions and problems may be a strictly derivative phenomenon based on an inability to comprehend or endure primary relationships. Distinguishing and uniting are both products of thought in any case and require the assumption of principles rather than a simple appeal to common sense or self-evident matters of fact. (And this consideration applies, *pari passu*, to any attempt to separate the theories of form—or to relate them.) The fact of the matter is that we do not yet know the boundaries of our discipline, nor can we establish those boundaries without calling on principles which implicitly take us beyond the discipline. In this way we are all subject to Hegel's maxim that "to be aware of limitations is to be already beyond them." Once we begin to reflect on the methodological bases of our activity, it is hard to escape the realization that criticism is a branch of philosophy, involved in philosophic questions and problems whether we like it or not. It appears that there can be no limits to our labors. Though it may appeal to

common sense and conform to the primary fact of academic life—the separation of disciplines and "fields" within disciplines— problematic thought is no less metaphysical than dialectical, and no less in need of giving a philosophic account of itself. The only way criticism can maintain itself is by becoming metacriticism.

2. To defend the pluralism of formal theories by showing that one cannot prove the universal truth of one of the three theories we have developed by arguing that it alone corresponds to the deep structures of language, the true nature of the human mind, or the one way in which we all necessarily experience the world. When faced with a plurality of contending views, the natural inclination of metacritical inquiry is to resolve that conflict by arguing that only one view rests on a secure logical or metaphysical foundation. We have found, however, that the grounds of coherence in thought are many rather than one. Rather than reducing the range of possibilities, a study of the modes of thought supports and reinforces the need for a plurality of formal theories. It is a pluralistic justification of pluralism and, as a consequence, instead of solving the problems of chapter 1 it reinforces and preserves those problems by revealing the philosophic reasons why they had to arise in the first place.

3. To put us in a position to confront the problems of literary interpretation once again, but in a manner more reflective and self-critical than was possible in chapter 1. Faced with the conflict of interpretations, we all crave some neutral court of appeal, some infallible signs, some apodictic canons of evidence and proof. Our examination of the modes of thought indicates that no such norms exist. The only way we can apparently establish binding canons of evidence and proof is by giving the principles proper to one mode of critical reasoning a covert force and then employing them to judge the merits of approaches which necessarily operate by other criteria. Such is the case, for instance, when R. S. Crane makes emotional response the index of form and proceeds to argue that his approach is the only one appropriate to mimetic works because it alone preserves the pleasure generations of readers have found in such works, while freeing us, in the process, from the need to interpret literature in "abstract existentialist terms." Conversely, when rhetorical and dialectical critics argue that the "Chicago" approach fails to account for the profound meaning and relevance modern readers find in literature, they fall into the same kind of self-confirming circularity. The different

solutions that are proposed to the conflict of interpretations are themselves part of the problem.

We must build this recognition into the method of multiple working hypotheses we are developing. In chapter 1 we faced the horns of the following dilemma: on the one hand we apparently had to choose one of the three interpretations offered, under the assumption that each literary work should be matched to the single theory appropriate to it; on the other hand, we entertained the possibility that the three interpretations might enact a process analogous to Hegel's *Aufhebung*, so that the third interpretation would cancel, preserve, and uplift the first two. Both possibilities are legitimate. The former, however, is a problematic response to the problems of interpretation, while the latter rests on dialectical assumptions. Therein lies the deep appeal of each—and the reason why neither can be given a privileged status a priori. If the method of multiple working hypotheses is to provide a genuinely pluralistic organon for literary interpretation, it must itself be established and employed in a genuinely pluralistic manner. Developing the contours of this problem with reference to the study of literature in general and to the solution of the problems we uncovered in interpreting "The Bear" is the task of chapter 4.

Some such activity as this of reforging the broken links between creation and knowledge, art and science, myth and concept, is what I envisage for criticism. Once more, I am not speaking of a change of direction or activity in criticism; I mean only that if critics go on with their own business, this will appear to be, with increasing obviousness, the social and practical result of their labors.

Northrop Frye, *Anatomy of Criticism*

One thing alone is needful. Everything. The rest is vanity of vanities.

W. H. Auden

4 The Language of Criticism and the Forms of Poetry

Introduction

One value of a pluralistic approach is that it enables us to resolve some of the unnecessary disputes among critics. Many of our conflicts arise simply from a paucity of concepts. Having only one way of thinking about all literary works, we are forced to make each work conform to our framework no matter how bad the fit. A pluralistic stance minimizes such embarrassments. Speaking ad hoc, it would probably not be too difficult to demonstrate that *Everyman*, "An Essay on Man," *Rasselas*, and *Catch-22* are rhetorical works; that *Tom Jones*, *Pride and Prejudice*, and *The Portrait of a Lady* are organized to produce a particular kind of emotional response; and that Mann, Joyce, and Proust are engaged in constructing a dialectic of art and reality.

With the resolution of such problems in mind, when I first began working on this project I sought examples that would be fairly easy to place. My assumptions were problematic. It seemed natural to assume that the only way one could resolve the conflict of interpretations was by establishing a strict correspondence between particular works and the single theory appropriate to them. The concept of form also appeared to demand such a solution, since the existence of more than one synthesizing purpose in a work would appear to go against the notions of artistic unity and wholeness implicit in it. That conclusion holds, however, only if artistic purposes exclude one another—and the assumption that they must is, once again, problematic and disciplinary.

By the time I began writing *The Act of Interpretation* I was concerned with works more difficult to place than those mentioned above, and a strict correspondence of theory to text had become only one possible solution to the conflict of interpretations. With some works we may have to choose one of the three theories we have discussed and exclude the other two. But in other cases we

121

may have to establish a more dynamic, formal relationship among the theories. A truly pluralistic use of the method of multiple working hypotheses requires that we consider a number of alternatives with the understanding that none has a privileged status but derives its force solely by reason of its adequacy to the particular text under examination. I will now try to show some of the ways in which this logic puts us in the most fruitful position to understand a number of different literary works, thus solving the two problems that most concern criticism: (1) the development of a general field theory of literature, and (2) the construction of an organon for the interpretation of particular texts.

The Modes of Dialectical Art

There are many modes of dialectical art. There is a purely ideational mode in which the poet as seer attempts, through the resources of paradox, ambiguity, and metaphor implicit in poetic language, to articulate an awareness of being which transcends the limitations of scientific and logical thought. (The attempt by Yvor Winters to find the rational statement such poems are trying to communicate—or the confusion they instance in failing to make such a statement—misses the distinctive effort of this art.) The purest forms of the dialectical lyric, such as "The Ode on a Grecian Urn" and "Sailing to Byzantium" (as well as the larger attempt at dialectical system building we find in a work like Eliot's *Four Quartets*) represent a philosophic agent engaged in the process of dialectical meditation. In such works the speaker, refined out of existence and become pure mind, is wholly taken up with the articulation of dialectical ideas in dense structures of images and symbols that affirm opposites.

In dialectical lyrics such as "Ode to a Nightingale," "Among School Children," and Rilke's *Duino Elegies*, on the other hand, speaker and situation are highly particularized. In such works the dialectical idea arises out of a passionate, mood-filled response to being and requires a complete appropriation of the concrete situation which gives birth to thought. Focusing on their mimetic character, Elder Olson has argued that since such works represent "the action of a speaker in a closed situation"[1] they should be interpreted emotionally along Aristotelian lines analogous to those R. S. Crane establishes for analyzing larger mimetic structures. Insofar as the New Critics tended to resolve such works into abstract structures of language and metaphor, Olson has a point.

But there is no reason to oppose dialectic and mimesis in abstract or exclusive terms. As Heidegger has shown, primary moods such as dread and love first put us in touch with the mystery of Being; authentic thinking consists in a lyric appropriation of the situation we find ourselves in when such moods announce themselves. The resources of dialectic in lyric art thus range from the representation of pure structures of dialectical thought to the impassioned articulation of the revelatory power of fleeting moods: the dialectic of the lyric realizes the kind of poetic activity Coleridge associated with the imagination, Eliot with the fused sensibility, the New Critics with the language of paradox, and Heidegger with the poetic thinking of Being.

Of unquestionable value for the interpretation of many lyric poems, the dialectical poetic outlined above is far from adequate for the dialectical interpretation of fiction and drama. Complex mimetic works are more than structures of language and imagery, and more than the representation of heightened states of mind. They represent actions, and the primacy of action defines them as forms. Preserving their integrity requires the development of a dialectical poetic which comprehends the imitation of action as an autonomous mode of dialectical knowing. That task is perhaps the major one dialectical critics face today. In addressing it I find it useful to distinguish the following kinds of works as stages in what one might term the dialectical movement of art toward the apprehension of concrete experience.

1. There are self-reflexive works that are wholly taken up with discovering the cognitive limits of art. Art is tested and proves wanting; its inadequacy forms the substance of the work. In works of this kind (*Malone Dies* and *The Unnamable* are cases in point) there is always a discontinuity between the artistic forms the work employs and the materials of experience which those forms fail to order—for that discontinuity is precisely what the work is about. Such works are not merely negative acts. In using art to criticize art one implicitly extends art beyond its previous bounds: the critique of art in and through art is at base an attempt to reconstitute the nature of art in order to bring it into closer contact with concrete experience. Thus the deepest significance of such works lies in the fact that they are radically open-ended: they call for a future work of art in which the new kind of artistic knowing they adumbrate will be concretely realized. In chapter 1 "The Bear" was interpreted as an instance of this mode of dialectical art: "The Bear" strives self-

reflexively to move from the dialectic of lyric knowing to a mimetic dialectic of concrete experience without achieving that breakthrough. (Shortly I will criticize this interpretation of "The Bear," without denying the general value of the theory behind it.)

2. The battle with the lyric principle won, the action of complex mimetic works and their dialectic becomes continuous. The simplest instance of this mode occurs in works in which the question of artistic cognition is the source and substance of the work's entire action. Here—and I am thinking primarily of Queneau, Robbe-Grillet, and the *nouveau roman*—the work of art is radically, though somewhat abstractly, about the process of its own coming to be. Mimetically, the work enacts a self-reflexive inquiry into the nature of aesthetic perception; the action of the work issues directly from that question and the development of the question constitutes the substance of the work. Such works are exercises in pure epistemology and are dominated, to the exclusion of other concerns, by the problem of knowing the external world and the immediate contents of consciousness.

3. The dialectical art of Dostoyevsky, Proust, and Mann is more concrete. Here self-reflexivity remains a constant, but it issues in a far more complex representation of human experience. Because art is seen as a fundamental principle of thought and action, and not merely of perception, the dialectical mimesis of concrete experience becomes possible. The forms of artistic cognition shape our entire lived relationship to the world. Artistic knowing is not only present in aesthetic reflection upon perceptual experience, but is the basic principle that informs the concrete projects in which existential agents attempt to give meaning and direction to their existence. Thus in a novel like *Doctor Faustus* the dialectical conflict between the aesthetic and the ethical is revealed as the source not merely of perception but of all modes of concrete engagement; the action of the novel thus becomes the concrete embodiment of a comprehensive dialectic. In a similar manner, the self-reflexivity of *Hamlet* is such that the action of the play turns on the question of what constitutes 'authentic action. Because Hamlet's interrogation of what it means to be and to act in the world is the source and center of its action, the play concretely negates all the conventions and aesthetic illusions (from revenge tragedy to the entire Elizabethan "world picture") which stand in the way of an authentic and tragic representation of human existence.

4. Finally, we have the dialectical mimesis of works such as *King*

Lear and *The Brothers Karamazov*. Here self-reflexivity is no longer a dominant problem or principle of structure. Assured of art's cognitive power, the artist particularizes that knowledge by constructing a comprehensive existential dialectic in which the fundamental structures of human existence are brought together in an action which dramatizes the working and teleology of fundamental projects in their concrete interaction.

The last two modes of dialectical art are especially significant because in them dialectic does not simply consist in processes of thought but resides in the concrete mimesis of character and event. Since that is so, it is possible to discover a coherent sequence of desires and expectations and a coherent rhetorical structure in such works yet find that both structures function in subordination to a controlling dialectical purpose. Thus it is no accident that one can interpret *Hamlet* in Cranian terms or give a successful rhetorical reading of *The Magic Mountain* while failing in both cases to enter deeply enough into the action. Rather than negating such structures, dialectical works of this kind preserve emotional and rhetorical forms within a larger artistic totality. Commenting on *The Magic Mountain*,[2] Thomas Mann expressed his delight over the deep emotional involvement of his readers in the "fate" of his characters, especially their concern for "the delicate child of life," Hans Castorp. At the same time he emphasized that producing such a response was not his controlling purpose in the novel. While stressing the rootedness of his novel in the dilemmas of bourgeois society, Mann also noted that he placed social and historical problems within a broader framework dominated by the awareness that Being-toward-death is the basis of human consciousness. In defining the scene in which an agent who becomes a "world-historical individual" must act, the work develops a rhetorical structure with a complexity worthy of close Burkean analysis; and for those who experienced World War I as the end of Western culture, *The Magic Mountain* remains a profound rhetorical experience. For Mann, however, the work's emotional and rhetorical structures are not autonomous, but contribute to a larger dialectical purpose. Mann's true subject is the dialectical relationship between art and reality: as he puts it, "the book itself is the substance of that which it relates ... its aim is always and consistently to *be* that of which it speaks."[3] That relationship constitutes both the matter and the form of the work and generates the major structures of experience it dramatizes. The understanding of self as Being-toward-death is the primordial aesthetic experience. Aesthetic fascination with disease, death, and the body initiates the self into a process of becoming which transcends the bounds of social, rhetorical, and conceptual thought as well as the alternatives offered by characters like Settembrini and Naphtha. Castorp's *Bildung* is a dialectical process—for him and for us—and in charting the necessary stages in the aesthetic education of man, *The Magic Mountain* records a dialectical ascent in which the mystery of the self is found to reside, as in the *Phaedrus*, in the psyche's appetitive relationship to the whole of things[4] and its responsibility (*Sorge*) for that totality.[5] A complete understanding of *The Magic Mountain* thus demands that we experience its coherent and complete problematic and rhetorical structures as functions within the architectonic of Mann's comprehensive dialectical purpose. And what is true of *The Magic Mountain* is true to an even greater degree in the more concrete mimetic activity we find in works such as *The Brothers Karamazov* and *King Lear*.

In the dialectic of a work like Mann's *Doctor Faustus*, on the other hand, rhetorical structures are relegated to a minor and local appearance, while from a problematic point of view the work breaks down and must be judged an artistic failure. By the time Mann wrote *Doctor Faustus* character was "fate," *mythos* was *dianoia*. The action of the novel is steadfastly focused on the dialectic of aesthetics and ethics to the exclusion of all other concerns. The "being" of both Leverkühn and Zeitblom lies solely in their response to that conflict. All other dimensions of "character" are practically nonexistent. The problematic and rhetorical resources of literary representation recede before the urgency of Mann's effort to dramatize the tragic issue of that terrible division of spirit he finds at the center of contemporary experience, thought, and culture. As he notes, his two characters have one thing to hide "namely, the secret of their being identical,"[6] an identity which derives from the fact that each strives throughout his life to mediate the dialectic of aesthetics and ethics; one from the aesthetic side of the coin, the other from the ethical. With an inexorable dialectical logic, the entire action of the novel issues from that problem; everything Leverkühn does in living his life and everything Zeitblom discovers in reflecting upon that life (which he admits "gives his own life its true content"), is a necessary moment or stage in Mann's effort to attain "the concrete" by bringing the conflict of aesthetics and ethics to its fullest tragic issue. In one sense the work is nonmimetic, if by mimesis we mean a realistic and quasi-empirical representation of the immediate contents of consciousness, the scattered projects, wishes, and desires that make up the dispersion of self we call our character, and the diverse contexts of interpersonal relationship that constitute "the splendid waste" of ordinary experience. In another and deeper sense the work is an ultimate development of mimetic art, if by mimesis we mean the artistic apprehension of reality and are willing to contend that genuine character, as *amor fati*, and significant action, as existential project, arise out of man's response to the comprehensive problems of human existence.

The Modes of Rhetorical Art

The modes of rhetorical art range from explicitly didactic works such as "An Essay on Man," *Everyman*, and the poetry of rational statement championed by Yvor Winters to complex mimetic works which communicate by involving us in symbolic actions. If one's primary concern is with narrative and dramatic art, it is especially important to distinguish these poles on the rhetorical spectrum. There are fictional apologues[7] such as *Rasselas*, *Candide*, and *Catch-22* in which action is organized to communicate the truth of a propositional statement; but there is also the far more complex and concrete rhetoric of works such as *Anna Karenina*, *The Golden Notebook*, and *The Rainbow* in which the *content* of communication is inherently dramatic and the process of communication depends, accordingly, on our emotional, attitudinal, and motivational involvement in symbolic actions.

The great value of Kenneth Burke as a rhetorical critic derives from his emphasis on the complex modes. Rational statement is, for Burke, the simplest instance of rhetoric. Because he sees attitudes and motives as the primary content of communication, and symbolic action as the primary process, Burke revolutionizes our understanding of the nature and resources of rhetoric. In so doing he takes us beyond the mimetic-didactic distinction R. S. Crane used to argue against the possibility of "rhetorical mimesis." As you will recall, Crane draws a sharp distinction between didactic works such as *Rasselas*, *Pilgrim's Progress*, and *The Divine Comedy*, in which events are organized to demonstrate a "theme" or propositional statement, and mimetic works such as *Tom Jones*, *Macbeth*, and *The Brothers Karamazov*, in which a complex human action is imitated for the sake of producing a particular kind of emotional response.[8] The distinction is valuable as far as it goes, only it doesn't go very far. Because he is intent on ruling out a rhetorical approach to "mimetic works," Crane conceives of rhetorical art in the narrowest terms, allowing for only its simplest instances. In works such as *Rasselas*, the novels of Hermann Hesse, and Robert Pirsig's *Zen and the Art of Motorcycle Maintenance*, characters are, indeed, walking concepts and action a series of exempla proving the truth of an abstract proposition that can be separated from the work. Because the sequence of events is arranged solely to demonstrate the truth of a theme or body of themes, the mimetic concreteness of character and action is deliberately suppressed. Such is not the case, however, in the still relatively simple rhetoric of works such as *The Shadow-Line* and *A Man for All Seasons*: moral instruction in the kind of experience one needs to undergo in order to pass from youthful romanticism to a mature attitude toward life and conduct in the one and the revelation of the way one has to act in order to maintain one's moral integrity in a world where compromise of principle is the order of the day in the other are rhetorical purposes that require the concrete representation of character and event. Dr. Johnson's rhetorical purpose is served as soon as each episode in *Rasselas* demonstrates the vanity of human wishes, but Robert Bolt's play collapses if Thomas More becomes a walking concept or his story anything less than an exceptional one, rhetorically powerful by reason of that very fact.

From whatever angle one traces the development of rhetorical art, one finds a constant movement toward the mimetic. The speaker dramatizes himself to prove his moral worth to his audience; Gerald Else argues, in fact, that Solon's style of public oratory was the example that gave birth to Greek drama.[9] Works where the satiric hand is uppermost, such as Barth's *The End of the Road*, Shaw's *Man and Superman*, and Mary McCarthy's *The Groves of Academe*, tend like the apologue to abridge the mimetic particularization of character and event, yet even in them a perceptible movement from abstract doctrine to concrete imitation is at work: the best way to prove men or institutions foolish is to represent them in all their folly. Mimetic realization is even more pronounced in works dominated by social and political concerns: examples include *A Doll's House*, *Mother Courage*, *The Grapes of Wrath*, and *The Plague*. Such works verify the paradox that character and event become representative in direct proportion to the degree to which they are individualized. Yet because these works are still fairly simple examples of that possibility, one can detect signs in them of a conflict between didactic and mimetic motives. At times *The Grapes of Wrath* reads like a sociological tract and the Christian symbolism of the work is forced and gratuitous; Ibsen's endings frequently serve his social thematic at the expense of his characters and the concrete possibilities contained in the situations he has constructed; *The Plague* tends toward abstract allegory far too often; and Brecht, of course, was always willing to sacrifice action for abstract doctrine once the audience was ripe for it.

By the time we get to an artist like Tolstoy, however, and Tolstoy at his best, rhetoric and mimesis are one and indistinguishable. Theme is completely realized in action and never operates at the expense of action. In *Anna Karenina* the thesis "all happy families resemble one another, but each unhappy family is unhappy in its own way" (and the moral fervor evidenced in Tolstoy's epigraph "vengeance is mine; I will repay") does not lead Tolstoy to create a gallery of types or a series of didactic episodes; on the contrary, it demands that he create a complete and objective historical world in which the constant juxtaposition of Anna and Levin—and it is hard to think of two more fully realized characters—will reveal the logic of spiritual and moral renewal or decline contained in the primacy of passion that defines Tolstoy's characters, their actions, and their world.

As Kenneth Burke shows, rhetoric and mimesis are also inseparable in the ritual symbolic action of works such as *The Oresteia*, *A Passage to India*, and "The Rime of the Ancient Mariner."[10] In works of this kind, as in "The Bear," a direct representation of the symbols and ritual patterns (defilement and cleansing, victimization, the principle of hierarchy) which structure the identity of rhetorical man forms the substance of the drama. Action thus dramatizes the rhetorical process in its purest form—the movement from a disruptive social situation to the restoration of a benign order of motives—and exploits the rhetorical resources of dialectical principles such as hierarchy and the desire for perfection as one of the primary means of effecting identification and persuasion.

The movement from *Rasselas* to *The Oresteia* is the progress toward a concrete rhetoric. It is a hierarchy of artistic complexity, though not necessarily of artistic value. As an outline of the essential moments that must enter into the definition or "notion" of rhetorical form, it records an evolution from the communication of abstract ideas and commonplaces to the communication of motives and attitudes in and through symbolic actions. As a result, it also traces the movement from a situation in which rhetorical form may be sharply distinguished from emotional and dialectical form to one in which the rhetorical artist finds both of those principles essential to the realization of his rhetorical purpose and incorporates them within it.

R. S. Crane apparently would have us believe that rhetoric and mimesis are exclusive, with the fact that we respond emotionally to an imitated action providing strong evidence that we are not in the presence of a rhetorical work. But Kenneth Burke has shown that there is no necessary conflict between the mimetic and the rhetorical impulses. On the contrary, our emotional involvement in "the fate of characters about whom we are made to care" forms an integral part of the process of identification which structures the art of "rhetorical mimesis." In terms of the overarching theory we are developing, the important point to grasp is that the process of emotional involvement Crane describes may be a constituent yet subordinate part of a larger rhetorical structuring of attitudes and motives. Just as Burke's conception of rhetorical art deepens and transforms our understanding of emotional involvement without canceling it, the kinds of literary works Burke is most concerned with are ones in which completely developed emotional and rhetorical structures are concretely synthesized, with the former subordinate to the latter.

For Burke there is no reason to oppose the poet as sayer and the poet as imitator. In seeing ritual, myth, symbol, and action as both the primary method and the primary content of communication, Burke has made the rhetorical tradition in criticism adequate to the concreteness of mimetic art. Thanks to Burke, it is no longer necessary for rhetorical critics to reduce mimetic works to a bundle of abstract themes, to short-circuit our emotional involvement in such works, or to destroy, in the search for thematic "meanings," the mimetic integrity of the object before us. The poet as sayer speaks in many ways, and if we would communicate effectively we must resort to all the rhetorical resonances of symbols and symbolic actions. What we do to and with one another through symbols is the primary way in which we shape and are shaped by the rhetorical process.

Burke, of course, thinks everything is rhetoric; and for what it is worth I have my own suspicions that the literary universe presents us with more instances of this kind of art than it does with anything else—for reasons that are philosophic and sociological as well as aesthetic. Operational thought defines and circumscribes human consciousness insofar as initially and for the most part man is and remains primarily a social being. Existential freedom is an achievement rather than a birthright; by and large the self is the generalized other, and our acts, including our creative ones, are most often shaped by the social process, the abiding drama in which most of us live and move and have our being.

On Problematic Art

Strictly speaking we don't have distinct modes here. Crane's mimetic-didactic distinction takes care of that. For Crane, emotional form is the sole purpose of mimetic art. Thus there is no question of establishing a dynamic formal relationship between equally coherent dialectical, rhetorical, and emotional structures; the problem, instead, is to show how rhetorical and dialectical materials—as parts and elements rather than as total structures— contribute to the realization of emotional form.

In his battle with the rhetorical and dialectical tendencies of modern criticism, one of Crane's major goals was to show that the primary function "thought" has in mimetic works is to increase our emotional involvement in action. "Thought" is one of the constituents of character and functions to help establish desires and expectations. For such a purpose many different kinds of ideas will be found useful. In a work like *Tom Jones*, Fielding uses the general intellectual commonplaces (or unit-ideas) of his time to help shape our moral estimation of Tom, thereby enhancing, through the philosophic wit of his narrator-commentator, the general perspective on human conduct needed to maximize our emotional participation in the comedy of the work. Jane Austen employs the social mores and psychological commonplaces of her day for a similar end. Had Crane considered contemporary writers, he would no doubt have found that "abstract existentialist themes" often perform an analogous function. Writers like Updike, Roth, and Bellow use popular existential and psychoanalytic commonplaces as a primary device of characterization; indeed, oblique reference to Sartre and Freud is one of the readiest means modern writers have of conveying the impression that something important is happening and that their characters are worthy of our deep emotional involvement.[11]

General views of man and human conduct are, of course, implicit in any mimetic work, which is why it is always possible for critics so inclined to abstract a general vision of man and the world from any piece of literature. If we wish, we can ransack the literary universe for world views just as easily as we can for unit-ideas, profound statements, or significant themes. As Crane sees it, however, the tacit or implied conceptions of time, reality, consciousness, and the like that are present in any literary work are not the purpose behind mimetic literature, but one of its props. Because mimesis proposes pleasure rather than thought as its end, in dealing with the question of ideas in literature the basic interpretive task is to show how thought functions to shape our emotional response to action.

In theory and in practice Crane always aspired to the utmost degree of particularity in his description of individual works and the variety of distinct emotional ends that may be realized in mimetic art. What he lacks in openness to other theoretical possibilities he more than makes up for here; they do him wrong who see Crane as an abstract Aristotelian bent on fitting the many varieties of tragic art, for example, into the single formula provided in the Poetics. Wayne Booth relates that whenever Crane taught Macbeth he forced his students to confront a simple but far-reaching question: "In what ways would Aristotle have been forced to revise or extend the Poetics if he had known Macbeth?"[12] Tragedy, for Crane, is and can be no more than a vague general term. The works we group under it range in form from the classical "catharsis of pity and fear" produced by the representation of characters better than us who are destroyed as a result of some mistake (hamartia) or defect in character, to the kind of "retributive tragedy" found in Marlowe and Shakespeare's Richard III, where the spectacle of a villanous agent brought to destruction relieves our horror over vicious deeds while satisfying our abstract sense of justice. Macbeth, Crane argues, is neither type.[13] Here emotional response is determined by the complex interaction in our feelings between sympathy for Macbeth and the demand that he be destroyed, not only for the sake of Scotland but for his own good. Macbeth, unlike Richard III or the Jew of Malta, is never a simple villain; he remains a moral agent, and an anguished one, throughout his tragedy. The inside view Shakespeare gives us through soliloquy of Macbeth's growing dread at his moral self-destruction is more horrifying, more human, and more profound than the rather abstract judgments of him offered by Macduff and others. As a result, *Macbeth* moves us in a way that *Richard III* cannot; indeed, the type of tragic emotion Shakespeare realized in *Macbeth* was of a new and unprecedented order, far beyond anything found in his sources or the conventions of his time. In a similar fashion, the tragic pleasure realized in a work like "The Bear" is of a special order: the story never degenerates into the kind of sentimentality one finds in a work like *The Catcher in the Rye*, nor does it ever attain the magnitude we associate with the masterworks of tragic drama. Its tragic pleasure, as we have seen, lies between the heroic and the pathetic, arising, as it does, out of our response to a character who strives to assume a responsibility of which he is incapable. As the examples above indicate, the basic effort of problematic theory is to formulate an exact definition of different principles of emotional synthesis in order to put us in a position to describe as exactly as possible the precise emotional form which unifies the action of individual works.

The same effort at individuation is evident in Crane's consideration of "comedy." Here the possibilities range from the serious comedy of Henry James and Jane Austen's *Persuasion*,[14] through the complex interaction of "faint alarm" and "friendly mirth" which constitutes the comic form of *Tom Jones*,[15] to the kind of simple comic pleasure Elder Olson describes as a "katastasis of concern through" the representation of "the absurd" and which Olson finds, as the polar opposite of tragic catharsis, in works such as *A Midsummer Night's Dream*, *The Comedy of Errors*, and *Love's Labour's Lost*.[16] Between the many types of "tragic" and "comic" art there are, in turn, a potentially unlimited number of possibilities.

Given the inadequacies of abstract discursive language to the concreteness and particularity of emotional experience, the common terms we use to describe distinct emotional forms will often prove unsatisfying and ambiguous. Crane's "serious comedy" and "retributive tragedy" are cases in point. But Crane is no Polonius. He is closer to Duns Scotus (*haecceitas*) and Husserl (the intuition of essence) than he is to any abstract theory of genre. His preeminent concern is to develop a theory directed to particular poetic structures and distinct emotional forms. At all times the effort of his criticism is to put us in a position to define the particular structure of desires and expectations realized in the particular work under examination. For Crane the primary task of critical theory is to make generic concepts such as tragedy and comedy, as well as the language used to describe the emotions, flexible enough to issue in a science of particulars. I do not think Crane has succeeded in putting that science into practice as well as he might. The language of common sense on which he relies to describe the emotions, and the commonplaces of eighteenth-century moralizing he uses to define the moral judgments that shape our response, are far too often vague and nondescript, generating the very abstractness and imprecision Crane wishes to overcome. (As cases in point one might cite "the feeling of faint alarm" from the study of *Tom Jones* and the description of Macbeth's character as that of "a basically good but incontinent man.") But if Crane does not offer us all that he might on these scores, it is the deed and not the attempt that confounds him; his call for a return to the particular remains an impressive one in an age of abstract theorizing.

When we turn to "lyric poetry," the need to give precise definitions of distinct emotional ends is more pressing and more difficult than it is with fiction and drama. The problems are also greater than with any other literary type because the triumph of the New Criticism has made it hard for most of us to think of lyric poems as anything other than structures of meaning. The possibilities of emotional form in lyric poetry are great, however, and range from the fitful expression of general feelings of longing and loneliness we find in poems like "To the West Wind" and "Stopping by Woods on a Snowy Evening" to the complex emotional structure of poems such as Shakespeare's "Sonnet 34," "The Flea," and "Fern Hill." Focusing on the latter kind of works, Elder Olson has defined "lyric poetry" as "the imitation of the action of a speaker in a closed situation"[17] and has argued quite cogently that such poems are not structures of statement or meaning but are organized mimetically for the sake of producing a particular emotional experience. Lyric poetry, for Olson, represents the process of choice, contingent on character and thought, which a particularized speaker makes when faced with a general situation. Analogous to the plot of larger mimetic works, the dramatization of choice is the imitation of what amounts to an action and is organized to produce in us the emotions proper to such an event. Rather than continuing to see lyric poems as abstract structures of poetic language or rhetorical statement, we must begin to focus our attention on their mimetic characteristics if we are to appreciate the special emotional forms they embody. In calling attention to the mimetic properties of lyric poetry, Olson develops a powerful argument. As a critique of dialectical and rhetorical approaches, however, it really signals the need for reform rather than a refutation. Cleanth Brooks may be fixated on the language of paradox, and Yvor Winters may see all speakers as orators and all poems as "what one should say."[18] But Heidegger's dialectical theory of the lyric and Kenneth Burke's rhetorical one are as mimetic as Olson's theory and remind us, once again, that the ends of mimesis are many.[19]

Thanks to Crane and "the Chicago critics," one important mode of mimetic art has been rescued from abstract didactic commentary. For many artists, producing pleasure (or, in more rigorous terms, embodying the universal principles of emotional response that determine our reaction to the representation of human actions) is a sufficient end for art. In our time, however, this understanding of art has become an almost forgotten language of criticism. While dialectical and rhetorical theories have an immediate claim on our attention because they speak directly to current needs and assumptions, problematic theory is a mode of critical reasoning we must labor to recapture by going against prevailing preconceptions and inclinations—which is all the more reason why one should make the attempt.

"The Bear"

Recalling William James' theory of the three stages through which an idea passes in its reception by the intellectual community, I can imagine a day when critics might contend that we have always been aware of the many different kinds of literary forms distinguished above and have always known, for example (though we would never put it in such terms) that *Tom Jones* is a problematic work and *The Magic Mountain* a dialectical one. In a general sense there would be some truth to the claim. In many ways the task of theory is to become adequate to perception, and to make a secure conceptual possession of what we already know in a vague, intuitive, and imprecise way.

At the same time all the examples used above remain open to debate and I can imagine readers taking issue with any and all of the placements. There are many arguments that might be advanced to show that *Tom Jones* is not a Crane-like structure at all; and one can imagine Crane's response to the suggestion that *Hamlet* and *The Brothers Karamazov* should be analyzed along dialectical lines. Rather than pursuing such arguments—which would merely repeat the debate of chapter 1, leaving us with the same general dilemmas—I will now return to "The Bear" and attempt to work out a solution to the problems uncovered in its interpretation. If we can solve the conflict of interpretations over a single text, that act will provide us with a paradigm for dealing with the debates that any of the placements made above could occasion. (It is, by the way, a paradigm of the reasoning process I went through in determining each of those placements.) To the critic who argues that *Tom Jones* (say) is not a Crane-like structure at all, the first thing I would reply is that he may quite possibly be right. To find out, however, he would have to be willing to subject both his interpretation and the ones he disagrees with to the following tests.

When viewed alone and subjected to its own criteria of verification, each interpretation constructed in chapter 1 provides a coherent reading of "The Bear." To go beyond that state of affairs we must now mediate the interpretations by one another, and prosecute each anew, beginning with the search for negative evidence. Our general canon of method is to try to find which interpretation of the three is hardest to eliminate, but we now know that a one-to-one correspondence of theory to text is only one possible outcome and that we must be prepared to establish a dynamic formal relationship among the three interpretations if the text under examination calls for such a resolution. While in chapter 1 the emphasis was on the interpretive power of each theory and the readiness with which the text could be assimilated to it, the focus now is on the text's resistance to our concepts, and the task is to bring as much evidence against each interpretation as we can find. The ingenuity upon which each interpretation prides itself has become the object of our skepticism; the "data" in the text which are recalcitrant have become "the knowledge most worth having."

Critique of the First Interpretation

Inquiry along these lines raises the following questions about the Cranian interpretation:

1. Given Faulkner's massive use of mythic, ritual, and Jungian structures in the tale, is it likely that those structures only function as devices of narrative magnification to establish and increase our desires and expectations for Ike? Or could the reverse be the case?

Is it possible that they are substantive, and that our feelings for Ike function within the broader context of action they establish?

2. Does the markedly incantatory and rhetorical nature of Faulkner's style and narrative manner, especially when he uses a generalized voice to comment on the significance of the action, serve primarily to shape the same structure of desires and expectations, or does it perhaps also indicate a larger intent?

3. Does the Cranian reading of section 4 as essentially a means of defining and magnifying our response to Ike offer a sufficient account of the broad historical context Faulkner there introduces into the tale? Does the convoluted time scheme Faulkner employs have a direct bearing on the problem of defining Ike's tragedy and creating the proper response to it, or does it instead lead us away from those concerns into questions of a fundamentally different kind? Granted "thought" remains subordinate to "character," do the elaborate theological, historical, and quasi-philosophic speculations Faulkner introduces in section 4 make a contribution to Ike's tragedy that is in any way proportionate to the amount of time and space given to them?

4. Finally, is section 5 really necessary? If our emotional experience is essentially complete at the end of section 4, why does Faulkner bother with it?

Crane frequently argues that the distinctive value of his method is that it enables us to reconstruct from our response the problems the writer faced in contructing the work: for that very reason there is no way to avoid these questions. They relate directly to the basic artistic choices Faulkner made in shaping the action. The second and third interpretations complicate the problem by indicating that the ritual, symbolic, and philosophic structures present in the work are even more complex and detailed than was apparent in the first interpretation.

To maintain itself, the first interpretation faces two alternatives. It can try to show how the structures revealed in the second and third interpretations function as yet further techniques of narrative magnification designed to shape and increase our desires and expectations. There is no reason a priori why the scene-agent ratio of the second interpretation and the lyric dialectic of the third might not so function. But it is difficult to render such an account without excessive labor—and without generating a basic inconsistency. The first interpretation views "The Bear" as a fairly simple tragedy of romantic confusion and willfulness, devoid of growth and recognition, and frequently verging on the pathetic. To pump up that action in the ways Faulkner does indicates an artistry in excess of the facts—an elaborate attempt, if you will, to confer upon his materials an emotional form that is inappropriate to them! Ike McCaslin is not Prince Hamlet, nor was he meant to be. To define his failure it is not necessary to invoke the entire history of the South, the mythos of the hero, and the grandest reaches of dialectical thought. It is far easier to maintain the first interpretation, in the face of the other two, by seeing "The Bear" as in many ways an artistic failure. As is so often the case in Faulkner, the striving for narrative magnification has gotten out of control. The discrepancy between Faulkner's narrative strategies and his materials is such that it is easiest to save the first interpretation by seeing the work as an example of emotional form, no doubt, but a bad instance of its kind. We will want to keep this option in mind in what follows. There is no guarantee of artistic success. The fact that an interpretation makes a work succeed where others see it failing does not, by itself, make that interpretation the correct one.

There is, however, another possibility. The first interpretation may break down because it is forced by its concepts to define the action of "The Bear" too narrowly. I deliberately concentrated on the mythic, ritual, and Jungian structures of the work in the first interpretation in order to show that the mere presence of such structures in a work does not necessarily indicate a rhetorical or dialectical intent. Myth is a powerful means of narrative magnification, and writers of fiction from Fielding to Updike have been quick to seize upon the potentialities it contains for maximizing our emotional response to their characters. With "The Bear," however, considerable effort and ingenuity is required to account for those structures in such terms. And at considerable cost! For Faulkner does not use those structures merely to increase our involvement in an action that could be understood independent of them. On the contrary, they define that action; in interpreting them in the way that his theory demands, the Cranian has to narrow not merely the context, but the very nature, of the action Faulkner is constructing. The same objection applies to the way the interpretation treats style, narrative manner, and the function of the broad historical and intellectual context developed in section 4. At all points we find that the first interpretation deliberately short-circuits Faulkner's action and the way technique may contribute not simply to its presentation but to its very constitution. Thus it should not surprise us to find that the explanation it offers of section 5 is of unrivalled ingenuity—in the solution of a self-imposed problem.

The major inconsistency throughout the first interpretation is that it has to go to great lengths to assign a minimal function to structures, techniques, and materials which are given a maximum development in the work. Far too often it explains by, in effect, explaining away. Throughout there is a continual narrowing of the scope of Faulkner's action with a consequent necessity of limiting the function of all the devices and structures Faulkner has used precisely in order to broaden the scope of that action. The ingenuity with which the first interpretation handles the problems it uncovers is not in question here. What it fails to recognize is that the very difficulties it faces may indicate the need for another approach. The main reason it is unable to consider that possibility is because its entire operation is determined by the assumption that the fact we respond emotionally to an action is an infallible sign that we are in the presence of a work where the problematic approach is the correct one, whatever the subsequent difficulties— an assumption that may be extremely powerful intuitively, but which must now be discarded.[20]

In rejecting the first interpretation I see no reason to deny the existence of the coherent structure of desires and expectations it reveals. The main problem we face in interpreting any mimetic work is not how emotional form by itself can account for the continuity of the entire action, but whether our desires and expectations function within a broader framework. On this question the possibility of mediating the first interpretation by the second serves us well, for the second interpretation provides a more direct, coherent, and functional account of Faulkner's basic artistic choices and techniques and does so in a way that preserves and deepens the emotional structure described in the first interpretation while overcoming its inconsistencies and dilemmas.

Critique of the Third Interpretation

In criticizing the first interpretation I have tried to show that its ruling concepts are too narrow to account for the action of "The Bear." At the opposite pole, it appears that the ruling concepts of the third interpretation may be too broad. The main question that can be raised about the third interpretation is whether it really cancels, preserves, and uplifts the first two, or whether it simply cancels them and does so at the expense of the work's continuity as a represented action. For the third interpretation to work it can't simply go beyond the first two or leave them behind. It must in canceling them also preserve and uplift them. It must show, in other words, that the structures described in the first two interpretations are in fact essential to the generation of the work's dialectic. Rather than rejecting the first two interpretations—as would be the case were Faulkner's dialectic the sort we find in the purely ideational structure of many lyric poems—it must integrate them.

Procedurally, of course, because the third interpretation supposes the first two, it appears at first glance to deepen them in a genuine interpretive synthesis. But is it really so? If we consider the third interpretation by itself for a moment, it becomes apparent that far too much that the first two interpretations show to be central to Faulkner's action is simply left out of account or plays no discernible function in the third. In setting up its dialectic the third interpretation levels off the structure of desires and expectations that forms our immediate interest in the action as well as the complex structure of attitudinal and motivational conflicts Faulkner has labored so mightily to construct. Rather than generating the dialectic of the work from those structures—thereby assuring the grounding of that dialectic in existence—the third interpretation finds the "plot" of "The Bear" finally of little importance to its dialectic.

Everything becomes an abstract counter in a purely intellectual drama. Ike's character is leveled off: he becomes no more than the representative of a way of knowing. While there is nothing to prevent a character's philosophic project from forming the basis of his psychological and social situation—as is so often the case in Dostoyevsky, Mann, and Sartre—the connection in "The Bear" is tenuous at best. In bearing "the dialectic of the lyric principle," Ike McCaslin is burdened with a weight too great for his frail shoulders—and Faulkner's supposed critique of the lyric principle suffers accordingly. To take that critique seriously we have to forget that Ike McCaslin is the Faulknerian representative of lyric knowing. He is not Marcel Proust; and rather than arising out of his character the lyric dialectic is imposed upon it.

Action, too, is leveled. Unable to find a dialectic inherent in the concrete action of the work, the third interpretation quite skillfully makes a virtue of necessity. Assuming that Faulkner's organizing purpose is to criticize the lyric principle, everything in the work that is not encompassed by that principle becomes, by definition, unintelligible—with its artistic function residing in that very fact. Faulkner supposedly sets out to represent all that the lyric principle excludes as a splendid waste of unformed matter—material represented *qua* material awaiting an art adequate to it. The discontinuity between the work's action and its dialectic becomes a positive characteristic which functions both as a critique of the lyric principle and as a call for the more concrete dialectical artistry which would order those materials for the first time. The self-reflexivity of Faulkner's art is such that the "discontinuity between moments of lyric contemplation and voids in narrative movement" in "The Bear" is thoroughgoing and extreme precisely in order to reveal the latter as a realm of experience that has not yet been mastered by art. The work becomes radically discontinuous—and that discontinuity becomes its purpose.

The third interpretation stands or falls on whether such is, in fact, the case. But the first two interpretations demonstrate that it is not. There are no voids in the narrative, mimetic movement of the work: coherent structures of emotional and attitudinal involvement shape the action with an inexorable regularity. Because it is unable to preserve and uplift those structures, the third interpretation is forced to cancel them.

Could the third interpretation overcome these defects? Theoretically, yes. As we have seen on pages 122–27, the general theoretical orientation it brings to "The Bear" places the kind of dialectical art it finds there within a much broader hierarchy of possibilities that is defined and ordered in terms of the movement toward a dialectical mimesis of concrete experience. It is not a question of whether it is possible to construct a concrete dialectical action, a possibility which a critic like Crane would be quick to deny. If the dialectician could find such a structure in "The Bear," he would be the first to call attention to it. But the fact of the matter is that "The Bear" presents us with no such thing. Having tried to find a dialectic in the action of the work and having failed to do so, the third interpretation "saves" the work by making it a necessary stage in the movement toward such a dialectic. As a result, however, the self-reflexivity of the work is after the fact rather than *in* the fact. Were a concrete dialectic present in "The Bear," it would have been possible to show how that dialectic gives birth to the action of the work and not only maintains but realizes itself in

the development of that action. But such is not the case. The only
dialectic present in "The Bear" is one which is neither direct nor continuous, and which finally has little to do with the action of the
work.

Procedurally, I arranged the three interpretations in the way I
did in order to dramatize how readily we assent to dialectical
readings, no matter how much they force us to leave out of
account. Our assent to a given interpretation is often based on our
prior, though usually unrecognized, assent to the metaphysical
framework or "metaphysical pathos" on which it is based. Convinced that the poet is a seer with a unified sensibility and poetry
the highest form of knowledge, many of us gravitate to dialectical
readings as if by impulse. My primary intention in structuring
chapter 1 was to enable us to catch ourselves in that act. Structurally, the chapter imitates the various principles of explanation that
are commonly employed in criticism today in order to bring out
their regulative presence—and all that fact implies. Many colleagues have assured me that they found the third interpretation of
"The Bear" convincing because it included the previous two and
gave them a deeper significance. We are now in a position to
recognize that we are predisposed to accept interpretations which
perform such operations because explanations of this kind satisfy
the principle of hierarchic integration which has a pervasive if
unrecognized hold over our thought (vide Kant's dialectic of pure
reason) while also conforming to the dialectical orientation which
pervades contemporary criticism. On close scrutiny, however, it
becomes evident that the third interpretation appears to preserve
and deepen the first two only because it comes after them. The fact
of the matter is that it does not cancel, preserve, and uplift the first
two interpretations in a truly concrete way, but simply supposes
them in order to move on to the construction of a dialectic which is
no doubt present in "The Bear" but is not the principle giving it
structure as a concrete whole.

In Support of the Second Interpretation

Yet what are we to make of the important structures revealed by
the third interpretation? It provides the deepest, most suggestive
reading of the first and fifth sections of "The Bear," and there can
be little doubt that the dialectical structures it finds there are of
great importance to the work. Is it possible to find a more direct
and dramatically coherent function for them?

In his study of communication, Kenneth Burke has always been fascinated by the rhetorical resources of dialectical terminologies and strategies. He sees the search for a supreme term (or god term) around which one might construct an essentialistic and ahistorical understanding of motives as a natural and recurrent response to the dilemmas of social life, especially when men see no way to resolve their conflicts on a purely human level. Though it is no more than one ideology among others, the rhetorical value of dialectic lies in the satisfaction it affords to our desire to attain a divine or transcendent perspective which remains secure above and beyond the seemingly insoluble conflicts that plague life in the cave.[21]

In "The Bear" Faulkner gives full play to that rhetorical strategy—in order to negate it. Every component of the lyric dialectic isolated in the third interpretation functions quite coherently as part of the rhetoric Faulkner uses to define the scenic grammar of the wilderness; and everything else in the work just as coherently dramatizes the inadequacy of that grammar to the historical conflicts that make up its larger action. As a purely intellectual explanation of one side of the conflict dramatized in "The Bear," the dialectical interpretation is unsurpassed. But the action of the work is far more concrete than its terms allow; the lyric-narrative dichotomy into which it resolves the action requires a single-minded focus on one side of the conflict dramatized in the work at the expense of any attention to the equally coherent historical action in which the desire for dialectic is contained and structured. The dialectical reading is only possible if one adopts Ike McCaslin's viewpoint and persists in seeing and judging everything in the work in terms of it. The irony of that fact spells its destruction. As a subordinate part of the work's rhetoric, however, the lyric dialectic has a direct function consistent with the action of the work: in describing structures that deepen and expand our understanding of Faulkner's rhetoric, the third interpretation makes a significant contribution to the second.

But what of the second interpretation? Can a case be made against it? After casting around for quite a while I must confess that I find no major objections to it, either within its own terms or when it is contrasted with the other two interpretations. It overcomes the characteristic defects of the other two readings while integrating their contributions functionally within an interpretation which stays in constant touch with the concrete movement of the work. In interpreting the structure of "The Bear" it finds no need to eliminate anything essential to its action, no need to short-circuit the explanation of Faulkner's artistic choices, and no need to minimize the important but subordinate function that the structures revealed by the other two interpretations play in the construction of the work. It explains the basic artistic choices Faulkner made in shaping "The Bear" in a way that gives a maximum functional relevance to those choices without calling upon extreme ingenuity in the devising of that explanation.

All of these considerations create a strong probability in its favor, and there is much that one could bring forward at this point to increase that probability.[22] Because it has overcome the tendency of most rhetorical critics to reduce the literary work to a bundle of abstract statements, it is not vulnerable to the charge of compromising action for theme. Because in its mediation by the other two interpretations it is able to preserve the coherent structures they reveal without separating those structures from the action, or compromising the concreteness of that action, it grows and prospers from the conflict of interpretations; rather than retreating to a defensive posture or trying to explain away what the other interpretations reveal, it is able to use the conflict of interpretations as an occasion for deepening its understanding of "The Bear" in a reading that is already implicit in chapter 1 and that could be extended indefinitely without ever losing touch with the phenomenon. It explains, while the others are forced to explain away. Within the terms of the present debate it appears on all counts triumphant.

Perhaps my critical powers have failed me here. The reasons for that are not personal however. Speaking in terms of my own interests and inclinations, I find myself most satisfied when in the presence of a dialectical work; when not so employed, I prefer to recreate myself in the world of emotional form. Although I suspect that the literary world presents more instances of rhetorical form than it does anything else, I am no great friend of rhetoric. If I had my way we'd all be dialecticians, as men if not as critics. The uses of pluralism are many, however, and one is as aid and prologue to choice. If we must be dialecticians, let us choose works that will enable us to develop a genuine dialectic of human existence; the first step toward that project being the recognition that dialectical art is a rare endeavor, though all the more valuable by reason of that fact.

If we conclude our study with a decision in favor of the second interpretation, we should recognize that the decision is not a result of its universal theoretical truth, interpretive power, or practical ingenuity. All three theories are true. The truth of each is a particular truth, however, rather than a general one. All are of unquestionable interpretive power: backed by sufficient ingenuity there is no way any of them can fail, in the teeth of whatever objections are raised to them—and that includes every objection we have here advanced against the first and third interpretations. Nor is our conclusion in favor of the second interpretation the product of either common sense or an existential hermenuetic. The first reading of "The Bear" corresponds most closely, I think, to the response of the ordinary reader; if our purpose as critics is to concur with the "pleasure that generations of readers" have taken and will take in works such as "The Bear," we must decide in favor of it. The third reading, on the other hand, comes closest to satisfying the conditions of an existential hermeneutic that would speak to the profound ontological significance so many of us want to find in literature: if our purpose as critics is to put art in touch with the ultimate reaches of human thought in its attempt to master the problems of human existence, we must decide the debate in its favor.[23] Neither decision, however, addresses the real issue, for the task of interpretation is not to satisfy some previously posited purpose all art must follow, but to discover the particular purpose at work in the particular text before us. Given that task, in the case of "The Bear" the second interpretation comes closest to satisfying the demands of self-critical reasoning.

There can, of course, be nothing definitive about that verdict. The fact that a given interpretation makes a work an artistic success while others are forced to see it as an artistic failure does not necessarily mean that the former is correct. Nor does a law of parsimony hold: if the simplicity of explanation were the primary criterion of verification, Crane would march like Sherman to the sea and dialectical readings would be ruled out a priori. The complexity of an interpretation is neither an argument for nor against it. The kind of ingenuity critics use, not the fact of ingenuity, is the proper object of skepticism. A truly pluralistic use of the method of multiple working hypotheses does not offer us abstract general rules, hard-and-fast interpretive procedures, or apodictic canons of evidence and proof that we can use to resolve all critical disputes. The primary rule, if we must have one, is to be self-critical in principle at all times, from all possible points of view, and all the way down the line. Fortunately, our problems will not always be as difficult as they were with "The Bear." Many texts are fairly simple—if we would only let them be. Many of the disputes among critics disappear once we understand, in a principled way, the manifold reasons why they need never have arisen in the first place. More often than not, however, we must be prepared to confront problems analogous to those we faced with "The Bear," for the interaction of forms rather than their mutual exclusion appears to be a primary characteristic of the literary universe, and is, I think, the new horizon our study has established—for theory and for practice.

Such a critical method offers little in the way of comfort to those who want to simplify the problems of interpretation or who assume that anything less than certitude convicts one of error. In criticism, as in life, truth lies in *a-lethia*[24] (that is, wresting from concealment) rather than in a system of rigid dogmas or clear and distinct ideas. Taking note of the ways in which the vagaries of human response frustrate "objectivity" in interpretation, I. A. Richards concluded that "any good interpretation is a triumph against odds." Theory attempts to shift the odds in our favor. But theory has its odds too—and its prisons. Theories are not only ways of seeing, they are ways of making oneself blind. To make theory adequate to perception and perception adequate to theory requires, as we have seen, that one accept a plurality of theories of form, trace those theories back to their philosophic bases, and then bring that total framework, in all its possible interrelationships, to bear upon a detailed and exacting attention to the text, in all its irreducible particularity.

The whole effort of our study has been to make criticism a science of particulars. Naturally our problems are greater now than they have ever been. The first thing such an approach requires, in fact, is a long silence in the face of the text—and keeping silence is for most of us the most difficult mode of discourse.[25] Until we have lived with and in the text for a long time, until we have considered it in detail from many points of view and criticized each in turn, we cannot begin to speak of it with any assurance that our discourse actually takes us into the text and deepens our understanding of it. The conquest of the text is a long march, and what Paul Ricoeur said of philosophy's attempt to become adequate to experience also applies to literary criticism: "If the route to the Concrete is so arduous it is because the concrete is the final conquest of thought."[26]

The phenomenon is all before us . . . .

The artist, like the God of the creation, remains within or behind or beyond or above his handiwork, invisible, refined out of existence, indifferent, paring his fingernails.

James Joyce, *A Portrait of the Artist as a Young Man*

But there exist more subtle behaviors, the description of which will lead us further into the inwardness of consciousness. Irony is one of these. In irony a man annihilates what he posits within one and the same act; he leads us to believe in order not to be believed; he affirms to deny and denies to affirm; he creates a positive object but it has no being other than its nothingness.

Jean-Paul Sartre, *Being and Nothingness*

Afterword:
Irony and Mimesis in
The Act of Interpretation

Two important characteristics of the mimetic method are irony and a distance between what an author represents and his own attitudes or position. When used in a theoretical work the method depends for its success on the reader's being alive to the constant possibility of reversals and complications in the apparent progress of the argument. Since the views dramatized are valid yet inadequate, their truth and their limitations must both be present in their representation and every statement must be apprehended from both perspectives. Each position is given full sway while it is on the stage, yet the seeds of its reversal are present within it. No matter how strong an argument may appear initially, the envolving structure of which it is a part is deliberately suspensive. The position that appears to triumph at one stage in the discussion is subject to reversal at a subsequent stage as a result of further reflections that are made possible by the consideration of other positions and possibilities. As the discussion proceeds, the untested assumptions and problems implicit in previously adopted views become apparent—thus the entire inquiry is always simultaneously progressive and reflexive.

I employed these procedures in a continuous fashion throughout the first chapter. In its overall movement the chapter appeared to enact a successful process of Hegelian *Aufhebung* in which the first two theories and the interpretations they offered were necessarily and successfully incorporated in the third. Subsequent considerations showed, however, that this result was only apparent, and when we returned to "The Bear" in chapter 4 the conclusion reached at the end of chapter 1 was reversed. The relationship between the conclusion of chapter 1 and the argument developed at the end of chapter 4 is one of the major ironies of *The Act of Interpretation*. I note it here to indicate that the irony of the book is not local and occasional, but structural and comprehensive.

There are both theoretical and rhetorical reasons behind my use of such strategies. One derives from the fact that I conceive the audience for whom the book is intended as the subject as well as the observer of my irony. I have tried to create a structure of thought in which critics of various persuasions will become caught up in a process of self-discovery as a direct result of finding themselves implicated in problems they had not anticipated and forced by the movement of the inquiry to pursue theoretical and philosophic issues most would prefer to avoid. Like Hamlet's mousetrap, *The Act of Interpretation* is designed to catch the reader in the act of assenting to assumptions and beliefs he is not aware he employs precisely because those assumptions and beliefs so pervade criticism today that they have become a second and unconscious nature to us; we are scarcely aware how thoroughly we depend upon them or how questionable they might appear to a reflective gaze. The effort throughout the book has been to make explicit the enabling assumptions and principles of explanation that characterize a number of different critical positions within an overarching context in which the questionable nature of those assumptions and procedures becomes apparent. Rather than directing my critique at a single critical audience or school, by covertly endorsing another, my purpose has been to call attention to the hidden dogmas and covert principles of reasoning that characterize the many distinct positions that make up the contemporary critical scene. Thus the effort in chapter 1, for example, is to imitate the different kinds of explanation that carry conviction for the adherents of each of the positions considered—a conviction dependent, as we subsequently discover, upon the fact that the principles on which those interpretations are based assume precisely what is to be proved.

Those who have studied it most closely have called attention to the great demands that the mimetic method places upon the reader. Joyce's *A Portrait of the Artist as a Young Man* was as old as its hero before critics began appreciating its ironies, and we are still far from completely understanding the structural rigorousness and unity of the ironic method Joyce developed in that novel. Many readers still identify with Emma Bovary and Frederic Morel, and many quite intelligent ones have found Stephen Dedalus and Serenus Zeitblom thoroughly reliable and have felt justified in assuming a close sympathetic relationship between the author, his central character, and the point of view through which the tale is represented, especially since that point of view appears to be what the story is primarily about. Many readers have shared Thomas

Merton's penitent response to the third chapter of Joyce's *Portrait*, have sided with the harsh wisdom of Thrasymachus against the pedantic humanism of Socrates, and have said "stay, thou art so fair" to many of the attitudes and positions the Hegel of the *Phenomenology* wants us to regard as way stations on the journey to absolute knowledge. The mimetic method offers the reader a mirror to himself: it is a chance, in watching oneself, to see oneself for the first time, but it always runs the risk of engendering a self-confirming narcissism.

When used in a theoretical work, the mimetic method requires a reader who is not only continually alive to ironic reversals but one who is capable of keeping his understanding of pivotal concepts flexible and suspended until he has experienced the movement of the entire argument. A mimetic work strives to be that which it is about: the attempt is to create a structure of thought which is at all times the expression of a single theoretical idea in one of the necessary stages of its development. Since that is so, nothing less than the movement of the entire work serves to define any of its central concepts. "The whole is all there is." As Hegel argued in the preface to *The Phenomenology of Mind*, there is no way to summarize the doctrines a mimetic work will propound because no concepts can be set down prior to the work or arrived at outside the process of continuous critique that shapes it. Because it works by dramatizing the limitations of different perspectives, the method subjects all formulations and "definitions" to a process of progressive reinterpretation. Thus it requires a reader possessed with the "negative capability" to restrain the desire for misplaced concreteness and fixed univocal definitions in favor of a movement of reflection which is essentially the search for a genuine beginning and for definitions of a fundamentally different order. Thanks to a shift in intellectual priorities that dates roughly from the time of Kant and Hegel, we are beginning to understand that many of our most important concepts are structures and can only be articulated and grasped by a similar act of understanding. Written in that spirit, *The Act of Interpretation* employs the mimetic method not merely as a technique, but out of a philosophic necessity—its irony, accordingly, is not merely a principle of style or tone, but an essential dimension of its content.

The primary virtue of the mimetic method lies, of course, in its compression. It is a way of saying through showing that reveals far more than one could state in any other manner. Represented in all of its dramatic immediacy, the virtues and the limitations of positions become apparent, as well as the deep and usually unrecognized bases of their appeal. When Joyce writes the third chapter of *Portrait* through what is, in effect, the official voice of the Catholic church, showing how that voice structures the consciousness of Stephen Dedalus and his experience at this stage of his development, he epiphanizes both the power and the trap Roman Catholicism represents. A passage such as the following can be read in two opposed ways, both of which are "correct":

> His sin, which had covered him from the sight of God, had led him nearer to the refuge of sinners. Her eyes seemed to regard him with mild pity; her holiness, a strange light glowing faintly upon her frail flesh, did not humiliate the sinner who approached her. If ever he was impelled to cast sin from him and to repent the impulse that moved him was the wish to be her knight. (*Portrait* [New York: Viking Press, 1964], p. 105)

We have here a perfect depiction of Stephen's spiritual state seen through the language of Catholicism, the kind of language one encounters again and again in devotional writing, even in writers like Chesterton, Belloc, and Mauriac. That language coincides with Stephen's viewpoint at this stage of his development, as do the other styles used in the course of the book. We can assent to the description, as we do, and I think are meant to do, in our initial reading of the work, or we can cast a cold ironic eye upon it. By the time we reach a passage like the following, however, the ironic perspective should have assumed command:

> He knelt to say his penance, praying in a corner of the dark nave: and his prayers ascended to heaven from his purified heart like perfume streaming upwards from a heart of white rose. (*Portrait*, p. 145)

Once one understands the intricate structure of *Portrait* and has experienced, for example, the point-for-point ironic parallel between Stephen's commission of the seven deadly sins at the beginning of chapter 3 and his repetition of precisely the same sins in his effort at "spiritual" purification at the beginning of chapter 4—Joyce's method of subjecting all experiences to ironic redefinition has become the dominant fact about the book—but that fact exists always as prelude to a more perceptive rereading. For Joyce is not simply giving the devil his due in chapter 3. While the chapter is one of the great representations of Catholicism as the model for

totalitarian propaganda—and a great act of ironic liberation from
that language—it is also a confession of the profound power of
Catholicism's aesthetic appeal and a recognition of the deep human
needs it satisfies. We are not meant to choose among these
readings: chapter 3 of *Portrait*, and it is one of the simplest
examples in the book, incorporates opposed responses, and does so
in a rigorous rather than eclectic fashion. Joyce's attitude toward the
religion of his youth always remained one of the utmost complexity—and his narrative method is the refusal of all single-
mindedness. To be fully understood *Portrait* has to be read
simultaneously from at least two opposed points of view. The
rituals of Roman Catholicism as well as its rhetorical and aesthetic
appeal address what were for Joyce essential needs of the psyche—
and those needs remain integral to Stephen's *Bildungsroman*. Joyce
never simply cancels anything. He performs, instead, the far more
complex act of *Aufhebung*, canceling, preserving, and uplifting the
essential forms of human experience that are structured by Catholic
ritual. As many have noted, Stephen's aesthetic creed (and in this
case Joyce's also) is the secular equivalent of Catholicism and
preserves the ritual needs and modes of experience the church once
fulfilled by relocating those structures in the world.

The virtues of the mimetic method imply its inherent pitfalls.
Carried away by their identification with what is represented,
flattered by what was intended as parody, many readers find
themselves confirmed in that from which the method was meant to
distance them. Which is why a man like Thomas Merton could,
with some justice, read the third chapter of *Portrait* as one of the
essential experiences on his way to Rome, yet why we read
Merton's account of his conversion, and of Joyce's place in it, as a
droll return to a language, and *ipso facto* a stage of experience,
which Joyce has liberated us from through his irony. (See *The
Seven Storey Mountain* [New York: Harcourt Brace, 1948], pt. 2,
chap. 1.) It is also why Wayne Booth is in one sense correct in his
strictures against the lack of clear focus and direction he finds
implicit in Joyce's narrative method, for Joyce's method both
depends on the natural responses of the reader and subjects those
responses to a continuous ironic critique. Contrary to the alternatives Booth proposes, *Portrait* must have it both ways.

Many readers, finding themselves the subject of ironic representation, are flattered rather than appalled. That risk is implicit in the
method because the dramatization—or immanent critique—of

ideas, attitudes, and "habits of mind and feeling" involves the reader in a way other kinds of writing do not. Indeed, the method recognizes misinterpretation as perhaps the reader's deepest need. Yet who would have things any other way? Knowledge is a difficult acquisition, dependent on painful reversals. If the Socratic method initially threatens to paralyze us when it abruptly turns us around, that is because it requires that we discover we are most in the cave when we think we are seeing most clearly. It is a dangerous, by definition a precarious, method, yet as Hegel argues it is the only method which is in fact organically one with its subject, the only method where form and content, the act of philosophizing and the content of philosophy, are joined in a way that is adequate to both the process and the nature of self-critical or reflective knowing.

The description of Joyce's method is, of course, a comment on my own. And as in Joyce, the irony is most intense and most revealing when experienced at the primary level of language. "Can you procure me a copy of the document?" The man who uses a word like *procure* rather than *get* has not refined his perception or purified the dialect of the tribe. He has embraced a corpse of dead language, the language of the generalized or socialized other, the language of a class expressing in its speech the contradictions of that class. It is a language of bad faith, the language of a man playing at being educated. But once one sees it as such, how can one make any statement that will not be an unconscious parody of itself? Isn't any attempt to criticize language simply a further instance of it? In a recent interview, Roland Barthes remarked that he talked about nothing but language because nothing disgusted him as much as language. In a similar spirit Adrian Leverkühn in Mann's *Doctor Faustus* asked, "Why does almost everything seem to me like its own parody?" Joyce's revolutionary idea (an idea shared in different ways by Hegel, the Marx of *Das Kapital*, Wittgenstein, and Mann) was that one could do a critique of language—and thereby extend language beyond its previous boundaries—by using existing language in such a way that its inadequacies called attention to themselves. It is an idea that should be kept in mind while reflecting on *The Act of Interpretation*.

In an earlier time the mimetic method may have asked too much of the reader. The continued failure of commentators to appreciate the dramatic complexity of Plato's dialogues as a complexity integral to his thought, and not merely a rhetorical device, is a case in point. But ours is the age of ironic discourse. Few notions are as prized by modern critics as irony, and when we read literature most of us find it everywhere. We are deeply attuned to a distance between the author and his characters or personae, the author and his style, the author and his narrative method. We prize ironic art because it answers our demand for a refined sensibility capable of making, in an orderly and progressive way, the infinite qualifications and discriminations that constitute a mature experience of the world. Isn't it about time we brought the same acts of intelligence into the house of criticism itself?

Notes

Chapter 1

1. My purpose in this section is to outline this logic in the most general terms: to articulate the preliminary conceptual understanding we need in order to approach the act of interpreting a text in a way that will make the nature of that activity and the substantive problems implicit in it stand out clearly. It is in interpretation alone, however, that theoretical concepts become concrete and thus the present discussion is and can be no more than a provisional scaffolding.

2. It will become evident that the concept of form I am developing has nothing to do with "formalism" and in no way entails an opposition of form and content. In *Beyond Formalism* (New Haven, Conn.: Yale University Press, 1972, p. 42), Geoffrey Hartman offers two convenient definitions of formalism, which I cite for purposes of contrast: "Bateson defined formalism as a tendency to isolate the aesthetic fact from its human content, but I will here define it simply as a method: that of revealing the human content of art by a study of its formal properties."

3. As we proceed it may be helpful to contrast the concepts of form, structure, and the method of close textual interpretation we are developing with the "structuralist" approach to literature made popular by the work of Claude Lévi-Strauss and based on the method of interpretation developed in *Mythologiques*. The structuralists agree with us that parts and elements must be understood in terms of their place in the whole, but their conception of structure is purely spatial (or synchronic) and is formulated without any reference to artistic purpose. In contrast, our concept of structure is based on a search for the immanent principle of purpose which exists in the temporal movement of the work. As a theory of language, structuralism formalistically abstracts language from the living speaker and the existential reference of his speech, as Paul Ricoeur has shown in a penetrating article, "New Developments in Phenomenology in France: The Phenomenology of Language" (*Social Research* 34 [1967]: 1–30). As a literary theory, structuralism in turn deprives the events in a work of any dynamic temporal connection, and resolves them into abstract spatial patterns. By thus depriving "structures" of their concrete development, structuralism becomes, ironically, a "formalism" of materials—a simple reverse of the formalism of pure aesthetic qualities it was designed to supplant. For a critical review of structuralism in the light of that history, see Frederic Jameson, *The Prison-House of Language* (Princeton, N.J.: Princeton University Press, 1972). To avoid any confusion on this score let me note my wholehearted agreement with the structuralist attempt to go beyond "formalism"; the theory I am developing is just as ardently opposed to

"formalism" in all of its guises. Rather than a stirring advance in critical interpretation, however, structuralism is a retreat from the logic of immanent purposiveness formulated above—a retreat no doubt facilitated by the fact that the logic of artistic purpose has seldom been made explicit. In this connection it may be worth noting that while structuralism is dominated by the image of the computer in its effort to spatialize literature, the criticism of forms relies on organic metaphors in its attempt to apprehend the literary work temporally in terms of an immanent principle of motion which is omnipresent in the phenomena but never there as a physical thing. Structuralist notation, with all its charts and graphs and spatial patterns, always falls short of the latter apprehension, for it cannot be had by Cratylean pointing but depends on those inferential and synthesizing acts of mind which have been variously termed insight, "the intuition of essence," the esemplastic power of imagination, or simply "an instinct for the natures of things" and which are one of the arduous ways in which man distinguishes himself from the machine. For the strict structuralist, of course, this book will resolve itself into a "deep structure" or "system" of parallelism and contrast arranged around the antinomies of identity and difference.

Structuralism, however, is a far-flung enterprise and the interpretive method derived from Lévi-Strauss is only one part of the whole story. Like so many other terms, *structuralism* is often no more than a vague label for a general orientation that has not yet made its principles clear to itself. See, for example, Roland Barthes, "L'activité structuraliste" (*Les Lettres Nouvelles*, no. 32, 1963). Here and elsewhere in *The Act of Interpretation* I am concerned with structuralism only insofar as it relates to the problems of holistic interpretation. There are many "species" or variants of structuralism that have nothing to do with these problems. Indeed, Jonathan Culler's *Structuralist Poetics* (Ithaca, N.Y.: Cornell University Press, 1975), a superb introduction to the topic, indicates that the primary impact of structuralism in literary theory might be in reviving and deepening our understanding of genre and of the generic expectations and learned rules that determine our responses to different literary types. My effort, in contrast, is to begin precisely where generic criticism leaves off; the concept of form I am developing grows in part out of a dissatisfaction with generic criticism, especially with the tendency of historical critics to reduce the literary work to its conventions and generic properties irrespective of function and of the way particular artists use the rules, forms, materials, and expectations of their time. Identification of conventions and rules is one thing, the study of function and purpose quite another. The structuralist poetic that Culler is concerned with is by and large taken up with the kind of critical considerations that are prior to the questions raised in this book and that need to be reinterpreted once all the consequences implicit in the primacy of form become apparent.

4. For the opposite argument see Jacques Derrida, "Force et signification" in *L'Écriture et La Différence* (Paris: Éditions du Seuil, 1967); "Differance," in *Speech and Phenomena* (Evanston, Ill.: Northwestern University Press, 1973); and *Of Grammatology* (Baltimore: Johns Hopkins University Press, 1976).

5. This problem is developed at length in chapter 2.

6. Three of the most interesting critics on this question, though of very different backgrounds and assumptions, are Sheldon Sacks, Stanley Fish, and Jonathan Culler.

7. The distinction, of course, is purely analytic and is advanced only in order to enable us to describe the logic that structures the interpretive process. That process, in turn, is the issue of experience and is determined, throughout its operations, by our response to the literary work as a totality which is, in Dewey's terms, "had, suffered, and enjoyed before it is cognized." We don't read in order to interpret; we read in order to read. The text grabs us and only then do we begin to ask the kind of analytic questions that will enable us to articulate what we already in a sense know. Any interpretation is no better or worse than the experience which gives birth to it. The logic shaping the interpretive process might be formulated, to borrow from T. S. Eliot, as the effort "to arrive where we started/And know the place for the first time."

8. For reasons that will become apparent I will not offer a plot summary of "The Bear" here or later. In order to focus attention on the fundamental problems of interpretation and the acts of mind that structure it, I assume that the reader has already read "The Bear" with care, has had the kind of perceptions discussed above, and is ready to move on to the question of how to synthesize one's understanding. Faulkner, however, is a notoriously difficult writer and many readers spend a lot of time simply trying to find out what happens in his works. So that we won't be deterred by such problems, a simple summary of the time scheme used in "The Bear" is in order. Ike's birthdate is 1867. Sections 1 through 3 take place in 1885. Section 4 takes Ike's story back in time to 1883 when he read the ledgers that record the history of his family and forward in time to 1885–86 when he made his trips to Tennessee and Midnight, Arkansas. The ledgers record events that go back in time as far as 1807, when Ike's grandfather, Lucius Quinters Carothers McCaslin, purchased the slave, Eunice, in New Orleans. At the end of Ike's discussion with his cousin, Cass (b. 1850), the section carries his story forward in time to 1895. Note that the death of Ben and Ike's investigation of the ledgers—his twin "nativities"—take place in the winter of 1883.

9. Since it is so dense and convoluted, a brief summary of section 4 may be helpful. All page references are to "The Bear," *Go Down, Moses* (New York: Modern Library, 1955). Section 4 may be divided as follows:

1. Pp. 254–61. Setting in the commissary on Ike's twenty-first birthday. Beginning of debate between Ike and Cass over Ike's relinquishment of the land. Ike introduces theological question of God's purpose in the South.

2. Pp. 261–82. Flashback. Ike at sixteen reads through the ledgers and discovers the burden of guilt he will try to expiate. Briefly: his grandfather has produced a daughter by the Negro servant, Eunice, whom he purchased in 1807 and married to his slave, Thucydidus. Later, by this daughter, Tomasina, he produced a son, Turl. He refused to recognize his son, yet leaves a provision for him in his will. Eunice committed suicide when she discovered her daughter's pregnancy. These discoveries are called facts of "Ike's own nativity." In an effort at expiation he attempts to give Turl's children their inheritance. He fails to locate the first child, James. Later he deposits one thousand dollars in a bank for the second child, Sophonsiba, whom he traces to Arkansas where he finds her living in poverty with her husband. At this point Ike is nineteen. Later, in 1895, the third child, Lucas, will present himself to Ike on his twenty-first birthday and ask for his money: with this glimpse forward in time the flashback concludes.

3. *Pp. 282-96.* The discussion resumes. Events of the Civil War and the Reconstruction period are recorded. Ike sees in them some manifestation of God's purpose and emphasizes the virtue of endurance.

4. *Pp. 296-98.* In an important flashback Ike remembers the discussion he and Cass had after Cass learned that Ike had run under Ben to save the fyce. Cass quoted from Keats' "Ode on a Grecian Urn." Ike was fourteen at the time.

5. *Pp. 298-300.* The discussion resumes. Ike emphasizes that Sam Fathers set him free from the curse of the South. By repudiating his inheritance he will become one of those who endures.

6. *Pp. 300-308.* Comic interlude recording Uncle Hubert's gift to Ike. Provides a contrast to Ike's repudiation of money.

7. *Pp. 308-15.* The discussion concludes. Faulkner then traces Ike's life in the next seven years and concludes with the attempt by Ike's wife, in offering her body to him, to persuade him to reassume his inheritance.

10. That view is, of course, debatable. One may recall the story of the admiring reader who expressed to Faulkner her gratitude that Ike had kept heroic faith with the wilderness by relinquishing his possessions. In asking her whether that choice was really a mature one, Faulkner suggested the need for a more attentive reading of the story. Attentive reading is the essential prerequisite to any act of interpretation and depends on a natural sagacity in perception that most likely cannot be taught. The willingness to be critical about one's perceptions and to resist the desire to be original simply for the sake of being original are somewhat different matters, and it is worth noting that the body of criticism that gathers around any important literary work usually presents what amounts to a series of precariously selective "readings" corrected by "new readings" based on an equally selective attention to isolated details. One of the best discussions of this kind of "conflict of interpretations"—which is far more characteristic of critical debate than is the genuinely philosophic conflict of interpretations that is my subject—occurs in the section titled "Deep Readers of the World, Beware!" in Wayne Booth's *The Rhetoric of Fiction* (Chicago: University of Chicago Press, 1961, pp. 364-74). Booth's discussion is a shrewd description of the motives that lead us to propound new readings, as different as possible from previous readings. Conforming to the model Booth there describes, in the early phase of its interpretation critics of "The Bear" emphasized Ike's heroic stature and Faulkner's use of myth. Then in an "ironic" phase, critics sought out everything in the tale that could be used to cast doubt on that interpretation. Recently we have entered phase 3. As we know, section 4 in "The Bear" was intended for publication only in *Go Down, Moses*; Faulkner has said as much, and that collection may be regarded as a unified "novel" or history of the McCaslin family. It is impossible to interpret "The Bear" by itself. But if we are to see *Go Down, Moses* as an artistic whole—and not merely as a collection of historical facts and abstract themes, as has been the case thus far—shifting from "The Bear" to it merely postpones the fundamental problem of interpretation or reintroduces it on a larger scale. It is, of course, revealing to contrast Ike in "The Bear" with Lucas in "The Fire and the Hearth" or to read "Delta Autumn" for its telling commentary on the aged Ike which we can then read back into the story of his youth. And as we all know Faulkner really

wrote only one work—the Yoknapatawpha saga. To understand any of his tales we must place it within that overarching context. I have no objection to such proposals. To carry any of them out, however, we must *begin* somewhere by treating one of Faulkner's works as an artistic whole. Otherwise we really have nothing to which to refer the others. If, out of frustration with that problem, we shift to a larger context, we have simply put off the day in which we have to confront the question of artistic integrity. For what is the nature of *Go Down, Moses* as an artistic whole (if it really is one) and what is the function of "The Bear" within it? In focusing on "The Bear" and in dealing with it as a work of art, my goal is to provide a paradigm of what is required to interpret any work as an artistic whole—and thus a model of what we would have to do should we decide to reopen the entire question and see "The Bear" as part of *Go Down, Moses.*

11. On Heidegger's conception of the hermeneutic circle, see *Being and Time,* translated by John Macquarrie and Edward Robinson (New York: Harper and Row, 1962, sections 14 to 18 and 21). For a history of hermeneutic theory from Schleiermacher to Gadamer, see R. E. Palmer, *Hermeneutics* (Evanston, Ill.: Northwestern University Press, 1969). The most important work of hermeneutic theory by a theorist working within the context of American criticism is *Validity in Interpretation* (New Haven, Conn.: Yale University Press, 1968) by E. D. Hirsch, Jr. In the course of the discussion I will have occasion at several points to contrast my hermeneutic with the existential hermeneutic of Heidegger and Gadamer as well as with the historical hermeneutic of Hirsch. Most of those contrasts derive from the fact that for me *the nature of the whole* is what has become the major hermeneutic problem. E. D. Hirsch, in contrast, constructs a hermeneutic which attempts to decide, on the basis of historical evidence, which reading of *particular lines* most closely corresponds with what was most likely the author's "meaning-intent" given the literary *type* his work instances. Much in the book is of great value, especially Hirsch's attack on wholesale endorsements of "the intentional fallacy" and his development of criteria of verification and the notion of intrinsic genre. As far as I can tell, however, Hirsch assumes that all literary works are "structures of meaning"—within a strictly and narrowly rhetorical conception of meaning—and never confronts the possibility of fundamentally distinct artistic purposes. Moreover, rather than seeking to discover the nature of works as artistic wholes through close textual analysis, Hirsch posits a rather abstract genre-theory and uses it to resolve critical disputes in a manner that is finally a priori: since it is always possible that a given writer is using a genre and its conventions in a fundamentally new way. For further discussion of alternate hermeneutic frameworks, see pages 57–59 and chapter 3.

12. The best statement of Crane's position is in *The Languages of Criticism and the Structure of Poetry* (Toronto: University of Toronto Press, 1953), especially chapters 2 and 5.

13. See "The Concept of Plot and the Plot of *Tom Jones,*" in *Critics and Criticism* (Chicago: University of Chicago Press, 1952, pp. 616–47) for the fullest discussion of Crane's interpretive methodology.

14. The phrase is from Sheldon Sacks' *Fiction and the Shape of Belief* (Berkeley and Los Angeles: University of California Press, 1964). Sacks' book

significantly deepens Crane's description of how the ethical representation of characters shapes our emotional response. My version of Crane's theory and practice is heavily indebted to numerous discussions with Mr. Sacks.

15. For an analysis of the *Poetics* from this methodological standpoint and for a provocative discussion of catharsis as a principle of structure, see Kenneth Telford, *Aristotle's Poetics: Translation and Analysis* (Chicago: Henry Regnery Co., 1961).

16. For an example of Crane's application of the method to a "tragic" work, see the discussion of *Macbeth* in *The Languages of Criticism and the Structure of Poetry*, pp. 169–79.

17. One of Crane's clearest discussions of this topic occurs in the essay "Ernest Hemingway: 'The Killers,' " in *The Idea of the Humanities* (Chicago: University of Chicago Press, 1967, vol. 2, pp. 303–14). While Crane tends to discuss this topic in a somewhat abstract manner, Wayne Booth's *The Rhetoric of Fiction* develops a detailed, and in many ways definitive, study of the way different narrative techniques function to shape our responses.

18. Faulkner, "The Bear," *Go Down, Moses*, p. 226.

19. Ibid., p. 254.

20. William Faulkner, "Speech of Acceptance upon the Award of the Nobel Prize for Literature." Delivered in Stockholm, 10 December 1950.

21. Strictly speaking, Cass is the one who introduces Keats. But the episode is presented as Ike's recollection and he recalls it, significantly, at the point in their discussion when he realizes that he can no longer communicate with his cousin because Cass is now so involved in his investments that Keats can have no meaning for him. Thus the main function of the episode, in relation to Ike, is to recall and magnify the values he has strived to affirm.

22. See "*Coriolanus*—and the Delights of Faction," *Language as Symbolic Action* (Berkeley and Los Angeles: University of California Press, 1968, pp. 81–97). To understand Burke's rhetorical theory of form, the following texts are essential: *A Grammar of Motives and a Rhetoric of Motives* (New York: World Publishing Co., 1962); *Attitudes toward History* (Boston: Beacon Press, 1961); *The Philosophy of Literary Form* (Baton Rouge: Louisiana State Press, 1941); and *The Rhetoric of Religion* (Boston: Beacon Press, 1961). Burke has never achieved in theory the systematic presentation of his basic position that I have tried to outline in what follows, and his practical criticism remains fairly casual and suggestive. The only time, to my knowledge, that he has tried to present his interpretive method systematically is in "*Othello*: An Essay to Illustrate a Method," now conveniently reprinted in *Perspectives by Incongruity*, edited by Stanley Edgar Hyman (Bloomington: University of Indiana Press, 1964, pp. 152–95). Burke has always had his doubts about the precise nature of his critical project. The reigning "formalism" of his day bequeathed a guilty conscience to anyone who found himself thinking about literature "sociologically." Caught in that dichotomy, Burke has often promised to supplement his rhetorical "approach" to literature with a poetic or symbolic of motives. As he conceives it, that poetic would be a pure "formalism" which would adopt an attitude of disinterested delight (similar to Kant's notion of the aesthetic as "purposiveness without purpose") in contemplating language patterns, symbols, and dramatic structures as if they were pure ends in themselves. But to arrive at such a poetic one must bracket all concern with a work's motivational "content" and social or rhetorical func-

tion—thus depriving the symbolic structures thereby studied of what is, for Burke, their *raison d'etre*. Fortunately, Burke has not pursued this line of inquiry very far, nor can he, without sacrificing what makes his grammatical and rhetorical inquiries into the social dynamics of literature so significant.

23. For examples of a traditional rhetorical approach to works of prose fiction, see Yvor Winters, *In Defense of Reason*, vol. 2, *Maule's Curse* (Denver: Alan Swallow, 1947), and for a general theoretical statement of the position and its representative voices, see Gerald Graff, *Poetic Statement and Critical Dogma* (Evanston, Ill.: Northwestern University Press, 1970). The "new rhetoric" initiated by Chaim Perelman and L. Olbrechts-Tyteca's *The New Rhetoric* (South Bend, Ind.: University of Notre Dame Press, 1968) is an important development in rhetorical theory, yet in many ways merely brings us to Burke's starting point. Perelman rethinks the nature of rhetoric from the perspective of a sociologist and argues that the rhetorician must focus on the motivational and attitudinal bases of persuasion rather than on intellectual tropes if he is to understand the real dynamics of the communicative process. Burke has always been aware of the identity of rhetoric and social theory, and his work is significantly related, by mutual influence, to the main trends in American sociology including, most notably, George Herbert Mead's *Mind, Self, and Society*, Talcott Parson's *The Social System*, and the recent work of Hugh Dalziel Duncan, Herbert Blumer, and Erving Goffman.

24. On this pivotal term, see *A Rhetoric of Motives*, pp. 543–53 and 573–83.

25. For Burke's systematic development of the pentad and its ratios see *A Grammar of Motives*, passim.

26. The above sentences indicate Burke's debt to Spinoza. In its attempt to find a neostoic intellectual peace in the methodization of "the human barn-yard," *A Grammar of Motives* has much in common, though in a far different time, with Spinoza's *Ethics*.

27. The last two sentences indicate Burke's debt to Marx, the complement to his Spinozism, which makes "substance" for him the historical drama of the social process.

28. See Herbert Marcuse, *One-Dimensional Man* (Boston: Beacon Press, 1964).

29. See Jacques Ellul, *The Technological Society* (New York: Vintage Books, 1967).

30. See Georg Lukács, *History and Class-Consciousness* (Cambridge: M.I.T. Press, 1971) and *Solzhenitsyn* (Cambridge: M.I.T. Press, 1970). The discussion of the "novella" as an artistic form in the latter volume and the relationship of that form to definite historical situations is quite germane to "The Bear."

31. On this concept see *Attitudes toward History*, pp. 34–107.

32. On this term see *A Grammar of Motives*, pp. 380–85, and "The Rhetoric of Hitler's Battle," in *The Philosophy of Literary Form*, pp. 164–89.

33. For a discussion of this crucial ratio and the related scene-act ratio, see *A Grammar of Motives*, pp. 3–21.

34. Even General Compson recognizes Cass' defects. See "The Bear," pp. 250–51.

35. See *A Grammar of Motives*, pp. 275–86, and the essay on Marshall McLuhan, "Medium as 'Message,' " in *Language as Symbolic Action*, pp. 410–18.

36. Burke's interesting "novel" (which he also calls a "series of declamations

or epistles") is titled *Towards a Better Life* and names what is for Burke the *end* of rhetoric; yet he describes his thought as neostoic resignation.

37. See "Lion: A Story" and "The Bear" (*Saturday Evening Post* version), in *Bear, Man, and God*, edited by Francis Lee Utley, Lynn S. Bloom, and Arthur F. Kinney (New York: Random House, 1964, pp. 132–64).

38. For Burke's most important discussions of "the scapegoat mechanism" and victimization, see *A Grammar of Motives*, pp. 406–8; *A Rhetoric of Motives*, pp. 776–91; "The Rhetoric of Hitler's Battle"; and the articles on *Coriolanus* and *The Oresteia* in *Language as Symbolic Action*.

39. I refer, among others, to the attempts by V. I. Lenin, *Philosophical Notebooks, Collected Works* (London: Lawrence and Wishart, 1961, vol. 38), Lukács, *History and Class-Consciousness*, and Jean-Paul Sartre, *Critique de la raison dialectique* (Paris: Éditions du Seuil, 1960) to recapture the Hegelian—and finally existential—Marx of the *Economic and Philosophic Manuscripts of 1844*. One should also consult Bertell Ollman, *Alienation* (Cambridge: Cambridge University Press, 1971). As we shall see in the next interpretation, however, moving in this direction takes us to the horizon of another mode of thought—takes us, indeed, beyond rhetoric, even beyond as rich and concrete a conception of rhetoric as we find in Burke.

40. A passive "endurance" characterizes Ike throughout section 4. Here, and for perhaps the only time, Faulkner shows the limitations of endurance as an organizing motive by placing it in a context that calls for action.

41. I employ the concept in Hegel's mimetic sense rather than in Wimsatt's restricted linguistic adaptation. See Hegel, *The Philosophy of Fine Art*, translated by F. P. B. Osmaston (London: G. Bell and Sons, 1920, vol. 4). As will become evident, my thought on dialectical poetics is most heavily indebted to Hegel and Heidegger; I have also derived much from Coleridge, Nietzsche, Auerbach, and the consciousness critics. The following theoretical statement is, however, my own formulation and in it I attempt to develop a conception of the dialectic of literary form that is not found in any of my sources.

42. Socrates refers in the *Republic* to an "ancient quarrel between philosophy and poetry." For such a quarrel to be a genuine one and a fundamental one, both activities must be regarded in the utmost seriousness and comprehended in terms of their broadest reach. Otherwise we get the rather contemptuous and uninformed dismissals that have too often characterized both participants in the debate: witness, for example, Bertrand Russell and the analytic philosophers on poetry and the New Critics on scientific and philosophic discourse. For a philosopher like Hegel, however, philosophy and poetry are both modes of Absolute Spirit; each, that is, is one of the self-grounding and self-reflexive ways in which "the whole of things," the totality of experience, may be apprehended in a genuine response to that problem—the reconciliation of inwardness and existence—which Hegel takes as the central problem facing a dialectical philosophy that would ground being in the unfolding of human freedom. Only if poetry and philosophy are both engaged in that kind of activity can they come into fundamental conflict or have a dynamic, reciprocal relationship to one another. On the relationship of the three modes of Absolute Spirit—Art, Religion, and Philosophy—in Hegel see *The Phenomenology of Mind*, translated by Baillie (New York: Macmillan, 1949, pp. 683–808) and *On Art, Religion, Philosophy*, edited by J. Glenn Gray (New York: Harper Torchbooks, 1970).

43. Although I put it to a new use here, Heidegger's distinctions of ontological and ontic inquiry and of *existentiale-existentiell* knowledge of *Dasein* underlies this paragraph. See *Being and Time*, sections 1 through 8.

44. For convenience I will use the traditional theory of rhetoric to introduce the basic distinctions. The argument applies to Burke also, but in a far more complex way. See below, pages 113–14.

45. See *Being and Time*, sections 33 and 34. Note, in this regard, the persistence since the New Critics of arguments for the metaphoric roots and nature of language. See, for example, Geoffrey Hartman, "The Voice in the Shuttle: Language from the Point of View of Literature," in *Beyond Formalism*, pp. 337–55; Colin Murray Turbayne, *The Myth of Metaphor* (New Haven, Conn.: Yale University Press, 1962); and Jacques Derrida, "White Mythology" (*New Literary History* 6 [1974]: 5–74).

46. See *Being and Time*, sections 29, 30, and 40. It is important to note that for Heidegger mood (*Befindlichkeit*) cannot be understood apart from the entire existence-structure of Being-in-the-World. Mood-understanding-discourse are *equi-primordial* in the *ec-stases* of human temporality, and the future, which is determined by one's project, is the informing mode of human time.

47. As R. S. Crane points out, L. C. Knights in his article "How Many Children Had Lady Macbeth?" takes this line of thought to its nadir when he argues that character and action are no more than "precipitates" from the reader's memory of the successive words he has read. Poetry becomes a bundle of words, self-referent ever inward toward a nonexistent center. For Crane's discussion of Knights, see *The Languages of Criticism and the Structure of Poetry*, pp. 14–16.

48. In *The Philosophy of Fine Art*, for example, Hegel orders the arts in a dialectical hierarchy determined by their progression toward an apprehension of concrete experience. His discussion in volume 4 on the evolution from the lyric to the dramatic mode is of special relevance to our argument.

49. On the equiprimordality of mood-understanding-discourse, see *Being and Time*, sections 31 through 34. In adapting Heidegger's analytic of the existence-structure to the analysis of literary actions I have found Ludwig Binswanger's article "The Case of Ellen West," in *Existence*, edited by Rollo May (New York: Simon and Schuster, 1958, pp. 237–364), particularly suggestive. In his seminal concept—World-Design—Binswanger highlights the projective nature of human existence and ties Heidegger's entire analytic of existence to the primacy of action.

50. For the development of this view of Plato's dialectical method, see Herman Sinaiko, *Love, Knowledge, and Discourse in Plato* (Chicago: University of Chicago Press, 1965) and Richard McKeon, "Philosophy and Method" (*Journal of Philosophy* 48 [1951]: 653–82).

51. Claude Lévi-Strauss, "The Story of Asdiwal," in *The Structural Study of Myth and Totemism*, edited by G. Leach (London: Tavistock Publishers, 1967, pp. 1–48).

52. In so doing it takes us to the horizon of a richer mode of dialectical art—and a further development of dialectical theory. "The Bear," of course, is merely one instance of the lyric-narrative dialectic; we find it more complexly dramatized, and with differing outcomes, in Sartre's *Nausea*, Powys' *Wolf Solent*, Proust's *Remembrance of Things Past*, and Joyce's *Ulysses*. One of the

major purposes of the present discussion is to move dialectical criticism from the lyric-linguistic dialectic of the New Critics to a dialectic of action.

53. For a definition of dialectic almost solely in terms of this procedure, see McKeon, "Philosophy and Method," and "Philosophic Semantics and Philosophic Inquiry" (unpublished ms., Chicago, 1967). I attempt to modify this conception of dialectic below on pages 94–97 and at length in *Inwardness and Existence: Hegel and the Dialectic of Subject* (forthcoming), passing reference to which will be made at appropriate points in the course of the discussion.

54. In section 5 the railroad and the timber company supplant the gun as the symbols of man's historical presence in the wilderness: the gun is still dedicated to the wilderness, whereas the latter are pure technological manifestations of man's desire to submit nature to his will.

55. All italics in the following quotations from "The Bear" are mine.

56. See the story "The Old People" in *Go Down, Moses*, pp. 163–87.

57. For a similar critique of dialectic from a philosophic perspective, and a similar recognition of its permanence, see Immanuel Kant, *Critique of Pure Reason*, translated by Norman Kemp Smith (New York: St. Martin's Press, 1965, pp. 297–307, 549–70).

58. See Freud, *Civilization and its Discontents* and Arthur Koestler, *Darkness at Noon*. Fortunately there is another primary mood—the mood of anguish or dread, which brings the self before the facticity of its existence. If properly appropriated (and doing so distinguishes genuine existentialism from the many things that parade in its name), anxiety is the basis of concrete projection, for it brings one back from lostness in the impersonal world of *Das Man* (the They) and places one before the responsibility for oneself which can only be carried out through a concrete project. Thus, in anxiety the lyric principle is directed beyond itself—to the actualization of self in action within the world in which one finds oneself thrown. See *Being and Time*, section 40. The central achievement of *Being and Time* lies in Heidegger's discovery of a new conception of the self, one that overcomes the Kantian antinomies of psychology. In the concept of authenticity Heidegger establishes the reflexive unity of the following existential structures: anxiety, being-toward-death, guilt, conscience, and resolve. The unity of those structures constitutes the total existential process through which the self becomes an issue to itself. Projecting upon those experiences in the totality of their essential connections constitutes the authenticity of the existential self. See *Being and Time*, section 64. The philosophic anthropology Heidegger thereby makes possible is, for the early Heidegger at least, a fundamental ontology which grounds Being in *Dasein* (human existence) and *Dasein* in nothing outside itself: see *The Essence of Reasons*, translated by Terrence Malick (Evanston, Ill.: Northwestern University Press, 1969, pp. 101–31) and *Kant and the Problem of Metaphysics*, translated by James S. Churchill (Bloomington: Indiana University Press, 1962, pp. 209–55). In this, as in so many other respects, *Being and Time* resembles Hegel's *Phenomenology*. There, too, absolute dread and the desire for recognition animate the dialectic of self-consciousness. But the study of such moods in their existential projection is preeminently the province of Dostoyevsky and Mann rather than of Faulkner.

59. On the primacy of the future in the *ec-stases* of temporality, see *Being and Time*, section 65. Heidegger defines *temporality* as "the primordial

'outside-of-itself' in and for itself" (*Being and Time*, p. 377). Such is the nature of human time because, as Hegel puts it in his favorite maxim, "consciousness is what it is not, and is not what it is."

60. In *The Critique of Judgment* Kant found in aesthetic experience the true roots of dialectical thought and in his *Letters on the Aesthetic Education of Man* Schiller found in play the basis for an integral humanism. Under the sway of the aesthetic, dialectical thought was reborn in the Romantic period. But from those lyric beginnings to the thought of Hegel, Marx, Nietzsche, Heidegger, and the existentialists, dialectic undergoes a number of transformations all determined by the movement from contemplation to *praxis*. I discuss this movement further in *Inwardness and Existence*.

61. Unfortunately, the later Heidegger in his *Seinsmystik* reverts to this position, for reasons political and "religious" as well as philosophic. In *Being and Time*, as in Hegel's *Phenomenology*, however, *Dasein* is grounded in its projective self-mediation; whereas in the later Heidegger (the Heidegger of the *Kehre* or of the *Umkehr*, depending on one's sympathies) we witness the hypostatization of "being." For a sympathetic interpretation of the later Heidegger and an attempt, following Heidegger's explicit directions, to read his later thought back into *Being and Time*, see William J. Richardson, S.J., *Heidegger Through Phenomenology to Thought* (The Hague: Martinus Nijhoff, 1967).

62. *Being and Time*, p. 29. Also see "What is Metaphysics?" in *Existence and Being* (Chicago: Henry Regnery Co., 1949, pp. 325–61). In this essay Heidegger shows how the activities of philosophy and poetry distinguish themselves from "science" by their ability to raise ontological questions.

63. See the epilogue of William K. Wimsatt, Jr. and Cleanth Brooks' *Literary Criticism: A Short History* (New York: Alfred A. Knopf, 1957, pp. 724–55).

64. See Kenneth Burke, *The Rhetoric of Religion*.

65. "Philosophic Semantics and Philosophic Inquiry," p. 1.

66. We find it, for example, in *Bear, Man, and God* and in a study of "critical methods" such as Stanley Edgar Hyman's *The Armed Vision* (New York: Alfred A. Knopf, 1947). It is the general fare of textbooks in critical theory which usually offer us some selection of the following "approaches": formal criticism, biographical and historical criticism, sociological criticism, Freudian criticism, and myth criticism—a rich plurality of ad hoc "approaches" jumbled together in search of a principle. See, for example, Harold P. Simonson, *Strategies in Criticism* (New York: Holt, Rinehart and Winston, 1971) and William J. Handy and Max Westbrook, *Twentieth-Century Criticism: The Major Statements* (New York: Free Press, 1974). For further discussion of this issue see below, pages 74–76, 89–91.

67. In both cases what Crane attacks, and I think convincingly, are the most vulnerable examples of both modes. He never considers the kind of dynamic rhetorical theory Burke develops, and as far as I can tell he remains benignly unaware of dialectical art as anything other than a rather extreme species of the "didactic."

68. It is only through that concession that Crane remains a pluralist with respect to the question of form. Didactic art in his system remains, however, an abstract counter which functions primarily to increase the polemical force of Crane's argument that his is the only valid theory of mimetic art.

69. The reasons why Aristotle only conceived one possible end for mimetic art derive from the general methodological and philosophic principles that underlie and shape his consideration of poetry. See below, pages 102–6.

70. For an attempt to substantiate Crane's theory of emotional form on the basis of innate "universal principles of human response" that are intuited in the reading experience, see Sheldon Sacks, *Fiction and the Shape of Belief*.

71. Although he is understandably cagey on the point, Crane suggests indirectly and rather repeatedly the precarious status of the other languages of criticism: for the "aspects" they discuss are only had by a thoroughgoing neglect of artistic function and artistic purpose. What, then, are they "aspects" of?

72. I hasten to add that such a pluralism does not cancel the situation Crane describes. They exist alongside one another. Moreover, the term *eclecticism* covers two quite different kinds of criticism, one of which is a valid mode of pluralism and a viable alternative to the theory I am constructing. The first and most obvious meaning of the term refers to the loose and ad hoc practice where a critic garners a bit from every available approach and makes it up as he goes along, with an eye at all times to the new "insight," the new "reading"—which is prized, whether it is good or not, simply because it is. The second is closer to what we find in R. S. Crane if we take seriously his notion that there are a number of different approaches which are finally complementary and which contribute in some not yet apparent way to a single understanding. I have tried to indicate some of the ways in which Crane contradicts this position, but that does not mean that it is not a legitimate possibility. In recent years, in fact, Wayne Booth has been developing precisely such a pluralism. Booth argues that there are some approaches (such as Burke's and Crane's) that can potentially be extended to cover all works without distortion and without ultimate essential conflict. In terms of the theory of form I am developing, that pluralism appears eclectic because it is not concerned to relate those approaches in a determinate manner. But in terms of Booth's pluralism, the concept of form is itself a dogma which limits the many different things we can say and do in discussing the many legitimate varieties of literary experience and critical discourse. Thus Booth gives us a "pluralism of pluralisms" while my effort is to construct a "dialectical pluralism" which will order the basic modes of critical discourse in a single context shaped by a single principle. The two views are not necessarily incompatible, for pluralism in general is based on the recognition that we can only know what our method enables us to know.

73. For an argument that historical interpretation provides the only way to resolve the problems of interpretation, see Robert Marsh, "Historical Interpretation and the History of Criticism," in *Literary Criticism and Historical Understanding*, edited by Philip Damon (New York: Columbia University Press, 1967, pp. 1–24). In one sense our arguments are complementary, though I am far more skeptical than Marsh concerning the nature and construction of historical evidence and far more confident than he concerning the possibilities outlined on pages 50–52.

74. From the start we have gone beyond generic criticism and have placed it within a more fundamental inquiry into the potentially distinct natures of works which may share conventions and generic properties. Suppose, for example, that one identifies *Notes from Underground*, *The Sorrows of Young*

Werther, and *Herzog* as instances of the confessional mode, or Spenser's *Amoretti,* Shakespeare's *Sonnets,* and Donne's *Songs and Sonets* as Petrarchan poems. Isn't it possible, perhaps likely, that close examination will reveal that these texts have fundamentally distinct artistic purposes? The theory of form is not a theory of genres; the distinctions it makes go far deeper than that. For a recent review of different types of generic criticism and concepts of genre, see Paul Hernadi, *Beyond Genre* (Ithaca, N.Y.: Cornell University Press, 1972).

75. See E. D. Hirsch, *Validity in Interpretation,* pp. 68–126. I am concerned with the philosophic and epistemological presuppositions that shape any kind of evidence, be it historical or textual. The different testing procedures that are constructed to adjudicate the conflict of interpretations are not independent of that prior order of inquiry. On this problem, see below, pages 84–86, 115–19. Thus, while I share the desire of R. S. Crane, E. D. Hirsch, and Robert Marsh to conceive of interpretation in terms of the testing of multiple working hypotheses, my skepticism about historical evidence extends much further than theirs because I am concerned with the prior philosophic assumptions and principles that enable us to construct history or test our hypotheses about it—and I find that those principles, too, are radically plural.

76. For an incisive critique of Gadamer's extreme endorsement of the circle, see E. D. Hirsch, "Gadamer's Theory of Interpretation," *Validity in Interpretation,* pp. 245–64.

77. For a detailed discussion of the three theories in terms of their philosophic and methodological bases, see chapter 3.

78. For my use of the term *operational* see below, pages 98–101. It will become evident that the meaning I give the term is somewhat different from its current use to describe a conception of philosophy, based on the work of Dewey, Korzybski, and others, which "views thought and action inseparable; which defines 'truth' in terms of the predictive content of assertions, and ethics in terms of action-directed goals" (Anatol Rapoport, *Operational Philosophy* [New York: Harper, 1954], p. 230).

79. This is the basic thesis I attempt to develop in *Inwardness and Existence.*

80. Most contemporary efforts to unify the "sciences of man" have really been little more than unexplicit returns to Hegel: difference is posited within the unity of a single principle. As Derrida points out, monism remains our deepest metaphysical pathos, and here, if nowhere else, I find myself in general agreement with him. *The Act of Interpretation* suggests that we consider difference in a far more radical way than we have done heretofore.

81. The phrase is used by Robert Marsh in "Historical Interpretation and the History of Criticism." I am trying to construct, on theoretical rather than on historical grounds, what Marsh there calls for. In *The Critique of Pure Reason* Kant endeavors to work out the a priori forms of intuition and the categories of understanding which make experience, as conceived by Newtonian science, possible. Those principles form for Kant the unified structure of human receptivity and spontaneity. What I have supplied for literary interpretation is only analogous: the concepts of artistic purpose which make it possible as a rigorous discipline. The reader can, if he wishes, regard those concepts as a description of the alternatives presented by contemporary criticism or as a product derived empirically from a study of the history of criticism rather than as universal forms of artistic creation.

82. See R. S. Crane, "The Houyhnhnms, the Yahoos, and the History of Ideas," and "On Hypotheses in 'Historical Criticism': Apropos of Certain Contemporary Medievalists," in *The Idea of the Humanities* (Chicago: University of Chicago Press, 1967, vol. 2). My development and use of the method of multiple working hypotheses is radically different from Crane's, however, and I discuss some of the assumptions that structure his problematic development of the method below on pages 84–86, 116–19 and in chapter 4.

Chapter 2

1. A note on method. There are two moments to every critical position I discuss—a moment of critique and a moment of incorporation. The two moments are put into operation in a variety of ways, but in general the second moment dominates in chapter 1 while in the present chapter the moment of critique holds center stage in keeping with an effort to get critics who are doing work of great potential value to recognize the unexamined assumptions and covert principles of explanation which limit their efforts, involving most in some form of reductionism. To dramatize the problem I focus on the way those principles control the direction and development of the position and deliberately exclude the kind of detailed treatment that would be involved were I after a purely descriptive presentation of each position. My concern is not to write a guide to contemporary criticism, but to offer critics already practicing the positions under scrutiny an insight into the underlying assumptions and tendencies that control their methodologies, even though many practitioners are not aware of those assumptions or the unintended consequences they entail. If we have straw men here, they are the straw men implicit in the positions surveyed, and with their consignment to the flames those approaches achieve a new direction and become integral parts of the overarching theoretical framework being fashioned in the course of the book. Rather than categorically rejecting anything, then, my intention throughout the chapter is quasi-Hegelian, to cancel, preserve, and uplift. Although our theoretical positions are quite different, like Paul de Man I find that much in contemporary criticism is an affair of blindness *and* insight: it is the particular character of the modern blindness that is my subject here.

For reasons that will become apparent, I also attempt in this chapter to situate contemporary criticism in a broad interdisciplinary context and to show how it participates in a social and philosophic crisis that in many ways defines modern life—the disappearance of man, the displacement of the purposive individual agent as a principle of explanation in accounting for human acts. One irony in the disappearance of man is how seldom the absence is recognized, but it is even more disconcerting to see how often those who proclaim respect for the individual as a basic article of faith actually compromise that principle continually in the explanations they give of human actions. To avoid an ambiguity that may arise in the course of the following discussion, it is therefore important to take note of the fact that many of those I will criticize for contributing to the displacement of the agent are among the most fervent in proclaiming the individual as their first and last concern. Jung's position is fairly representative:

> The individual is the only reality. The further we move away from the
> individual toward abstract ideas about *Homo sapiens*, the more likely we are

to fall into error. In these times of social upheaval and rapid change, it is desirable to know much more than we do about the individual human being, for so much depends upon his mental and moral qualities. But if we are to see things in their right perspective, we need to understand the past of man as well as his present. That is why an understanding of myths and symbols is of essential importance. (Carl G. Jung, "Approaching the Unconscious," in *Man and his Symbols* [New York: Doubleday, 1968, p. 45])

Though this is a popular statement of Jung's views it is also a fairly typical one, repeated frequently throughout his work and canonical among his followers. Jung's humanistic sentiments are beyond question; indeed he often strikes one as a storehouse of humanistic commonplaces. But saying one believes in the individual and making the individual a genuine principle of explanation in accounting for human phenomena are two very different things. It is the latter question that will concern us—a question before which any humanism earns itself at the level of principles or flounders in sentimentalism and nostalgia.

2. See Paul Ricoeur's penetrating discussion of Freud's method in *Freud and Philosophy* (New Haven, Conn.: Yale University Press, 1970, pp. 87–115). For representative examples of Freudian criticism one should consult *Art and Psychoanalysis*, edited by William Phillips (New York: World Publishing Co., 1963), and Morton Kaplan and Robert Kloss, *The Unspoken Motive* (New York: Free Press, 1973), along with the standard works of Ernest Jones, Ernst Kris, and Norman Holland. In considering each of the approaches discussed in this chapter I have three groups in mind: (1) the founders of the positions considered and their relationship to the philosophic crisis I am discussing; (2) the literary theorists who have attempted to adapt those positions to literary criticism; and (3) the practical critics who set out to apply these general orientations to the interpretation of particular literary texts. With each position interrogated, moreover, the basic attempt is to construct an essential formulation of the position and the method of literary interpretation implicit in it. Though they stand back from particulars, these formulations are not hypothetical entities in any arbitrary, conjectural, or imaginative sense. Each description is derived from the practice of a number of critics, but what I have tried to offer is precisely the kind of conceptual distillation that would not have been possible had I committed "the fallacy of misplaced concreteness" and attempted to describe all the different things which practitioners of the different critical methods under investigation have said, a procedure that would be like trying to number the streaks of the tulip. The fact that many "Freudian" critics, for example, are not really very rigorous Freudians but play fast and loose with the selected concepts they borrow from Freud is certainly distressing but is not really germane to the study of critical methods. The same consideration applies to the popular notion that "metacriticism" should begin with the description of extant criticism, as if the body of critical writings on a text like 'The Bear" were a primary datum that is somehow indicative of what criticism can or should be, an assumption exemplified in an inadvertent *reductio ad absurdum* by Morris Weitz's book on Hamlet criticism. Since my purpose is to construct—not describe—the conditions that must be met if criticism is to become a rigorous discipline, I have necessarily bracketed such matters.

3. Jung, of course, is the archetypal example. In the Jungian metapsychology it is the "self," the collective unconscious, and the archetypes which provide the

substantive principles that shape the psyche: the process of "individuation" is a gradual surrendering of oneself to those principles or a remaking of oneself in terms of adherence to their directives. Jung's horror of modern life is genuine; his solution nostalgic. Even the most sympathetic construction of the Jungian metapsychology would be forced to recognize that the existential, historical individual is peripheral at best in the Jungian scheme; the sole function of the individual appears to be to adapt the universal principles of the collective unconscious to particular circumstances. It is a Platonism of the psyche—and is, as we shall see, a far cry from the constitution of the individual as a genuine principle of causation; which does not deny the fact that there are insights and concepts of great value in Jung, who so often calls attention to drives of the utmost importance but gives explanations that are ultimately mystifying. The most unqualified endorsement of the power and value of mythic criticism is in Richard Chase, *Quest for Myth* (Baton Rouge: Louisiana State University Press, 1949).

4. Joseph Campbell, *The Hero With a Thousand Faces* (New York: World Publishing Co., 1956).

5. Northrop Frye, *Anatomy of Criticism* (Princeton, N.J.: Princeton University Press, 1957, p. 190).

6. What is Frye's "Theory of Modes" other than an abstract way to classify an exhaustive collection of plot summaries? In this, as in so many other things, Frye anticipates the interpretive methods of Lévi-Strauss.

7. Few critics have insisted as explicitly as has Frye on the autonomy of criticism and on its need to become an independent science directed toward the "formal" understanding of its object "as art and not another thing." Frye's announced intention is to found a "systematic study of the formal causes of art" (*Anatomy of Criticism*, p. 29); indeed, he is one of the main sources for the opposition between a formalist understanding of literature and a reduction of the literary object to sociology, biography, psychology, or the history of ideas. In many ways the elaborate system of classifications and cross-references developed in *Anatomy of Criticism* is an attempt to exhaust the formal knowledge we can have of a literary work prior to raising "extra-artistic" questions about it. There can be little doubt that Frye develops a number of purely aesthetic categories, especially generic ones; and it would be hard to imagine a system with more distinctions and methods of multiple classification, with the exception, of course, of Aristotle's. However, an exhaustive classification of the literary work and an apprehension of its form are two very different things. And insofar as Frye attains the latter, it is the categories of cultural anthropology rather than aesthetic categories that enable him to do so. Consider the following specimens from "The Archetypes of Literature," *Fables of Identity* (New York: Harcourt, Brace and World, 1963, pp. 7–20): "here we glimpse the possibility of seeing literature as a complication of a relatively restricted and simple group of formulas that can be studied in primitive culture. If so, then the search for archetypes is a kind of literary anthropology, concerned with the way that literature is informed by preliterary categories such as ritual, myth, and folktale. We next realize that the relation between these categories and literature is by no means purely one of descent, as we find them reappearing in the greatest classics—in fact there seems to be a general tendency on the part of great classics to revert to them" (p. 12); and: "We cannot study the genre without the help of the literary social historian, the

literary philosopher and the student of the 'history of ideas,' and for the archetype we need a literary anthropologist. But now that we have got our central pattern of criticism established, all these interests are seen as converging on literary criticism instead of receding from it into psychology and history and the rest. In particular, the literary anthropologist who chases the source of the Hamlet legend from the pre-Shakespeare play to Saxo, and from Saxo to nature-myths, is not running away from Shakespeare: *he is drawing closer to the archetypal form which Shakespeare recreated"* (p. 13, italics mine). I recently discovered a somewhat similar critique of this aspect of Frye's system. In *The Fantastic* (Ithaca, N.Y.: Cornell University Press, 1975, p. 16), Tzvetan Todorov makes the following comments on Frye's categories:

> We cannot fail to notice a characteristic common to these categories: their non-literary nature. They are all borrowed from philosophy, from psychology, or from a social ethic, and moreover not from just any psychology or philosophy. Either these terms are to be taken in a special, strictly literary sense; or—and since we are told nothing about such a sense, this is the only possibility available to us—they lead us outside of literature. Whereupon literature becomes no more than a means of expressing philosophical categories. Its autonomy is thus profoundly contested—and we again contradict one of the theoretical principles stated, precisely, by Frye himself.

Unfortunately, Todorov's argument reintroduces the very dichotomy it should have surmounted. What I will try to show in this chapter is that literary criticism is both autonomous and not autonomous; if it tries to be only the former it becomes "formalism," whereas if it relies on other disciplines for the substantive categories of interpretation it reduces the work of art to its materials. Like so many of the dichotomies that structure our discipline, the option is a false one.

What was noted earlier with respect to Jung applies also to Frye. Proclaiming humanism and making the human being an autonomous—or potentially autonomous—force in the constitution and explanation of phenomena are two quite different things.

8. Lévi-Strauss' essay on the Oedipus myth, "The Structural Study of Myth," in *Structural Anthropology* (New York: Basic Books, 1963) remains a paradigm of the method developed at length in *Mythologiques*.

9. Claude Lévi-Strauss, *The Savage Mind* (Chicago: University of Chicago Press, 1966), chapters 1 and 9, and "The Structural Study of Myth," in *Structural Anthropology*, p. 227.

10. Paul Ricoeur, "New Developments in Phenomenology in France: The Phenomenology of Language" (*Social Research* 34 [1967]: 1–30).

11. Stanley Fish is the most noteworthy recent example of these practices. For a critique of Fish's method, see Ralph W. Rader, "Fact, Theory, and Literary Explanation" (*Critical Inquiry* 1 [1974]: 245–72).

12. For a clear and often impassioned example, see Murray Krieger's discussion of "thematics" in *The Tragic Vision* (Chicago: University of Chicago Press, 1966).

13. René Girard, *Deceit, Desire, and the Novel* (Baltimore, Md.: Johns Hopkins University Press, 1966).

14. See George Poulet, *Studies in Human Time* (Baltimore, Md.: Johns

Hopkins University Press, 1956); J. Hillis Miller, *Poets of Reality* (Cambridge: Harvard University Press, 1965); and *The Form of Victorian Fiction* (West Bend, Ind.: University of Notre Dame Press, 1968). For a review of the entire movement, see Sarah Lawall, *Critics of Consciousness* (Cambridge: Harvard University Press, 1968).

15. I know of no Freudian critic who has articulated the position this explicitly. What I have tried to do in this paragraph and the one that follows is construct the position to which a strict adherence to Freudian principles necessarily leads. On philosophic grounds this is the Freudian position and there is no way a genuine Freudian can avoid the dilemmas it entails. To show how this understanding of Freud might relate to the problems of literary interpretation I have constructed a position which attempts to describe the methodological bases of the work in progress of my colleague Stephen Lacey. For a critique of traditional Freudian criticism somewhat similar to the one I develop (and by a Freudian), see Frederick Crews, *Out of My System* (New York: Oxford University Press, 1975).

16. My own view is that an existential philosophic anthropology, derived from Hegel's *Phenomenology* and Heidegger's analytic of *Dasein*, and containing Freud as one of its moments and Marx as another, provides the only theoretical framework adequate to the complexity of human existence. But we are still a long way from such a framework, even in principle. In *Inwardness and Existence* I try to formulate the philosophic grounds for such a project. The final chapter of Ricoeur's *Freud and Philosophy* is an important document indicating the need to ground psychoanalysis in a broader philosophy of reflection based on the possibility of self-consciousness and achieved freedom. Continuing interest in Marx's *Economic and Philosophic Manuscripts of 1844* and their Hegelian roots indicate the desire of many thinkers to ground Marxism in a broader existential understanding of the human subject.

17. I know the argument well because I have made it myself on numerous occasions and would still contend that there are issues where it is quite appropriate—ethical issues and issues where we face what Paul Tillich calls questions of ultimate concern. The following paragraph places this dialectical conception of the subject within a pluralistic and disciplinary context. For a contrasting attempt to construct a dialectic of freedom which includes all human activities, see below, pages 113–14, and *Inwardness and Existence*.

18. Freudianism, Marxism, Jungianism, and existentialism are, of course, shorthand significations for the instinctual, sociological, religious, and self-reflexive bases of human action. I would argue that the four movements I discuss give us the most powerful theories of those contexts of existence and conduct, but that argument would take us far afield and I will not pursue it here. I should also point out that I take Hegel's *Phenomenology of Mind* and Heidegger's *Being and Time* as the most important books in the development of existential thought.

19. The other frameworks that suggest themselves as well as the "truths" about human nature that common sense regards as its special prerogative can only play a minor part in our inquiry, for strictly speaking they do not address the fundamental problem that concerns us here: the "materials" they identify do not provide what is needed to construct the action of complex mimetic works. If one's task is to represent agents in action, all the unit-ideas in the

world, all the intellectual commonplaces and cross-currents of the day, all the general values and beliefs of traditional morality will not be sufficient. They may, of course, play a subordinate part in one's plan, as when an artist uses the intellectual commonplaces of his time as one of the constituents in the "thought" of his characters. And in nonmimetic works, such as Pope's "Essay on Man," commonplaces and abstract ideas become substantive. But insofar as one's primary concern is with "mimetic art," the problem is to develop an understanding of the basic forms of existence and experience that determine our lived relationship to the world, what Heidegger calls the *existentialia* (analogous to the Kantian *categoria*) which make it possible for human life to be experienced in terms of the primacy of action or projection. In terms of this problem I find Jung's theory a noteworthy one—even though I have little sympathy with Jungian psychology either as a philosophic view of man or as a means to health—because Jung articulates desires and needs that shape many human projects. Despite their failure to satisfy the demands of existential authenticity, myth and the religious quest remain major existence-structures, key sources of drama.

20. See pages 50–52.

21. I return to this problem in chapter 3, where I deal with it from a pluralistic standpoint. I attempt to work out the principles for a dialectical understanding of human existence and of the hierarchy of possible integrations that constitute existential freedom in *Inwardness and Existence*.

22. This is not, by the way, Faulkner's usual practice: in works such as *The Sound and the Fury* and *Absalom, Absalom!* Freudian and existential frameworks dominate.

Chapter 3

1. Stanley Edgar Hyman, *The Armed Vision* (New York: Alfred A. Knopf, 1947).

2. René Wellek, "The Main Trends of Twentieth-Century Criticism," in *Concepts of Criticism* (New Haven, Conn.: Yale University Press, 1963, pp. 334–64). See also the essay "Concepts of Form and Structure in Twentieth-Century Criticism" in the same volume, pp. 54–68.

3. William K. Wimsatt, Jr. and Cleanth Brooks, *Literary Criticism: A Short History* (New York: Alfred A. Knopf, 1957). For a critique of the method used in the book, see Robert Marsh, "The 'Fallacy' of Universal Intention" (*Modern Philology 55* [1958]: 263–75). As far as I know this is the only essay-length review of the book. It is interesting to note that Wellek's definition of "the mode of existence of the literary work" is essentially a sociological one in which the present consensus or ruling mind of the profession determines the nature or "meaning" of the literary work. See René Wellek and Austin Warren, *Theory of Literature* (New York: Harcourt, Brace, 1942, pp. 143–45).

4. For a contrast of the methods of Plato and Aristotle, see Richard McKeon, "Imitation and Poetry," *Thought, Action, and Passion* (Chicago: University of Chicago Press, 1954, passim). For further discussions of the method Aristotle uses in the *Poetics*, see Richard McKeon, "Literary Criticism and the Concept of Imitation in Antiquity," in *Critics and Criticism,* pp. 147–75; R. S. Crane, *The Languages of Criticism and the Structure of Poetry*, pp. 39–79; Kenneth

Telford, *Aristotle's Poetics: Translation and Analysis;* and the articles by McKeon and Elder Olson in *Aristotle's Poetics and English Literature* (Chicago: University of Chicago Press, 1965).

5. Crane's most important discussions of method occur in the "Introduction" to *Critics and Criticism, The Languages of Criticism and the Structure of Poetry,* and "Critical and Historical Principles of Literary History," in *The Idea of the Humanities* (Chicago: University of Chicago Press, 1967, vol. 2, pp. 45–156).

6. The following essays are the most important formulations by McKeon of the philosophic bases of pluralism: "Philosophic Semantics and Philosophic Inquiry," "Philosophy and Method," and "Being, Existence, and That Which Is" (*Review of Metaphysics* 13 [1960]: 539–54).

7. My debt to McKeon is profound; our differences, however, are substantial. For convenience they may be summarized under three topics. The significance of these differences will only become clear in the course of the chapter, but their statement here will provide a reference point for subsequent reflections while also serving as a concise summary of what I take to be the most important implications of McKeon's work for the problems of critical theory.

1. *Methodological Differences.* The distinction of four modes of thought is merely the beginning of McKeon's elaborate attempt to construct a schematism of semantic distinctions which will enable him to describe all the ambiguities that have arisen in the history of philosophic controversy. The continuing expansion of that scheme shows no signs of abating: in its latest version ("Philosophic Semantics and Philosophic Inquiry") McKeon provides sixteen distinct categories of semantics and sixteen categories of inquiry. For my purposes I continually collapse that elaborate schematism into the four modes of thought that are used to generate it. As a result the account of the modes I will develop brings together concepts and principles which McKeon separates and places at different points in his schematism, a development no doubt in conflict with McKeon's basic intentions. McKeon is concerned primarily with the history of philosophy and with the clarification of ambiguities that is necessary if one is to describe the wealth of differences that make up that history; my concern, in contrast, is to work out the fullest *contemporary* realization of the four ways of thinking that appear to be at the base of that history. To put it in stronger terms, McKeon is interested in the different ways in which the four modes of thought have been combined by different thinkers in the history of thought, whereas I am after a philosophic articulation of the essential content or world view dictated by each mode. I would readily concur with McKeon that the modes can and have been combined in a number of ways throughout the history of philosophy: for descriptive purposes McKeon's elaborate schematism is invaluable. However, the only way one can combine modes in a coherent manner is by adhering to one of them and using it to organize what one borrows from others. Thus we confront the question of form once again: no matter how manifold a discourse may be, the problem of interpretation is to discover the ground principle which structures it.

It will become apparent that the methodological differences summarized above derive from the fact that while McKeon employs an operational method to construct his system, my appropriation of his thought proceeds from dialectical motives. Using McKeon's scheme, the distinction might be described in the following terms: McKeon employs *actional principles* as starting points to focus on the different ways common terms have been used historically and to identify the unrecognized ambiguities which frustrate communication in any context of social debate; I use *reflexive principles* to establish the fundamental starting points that are possible on any question, regardless of the confusions and ambiguities surrounding the semantic and social context out of which thought arises. McKeon's *interpretations*, accordingly, are *existentialistic* because in attempting an exhaustive description of all the procedures that enter into the construction of discourse, the only classificatory scheme he can establish is one that describes all the different "types" of discourse that are possible given all the different ways in which the modes of thought can be combined. My *interpretations*, in contrast, are *essentialistic* because I focus upon the root principle which makes any combination of modes of thought possible; thus I reinterpret the various procedures that typify a given discourse in terms of the formal cause that shapes them.

2. *Aesthetic Differences.* The attempt to establish a necessary connection between modes of thought and theories of form is also my responsibility. As far as I can tell there is little precedent for it in McKeon. McKeon's contributions to the history of criticism, especially in "Imitation and Poetry," are far-reaching. When it comes to the application of critical theory to literary works, however, McKeon either discounts the whole question of form or assumes, with R. S. Crane, that since pleasure is the distinguishing end of art, Aristotle's *Poetics* is the only language of criticism capable of dealing with literary works as artistic wholes. While "Imitation and Poetry" offers us a complex system for discriminating the various "themes" and shifts in attention that have characterized the history of criticism, the implicit conception of how those languages relate concretely to the interpretation of literary texts remains eclectic at best. Since there is no developed concept of form to which those languages might be related, nor any order of questions to which they might be referred, there is no way to prevent them from becoming diverse types of qualitative criticism equally valuable for the insights they give us into a Lockean "I know not what supposed support of sensible species."

Thus the general theory of form developed in chapter 1 as well as the pluralistic theory of literary interpretation being fashioned in the course of the book are in no way derived from McKeon. In fact McKeon would most likely reject all of these developments because literature for him is no more than the multiplicity of different and quite possibly contradictory things that can be said about it. In contrast, I relate the many languages of criticism to a single order of questions and a single object of study—which is, of course, a further manifestation of the difference between McKeon's operationalism and my dialectical appropriation of his thought.

3. *Ontological Differences.* While McKeon is concerned with reality as it is mirrored in our discourses about it, in my program mode of thought serves as an ultimate epistemological principle with existential as well as cognitive and discursive significance. As a result of the different modes of thought they adopt, different human beings experience the world in fundamentally different ways: mode of thought is the formative cause of any discourse because in a radical way the mode of thought each thinker employs is what constitutes for him the nature of things, facts, values, and experience. In opposition to such a

radical epistemological and existential reorientation of his thought, McKeon regards his labors as a contribution to the linguistic emphasis of modern philosophy—the tendency to center all problems on the nature of language and the ways we use it. McKeon is always careful to distinguish between discourse about reality and reality itself: in fact the elaborate schematism he develops may be seen as a direct consequence of the primacy he gives to the analysis of statements. His goal has been to construct an exhaustive understanding of the language of philosophic discourse that would be analogous in a linguistic age to Kant's earlier epistemological attempt to gain an a priori understanding of the basic structures of mind. It is a project that has much in common with Wittgenstein's; my directions, in contrast, are Hegelian, phenomenological, and existential. McKeon's is a world of discourse, whereas mine is a world of discourse about the world. As a result, I extend McKeon's controlling distinction between discourse and the realities to which it refers into a productive opposition; and in place of his implied bracketing of reality as an unknowable *ding-an-sich* and his consequent reduction of phenomena not simply to their appearances but to their appearances in discourse, I attempt to develop a phenomenological way of evaluating hypotheses in terms of their adequacy both to the phenomenon before us and to the ways we can criticize our knowing of it.

The consequence of these differences is, of course, two radically different pluralisms, one linguistic and historical, the other existential and epistemological; one concerned with the possibility of communication and difference of opinion, the other with the possibility of conflict and error. The two pluralisms are not necessarily incompatible, nor is an absolute decision about their respective merits necessary. They are simply different and in operational terms each must be judged on its ability to solve the problems it is designed to handle.

8. The first quotation is from Hegel, passim; the second from Plato, *Republic*, 532–41. One of my major differences with McKeon is over the concept of dialectic. His conception, which I find static and contemplative, is based primarily on Plato and Spinoza and stresses the transcendent goal of dialectical thought; my view is derived primarily from Hegel and Heidegger and seeks to establish an immanent dialectic of existence. I discuss these differences at some length in chapter 2 of *Inwardness and Existence* where I trace the inner and historical movement of dialectical thought from transcendence to immanence, from contemplation to tragedy. In Hegel's *Phenomenology* and Heidegger's *Being and Time* the ground and possibility of dialectic is sought in the self-motion of the human subject. With the shift from a changeless model somehow rooted in the nature of things to a principle of creative unrest which *is* only insofar as its very being remains an issue for it, dialectical thought undergoes a transformation from the abstract to the concrete infinite, a shift from the universality of being to the universality of becoming. Throughout, my discussion of dialectic is oriented toward the latter possibility.

9. See George Santayana, *The Sense of Beauty* (New York: Charles Scribner's Sons, 1896).

10. See pages 66–67, 157–58n. The present discussion makes explicit the philosophic principles that underlie the "structuralist" interpretive methods discussed previously.

11. Thomas Kuhns, *The Structure of Scientific Revolutions* (Chicago: University of Chicago Press, 1962); Jürgen Habermas, *Knowledge and Human Interests* (Boston: Beacon Press, 1971).

12. The following three paragraphs summarize one of the main arguments of *Inwardness and Existence*. In Hegel and Heidegger (and also in Sartre) we find significant attempts to go beyond the actional principles of operational thought in order to ground the social in a broader existential dialectic. Both thinkers strive to get behind arbitrary social givens in order to discover a prior order of existential self-reference. That beginning, in turn, directs their thought to the fundamental experiences of self-mediation through which the self-reference of subject announces itself and achieves maturation. Both thus base their thought on a radical human inwardness, and in the present context it is significant to note that both thinkers focus on precisely those experiences—alienation, unhappy consciousness, desire, dread, death, conscience, and the need for recognition—which sociological thought has difficulty explaining, since the existential subject is not simply the by-product of collective tensions. But in developing a dialectic of the existential subject there is no need to drive a wedge between the existential and the sociopolitical. The real task, on the contrary, is to synthesize the two in a concrete way by referring the world of thrownness, the world of social, operational thought to the dialectic of human reflexivity, thereby grounding *praxis* in the understanding of self as Being-in-the-World. In developing that possibility, the basic direction of dialectical thought is to develop an ontology which will establish the coincidence of the existential subject and "the whole of things," the grounding of being in man and the projecting of man in the totality of his historical and political responsibility.

13. The development of Freud's thought is one of the most concrete examples of the movement from a logistic to a dialectical understanding of instinct.

14. Admittedly, existential-dialectical man is the exception to the rule of human complacence. But the substantive issue remains this, is authenticity only one of the ways men behave or does Heidegger have a cogent argument when he derives the possibility of inauthenticity from a failure to make an authentic appropriation of one's existence? See *Being and Time*, p. 234.

15. Sections 3 through 6 in effect trace the breakup of dialectic—the movement to particularity—while section 7 resumes the upward path.

16. Heidegger and Gadamer argue a similar conclusion—but within a dialectical rather than pluralistic context.

Chapter 4

1. Elder Olson, "An Outline of Poetic Theory," in *Critics and Criticism*, pp. 546–66.

2. Thomas Mann, "The Making of the Magic Mountain," *The Magic Mountain* (New York: Alfred A. Knopf, 1965, pp. 719–29). The following two paragraphs are an extrapolation from Mann's remarks.

3. Thomas Mann, "The Making of the Magic Mountain," p. 725. For a similar statement of Mann's intention in *Doctor Faustus*, see *The Story of a Novel* (New York: Alfred A. Knopf, 1961).

4. Thomas Mann, *The Magic Mountain*, pp. 469–98.

5. Thomas Mann, *The Magic Mountain*, pp. 706–16.

6. Thomas Mann, *The Story of a Novel*, p. 90.

7. Sheldon Sacks, *Fiction and the Shape of Belief*, pp. 1-31, 49-60. Sacks defines an apologue as "a work organized as a fictional example of the truth of a formulable statement or a series of such statements."

8. On Crane's mimetic-didactic distinction, see especially *The Languages of Criticism and the Structure of Poetry*, pp. 47-49, 156-58, and in *Critics and Criticism*, Crane, 16-18, 620-21, and Olson, 65-58, 588-93.

9. Gerald F. Else, *The Origin and Early Form of Greek Tragedy* (Cambridge: Harvard University Press, 1965, pp. 33-48).

10. See Burke's analyses of the first two works, and similar analyses of several other works, in *Language as Symbolic Action*. Burke's fascinating though sketchy discussion of Coleridge's poem occurs in *The Philosophy of Literary Form*.

11. In our time it should surprise no one to find many rhetorical works full of existential and dialectical commonplaces and themes. Robbe-Grillet's basic objection to the novelistic methods of Sartre and Camus was a dialectical one: in criticizing both writers for giving such an orderly form to their vision of chaos, Robbe-Grillet called for a dialectical correspondence between existential thought and existential art. As novelists, however, Sartre and Camus have no such pretense; Sartre is particularly clear on the popular and rhetorical nature of his literary works. Far more is needed for a dialectical work of art than dialectical ideas.

12. Wayne Booth, "How Not to Use Aristotle: *The Poetics*," in *Now Don't Try to Reason With Me* (Chicago: University of Chicago Press, 1970, p. 115).

13. R. S. Crane, *The Languages of Criticism and the Structure of Poetry*, pp. 169-79.

14. R. S. Crane, "Jane Austen: *Persuasion*," in *The Idea of the Humanities*, vol. 2, pp. 283-302.

15. R. S. Crane, "The Concept of Plot and the Plot of *Tom Jones*," *Critics and Criticism*, pp. 616-47.

16. Elder Olson, *The Theory of Comedy* (Bloomington: University of Indiana Press, 1968).

17. Elder Olson, "An Outline of Poetic Theory," in *Critics and Criticism*, pp. 560, 563-66.

18. See Yvor Winters' poem "On Teaching the Young," *The Giant Weapon* (New York: New Directions, 1943). It is, perhaps, the best statement of Winters' critical theory.

19. Thus pages 122-35 trace a circle from the dialectical to the problematic lyric, a circle which defines the distinct kinds of works the general theory we have constructed enables us to distinguish.

20. See especially the following pages in *The Languages of Criticism and the Structure of Poetry*: 56-57, 146-48, 153, 179, 185; *Critics and Criticism*, p. 18; and Sheldon Sacks, *Fiction and the Shape of Belief*, passim.

21. I know of no rhetorician, with the possible exception of Richard McKeon, who has spent as much time as has Burke studying dialectic and attempting to incorporate it into a rhetorical view of things. In *Inwardness and Existence* I attempt to reverse the process by situating operational-rhetorical man within the context of an existential dialectic.

22. Such as historical evidence about the backgrounds of Faulkner's art,

statements from Faulkner regarding his artistic intentions, and the use of other stories from *Go Down, Moses*.

23. The main defect in an existential hermeneutic such as Gadamer's is that it collapses fact and value, history and authenticity. The deepest reading of a text is not, by reason of that fact, the best one. Significance becomes insignificant if everyone necessarily participates in the disclosure of truth.

24. On the concept of Truth as *a-lethia*, see *Being and Time*, section 44; the essay "On the Essence of Truth," in *Existence and Being*, pp. 292–324; and the essay "Plato's Doctrine of Truth," in *Philosophy in the Twentieth Century*, edited by William Barrett and Henry D. Aiken (New York: Random House, 1962, vol. 3, pp. 251–70).

25. On silence as a mode of discourse, see *Being and Time*, p. 208.

26. Paul Ricoeur, *Freud and Philosophy*, p. 343.

Index